A BILLION

An Eyewitness Report from

LIVES

the Frontlines of Humanity

JAN EGELAND

SIMON & SCHUSTER   New York • London • Toronto • Sydney

SIMON & SCHUSTER
1230 Avenue of the Americas
New York, NY 10020

First Simon & Schuster hardcover edition March 2008

SIMON & SCHUSTER and colophon are registered trademarks
of Simon & Schuster, Inc.

For information about special discounts for bulk purchases,
please contact Simon & Schuster Special Sales at
1-800-456-6798 or business@simonandschuster.com.

Designed by Dana Sloan

Manufactured in the United States of America

10   9   8   7   6   5   4   3   2   1

Library of Congress Cataloging-in-Publication Data

Egeland, Jan.
    A billion lives : an eyewitness report from the frontlines of humanity / Jan Egeland.
    —1st Simon & Schuster hardcover ed.
        p.   cm.
    Includes bibliographical references and index.
        1. Social history—21st century.   2. Social problems.   3. Violence.   4. Disasters.
    I. Title.
    HN18.3.E44   2008
    909.82'5—dc22   2007045913

ISBN-13: 978-1-4165-6138-5

To Anne Kristin,
our daughters, Ane and Heidi,
and my mother, Margot

We—even we here—hold the power and bear
the responsibility.

—ABRAHAM LINCOLN

A community is like a ship. Everyone ought
to be prepared to take the helm.

—HENRIK IBSEN

Contents

Preface

THIS BOOK is an eyewitness account from many years of travel and work in the disaster and war zones of our time. Both in the field and the world's capitals I have met the best and worst among us. I have confronted warlords, mass murderers, and tyrants, but I have met many more peacemakers, relief workers, and human rights activists who risk their lives at humanity's first line of defense.

I am convinced that for the majority of people, the world is getting better. There is more peace, more people are fed and educated, and fewer are forced to become refugees than a generation ago—in spite of the halfhearted investment by rich and powerful nations.

During my years in the United Nations as undersecretary-general, emergency relief coordinator, and special adviser for Secretary-General Kofi Annan, I saw firsthand how effective multilateral action saved vulnerable communities who were at the edge of the abyss. I saw how local and regional efforts, aided by the UN, brought a measure of progress and peace in war-torn societies. Millions received relief and even more got security as wars were ending in Liberia and Sierra Leone, Eastern Congo and Burundi, Angola and South Sudan, Northern Uganda and Lebanon, Kosovo, East Timor, and Nepal.

The UN coordinated and facilitated massive international relief for the victims of the Indian Ocean tsunami, the South Asian earthquake of 2005, the droughts at the Horn of Africa, the hunger of Southern Africa, and the ethnic cleansing campaigns in Darfur. In all of these emergencies hundreds of thousands of lives were predicted to be lost. These somber predictions were, against all odds, averted because multilateral action that builds on local capacities is effective.

Still, lives saved through emergency relief are too often not protected thereafter. The victims receive food and blankets, but not security, not peace, not human rights. We can succeed in ensuring real change only when we have unreserved political support from the leaders of the world's powerful capitals and sufficient resources from its richest nations. We fail when there is no political unity of purpose among the member states. We fail, tragically and repeatedly, when the UN and regional organizations are not provided with the economic and security resources needed.

A billion lives are still at stake at humanity's front lines. This is the number of fellow human beings without drinking water, daily food, or even a dollar a day to survive on.

Climate change makes all nations more vulnerable to extreme weather hazards. Only collective, multilateral efforts can prevent, respond to, and mitigate the effects of the "once in a generation" disasters that will increasingly strike in the south as well as the north. The vulnerability of even the strongest industrialized nations was amply proved in 2005 when Hurricane Katrina overwhelmed local and national emergency response systems in the United States.

On the following pages I offer a firsthand report from communities and crisis areas where much is still at stake and more needs to be done. I am not in any operational position in the United Nations and can reflect now on what I saw and what I learned. The most important thing I learned is that our generation has the resources, technology, and institutions to end the massive suffering that is taking place on our watch. It is a question of will.

A BILLION LIVES

1.
Always Speak the Truth

G UIGLO IS a small town in the lush western province of Ivory
Coast, which in 2006 was engulfed in crippling fear. For many
years it had been among the most prosperous areas of West Africa,
with profitable cocoa plantations and a booming forestry industry.
But behind the façade of peaceful economic growth there was
mounting tension between those who considered themselves the
original inhabitants, and the descendents of those who came from
the north to find work. The few countries interested in western Africa woke up late to the fact that the former French colony was not
the success story it had been promoting itself as. Ivory Coast was a
nation torn by ethnic discrimination, war, violent youth gangs, and
spectacularly bad government. Liberia and Sierra Leone lie to the
west—places of child soldiers, mutilations, and massacres—and the
poorest desert nations on earth are to the north. Consequently, few
wanted to face the truth about a nation that had come to symbolize
African recovery from generations of colonial rule. In 2002 and
2003 the country had been split in two, with the rebel New Forces
movement in control of the northern half of the country and continuing strife in the south and west.

I came to this remote region in February 2006 as UN undersecretary-general and emergency relief coordinator. Our humanitarian

operations had been attacked and our buildings in Guiglo had been burned down four weeks earlier. As world public opinion was focused on the growing carnage in post-invasion Iraq, another emergency was allowed to develop. It was my job, as head of the UN Office for the Coordination of Humanitarian Affairs (OCHA), to mobilize attention, gather resources, and promote positive change when disasters occurred. Coordinating humanitarian action within the United Nations and between the UN and other governmental and nongovernmental humanitarian organizations meant I had access to all the actors, good and bad, but could not order anyone to do anything unless they were convinced it was right. The pattern of the violence and the atrocities in Ivory Coast was too familiar to me from previous travels to the Congo, Kosovo, Darfur, Chad, Colombia, the Middle East, and too many other places where fighting takes place amid the civilian population and is often waged directly against them. The anger builds when I see, time and again, how in our age it is more dangerous to be a woman or a child in these battlefields than an armed, adult male soldier.

With the help of hate radio, the "Jeune Patriots," the "young patriots" of President Laurent Gbagbo's dominant political party, had specialized in beating, raping, and killing defenseless people, primarily those from the Burkinabe ethnic minority, and the political opposition. The United Nations was provided with peacekeepers from its member states to go to Ivory Coast and Guiglo to try to prevent further ethnic violence, but it was too late. And the troops were ill prepared and ill equipped to confront fanatical thugs.

When a young man was killed in a confrontation between the gangs and the UN force, hate radio immediately called upon "all patriots" to "avenge the death" by attacking the minorities, the opposition groups, and "all foreigners," especially peacekeepers and humanitarian workers. In the violent chaos the peacekeepers, who were there to protect civilians and humanitarian operations, fled.

The government forces and police, as usual, did nothing to stop the "young patriots."

We walk amid the charred ruins of our local OCHA office and the destroyed offices, vehicles, and warehouses of the other UN agencies. The Save the Children compound and many other centers of relief have been looted, burned, and destroyed. The relief groups here have done effective humanitarian work for tens of thousands of vulnerable civilians for years. Now all international staff have been evacuated and most humanitarian services are at a standstill. The terrorized minorities who have fled to overcrowded camps receive no supplies and no protection.

I end the sad tour with an open-air meeting under a straw roof erected next to town hall. All the local dignitaries are there, sitting at a long table with a white cloth: the mayor, the government prefect, the military and police commanders, and the community leaders, including the chief of the dominant local tribe. They have come to meet me and my delegation from UN headquarters in New York, Geneva, and the capital, Abidjan, reluctantly. They know that I represent Secretary-General Kofi Annan and that I will report back to the powerful Security Council, which, after much time lost on futile discussions, has finally decided to impose sanctions on the head of the Jeune Patriots, on another leading politician working for President Gbagbo, and on a commander in the New Forces in the north. These men cannot leave the country without being arrested and will have their foreign assets frozen.

After the initial introductions, I get straight to the point: "I am the envoy of your fellow West African, the United Nations secretary-general, and I have come from the other end of the world to speak the truth and to seek justice. You all know that my UN and humanitarian colleagues came here because there was violence against defenseless women and children here and many unmet human needs. We came here in good faith and as your guests. The attacks, the burning, and the pillaging I have witnessed today is criminal behavior of the worst kind. I know that you know who did this, as I know you know the voices of Radio Guiglo who spoke hate and started the violence. They have to be severely punished and you are accountable for making that happen. I have a letter to President Gbagbo from Kofi Annan asking for three million dollars in compensation for the losses we sustained. If there is continued impunity I will ask for more sanctions against your leaders from the Security Council."

My French isn't perfect, but a simple, straightforward, and angry message is not difficult to get across even with errors in grammar. Looking at the embarrassed mayor, prefect, police chief, and military commander, I can see that I have been understood. So why are the twenty or so young men who marched in as I was speaking apparently having trouble getting the message? A number of them stand and start shouting at me: "What about the UN soldiers who shot our comrade? What about the foreign tribes who came to take our jobs and our land? Who are really the criminals?"

I prepare to respond—they all know that the violence and pillaging was unprovoked—but the UN humanitarian coordinator for Ivory Coast, Abdoulaye Mar Dieye, who is Senegalese, leans over to whisper in my ear: "This is definitely when we take our leave. Those guys are the rank and file of the local Jeune Patriots, who you rightly labeled dangerous criminals." As we go to our cars I notice the tribal chief engaging some of the young men in a shouting match. The policeman from Benin who is assigned as my one and only bodyguard, and who sat in a chair in front of my hotel room all last night, bravely takes a position in front of the car, his revolver in hand. Another large group of "young patriots" has arrived and now surrounds our four vehicles.

After a long twenty minutes inside our locked cars, the chief pushes himself through the mob and shouts some orders and a narrow opening is provided. Our local Ivorian colleagues later confirm that the paramount chief had single-handedly managed to convince the young thugs that it was a bad proposition to smash our cars and beat us up, as the leaders of the Jeune Patriots had wanted. They confirm that the chief is scared of sanctions and took it to heart when I said the community leaders are accountable for what happened. He says he will control the 'patriots' in the future and urges me to get the humanitarian organizations to return to the area.

We drive to the nearby camp where seven thousand displaced Burkinabe victims of the violence have taken refuge. Several hundred men, women, and children are waiting in an open space. Their greetings are formal and cordial, but the questions posed by their gray-haired leaders are honest and heartbreaking: "We have no protection nor supplies if we do not get it from the international community. So why did you all flee with your peacekeepers and aid workers and leave us behind to our fate?" A mother of three raises her hand: "The president, his tribe, and his Jeune Patriots have forced us away from the plantations that have been our homes for generations. If we cannot stay where our fathers and grandfathers lived, where can we go to live in safety and dignity?"

We are the only representatives of the international community that they will see during many days and nights of fear. And the only thing we can offer is to send new supplies by convoy in the coming days. With no security guarantees from the authorities and with no new peacekeepers from UN member states, we cannot call back our international staff. We cannot prevent future attacks nor guarantee that the meager supplies we may get through will not be looted.

The new millennium is six years old, man walked on the moon a generation ago, but we cannot provide these desperate civilians with even the most basic protection. As we prepare to leave the camp to drive back to Abidjan and then return to our comfortable safety in New York, Geneva, and Oslo, one of the camp spokesmen, who has a baby girl on his shoulder, will not let go of my hand: "You say you will not forget us. Will you remember? Do you realize that our destiny is in your hands? That tonight we will again be alone with no one to protect and to help us?"

The only promise I can make is that I will speak the uncensored truth about their plight to the powerful members of the UN Security Council next week.

Four days later I do exactly that in my briefing in New York. The ambassadors are attentive and share my concerns. The council condemns the indiscriminate violence, pledges increased humanitarian support, and promises to study my appeal for protection of the civilians through immediate deployment of a well-resourced peacekeeping force, more sanctions against the abusers, and more intensive mediation efforts. They know I will walk a few paces from their chambers to where the leading international news media are staked out. In a few hours, hundreds of millions all over the world will receive the message of the refugees in western Ivory Coast and hear who are accountable and why the member states must take action.

No nation can afford any longer to be seen as insensitive to mass murder or mass hunger. We who witness the unmasked realities have a responsibility as never before to shake up and embarrass the powerful. This generation has more economic, technological, and security potential than any in human history. Our only option is to speak the truth, always.

2.

The Bombs in Baghdad

THE LINES in front of passport control appear endless. It is August 19, 2003, and thousands of tourists have arrived at Newark Airport for a summer visit to New York City, the world's most exciting metropolis. My summer break is over. This afternoon I will start four days of briefings at the United Nations before taking up the job as undersecretary-general for humanitarian affairs on September 1. I join the line for non–U.S. citizens behind a planeload of Chinese visitors and edge toward the first of several television monitors providing distraction for the slow post-9/11 immigration lines. It is 1 P.M. and I can afford an hour in passport and customs control and make the 3 P.M. meeting with my new colleagues in the UN Office for the Coordination of Humanitarian Affairs (OCHA).

CNN is onscreen with the banner headline: BREAKING NEWS— UN BOMBED IN BAGHDAD. We fall silent as we see and hear the CNN Baghdad bureau chief say, "In the darkness behind us the effort is continuing to reach people who are trapped in the rubble from what appears to be a massive car bomb set off in a cement truck when this building, the headquarters of the UN here for many years, was crowded with UN people and others as well." She goes on to say that the UN special envoy, Sergio Vieira de Mello, is trapped in the debris. The reporter then turns to a grief-stricken UN spokesman, Salim Lone, who confirms that they are "desperately trying to remove Sergio from the rubble. But, at the moment, all I can say is he's very gravely injured, and we are praying for him and for some others who are trapped with him. But, you know, we have already lost some wonderful, wonderful people ... amongst them friends of mine who came here to help the people of Iraq."

I numbly follow the Chinese tourists toward the next monitors, where new horrific details of the bombing are shown. The death toll has grown from thirteen to seventeen. And then, just before I present my Norwegian passport to the security officer, the CNN news anchor pauses and announces, "We know now the dead include the UN special representative, the man in charge there, Sergio Vieira de Mello."

At that moment I realize that everything has changed. The UN and its mission, its work, and its environment will not be the same again. The age of innocence has gone. I had expected to spend all my energies in the UN on the security and survival of disaster and conflict victims, not the security and survival of our own UN staff. Humanitarian work has always been risky in the crossfire between armies, militias, guerrillas, and child soldiers. From Colombia to Cambodia I have seen for many years how our field colleagues learn to live with the risks in danger zones. But it is something entirely different when well-organized terrorists callously plan for weeks and months to kill and destroy those who have come to help. The emotional and bewildered Salim Lone sums it all up before he goes off the air: "We are unarmed. We don't have a lot of security, as this bomb shows. We don't want a lot of security, because we are here to help the people of Iraq who have suffered so much for so long."

Sergio Vieira de Mello has been my friend for many years, and is one of my predecessors in the job that I am to assume. We were both deeply involved in the humanitarian challenges of the Balkans, Central Africa, and Cambodia. Because of that experience, Kofi Annan called to ask me if I was interested in the job of emergency relief coordinator in 1997, but in the end Sergio was appointed. Three months ago Annan had again called to say he wanted me for this job, this time to succeed Japanese Kenzo Oshima, who had taken the position after Sergio and would be leaving at the end of June. When I got the offer from Kofi Annan, whom I so much admired as a principled UN leader, my wife and I agreed that our children were big enough for me to accept the challenge. Sergio had called me twice in recent weeks from Baghdad to give me advice and pledge his support. He said jokingly that it was not easy to get the large UN humanitarian agencies in line, and quoted Lenin: "Coordination must mean subordination!" He offered to rent me his apartment in New York but also had this request: "Please let me keep your soon-to-be personal assistant, Lynn Manuel, whom Oshima kindly let me borrow to start up work here. Lynn really looks forward to working for you in New York, but she is so important to me that I really need her here for a few more weeks, as I am wrapping up my mission in Baghdad at the end of September."

I get a ride to town with Mark Malloch Brown, administrator of the UN Development Programme (UNDP), who has come to meet his mother who is visiting from London. The UNDP, like OCHA, has many staff members among the three hundred in the bombed UN building and Mark is on his phone trying to see if his staff is safe. "There will be a crisis meeting in the Steering Committee on Iraq at 4 P.M.," he says as I get out of the car. "You should come there, because you can forget about your briefing program." All 191 flags of the member states have been taken down when I enter the familiar UN building on First Avenue along the bank of New York's East River. Only one flag is flying, half-mast: the blue UN flag. In the hallways and offices I see my new UN colleagues clustered around every available TV set. Some are sobbing, others hugging one another. Virtually everyone has friends or colleagues who are part of the large and growing UN mission in Iraq that was reestablished after the United States–led invasion had crushed the Saddam regime.

"What a terrible day to start," says Carolyn McAskie, the acting head of OCHA, as she greets me in my new office on the thirty-sixth floor, with a stunning view over the East River to Queens and Brooklyn. Carolyn was herself recruited by Sergio Vieira de Mello as his deputy. In Sergio's and now in Kenzo Oshima's absence she has ably led the department. We agree to scrap the briefings and the Iraq Steering Group meeting. The secretary-general is in Finland, where he had spoken as recently as yesterday with Sergio, his close friend and colleague of more than twenty years. Annan had persuaded him to take the difficult and controversial mission to help build a new Iraq after a war that had severely divided the UN Security Council and the international community at large. Annan had warned of the consequences of an attack by the United States and a coalition of like-minded nations acting without a mandate from the world body. Now he is suffering the worst blow of his many years at the helm of the organization, for going in and helping to pick up the pieces after an invasion he had opposed.

The meeting is chaired by the group's regular leader, Deputy Secretary-General Louise Fréchette, an impressive woman who was formerly deputy minister of defense for Canada. The briefings in this and subsequent twice-daily meetings over the next few days confirm that August 19, 2003, is the worst day in the history of the United Nations. Twenty-two colleagues have died in the blast. More than a third of the three hundred UN staff members who serve in the old Canal Hotel, which constitutes UN headquarters, are wounded. Many are maimed for life. The main topic at this first grim crisis meeting is how to ensure that the dead, the wounded, and the remaining staff are handled or cared for properly in Baghdad or evacuated to Amman, Jordan, or elsewhere. We hear that the American forces arrived quickly at the scene and took the wounded by helicopter and ambulance to hospitals. Many of the wounded have horrific scars from the thousands of pieces of glass that flew from the shattered windows. Only a core group is to remain in Baghdad. OCHA is sending a four-person team from New York and Geneva to help manage the crisis; it will be led by Kevin Kennedy, a former U.S. Marine colonel who directs our Humanitarian Emergency Branch. He had returned a few weeks earlier from Baghdad, where he served as deputy humanitarian coordinator.

Near the end of the meeting, the global UN security coordinator reads from new lists with the names of the killed and the wounded. He reluctantly confirms what we already have heard rumors of: "I am afraid that Lynn Manuel is on the list from Baghdad of colleagues who did not make it," he tells Carolyn and me. In a hastily convened OCHA staff meeting the terrible news is presented and reflected on. As I enter the packed meeting room next to my new office, Kevin Kennedy comes forward to introduce himself: "Welcome. I look forward to working for you, but now have to excuse myself to go and pack. I am leaving for Baghdad in a few hours."

One of the main tasks of the United Nations in Iraq is humanitarian work and there are many colleagues from OCHA in Baghdad. Immediately below Sergio's office, which was the direct target of the one-ton bomb, was OCHA's Humanitarian Information Center. There the manager, who was from Iowa, died along with the Iraqi information assistant and the twenty-five-year-old Iraqi driver. In Sergio's office a former OCHA staff member was also killed. And then there is the devastating news about Marilyn (Lynn) Manuel, who had worked for all my predecessors and whom everyone knew and loved.

Carolyn, who knows Lynn's family, volunteers to go to their home. In the late evening a Catholic priest comes to the grieving family to hold an emotional wake. But two nights later the phone rings. "It is me. I am wounded and in the hospital. I couldn't call before. Have you been worried?" Lynn had been found after the blast by a Palestinian colleague, Marwan Ali, who had gone back into the building to see if anyone needed help. On what remained of the second floor, he found Lynn staggering around, with multiple face wounds, in the hallway outside Sergio's destroyed office. She was brought by the Americans to an intensive care unit at one of the U.S. military hospitals. Her Filipino name had been confused with the name of a Spanish military man who had died. I meet Lynn many times after she comes back to New York. The scars slowly heal, but the glass fragments in her eyes cannot be removed, and so even though she will take up important work within OCHA, she will not be able to take on the intensive job of personal assistant.

In the daily Iraq Steering Group meetings, the department heads and other undersecretaries-general sit around a mahogany table that dates back to the legendary secretary-general Dag Hammarskjöld. Support staff sit along the walls to take notes and provide information. These will be the first of hundreds of meetings on the secretary-general's famed thirty-eighth floor, where Iraq and later Darfur, Congo, Lebanon, and other countries or issues will be discussed. The challenges often seem overwhelming: the participants are often eloquent, but the outcomes of the meetings are often underwhelming. Because I come from a tradition where the chair always starts by defining the purpose and expected outcome of a meeting, and ends by dictating a conclusion and expected follow-up, these top-level Secretariat meetings seem more like a debating society to me, in which participants discuss small and big issues alike. The actual conclusions and responsibilities for follow-up will remain unclear until Secretary-General Annan finally decides in 2005 to establish a more cabinet-style Policy Committee with proper procedures and decision making.

I have decided to lie low during the first months when the senior management of the UN is meeting on Iraq and other sensitive issues. I am the newest and youngest of the undersecretaries-general and my colleagues are more experienced in dealing with intergovernmental work from a multinational and multicultural headquarters. But the issue at hand is one that I cannot be silent about: Should the UN leave Iraq altogether or should our focus be on how to stay while still being the target of deadly attacks? I quickly see how deeply this issue resonates in the steering group, all the way back to its first meetings during the slow buildup to the war in late 2002.

After American forces took Baghdad in April 2003 and the Coalition Provisional Authority (CPA) was set up, there was acrimonious debate in the UN on whether and when to return the international staff that had been evacuated before the invasion. Colleagues from the two heavyweight Secretariat departments for political affairs and peacekeeping generally favored staying away until a clearer picture emerged and security would be better. The UN humanitarian agencies and OCHA in the Secretariat of the Secretary-General wanted to go back as soon as possible. Secretary-General Annan also felt that the UN should be present in this most important and difficult of international dramas and so on April 28 the decision was made to go back with humanitarian staff. On May 22, the Security Council passed the now-infamous Resolution 1483, giving a weak and ambiguous political mandate to a new special representative who was supposed to "assist" and "facilitate" the work of the CPA, United States, and United Kingdom, with the resolution explicitly recognizing the two states as "occupying powers." Thus between May and August the number of international staff assigned to Iraq has grown to well over six hundred even though the U.S.-led CPA is not willing to give the UN or Sergio Vieira de Mello a meaningful political role.

After the bombing the mood in the steering group changes completely from April's reluctant support for an Iraq presence to a nearly unanimous opinion that we should leave Baghdad and probably the northern Kurdish and southern Shia areas as well. Throughout the fall of 2003, the strongest dissenting voice is mine. I came to the job with a deep conviction that organizations such as the United Nations and the Red Cross, and humanitarian groups in general, have a moral and political obligation to try to stay where there is crisis and unmet basic needs. If able-bodied people in international agencies rush to the lifeboats when the situation becomes critical, what then of our obligation to seek to protect and provide for the women and the children who are left behind without international aid and without witnesses? In the weeks before I took up my new job I had watched with growing frustration how the UN country team evacuated twice from war-torn Liberia during the summer of 2003, while the International Committee of the Red Cross and Médecins Sans Frontières (Doctors Without Borders), among others, stayed behind and provided physical and moral support to the needy caught in the crossfire.

There are many advocates for evacuating all international staff from Iraq, especially Baghdad, but the strongest among them is probably Sir Kieran Prendergast, the British diplomat heading the UN Department of Political Affairs (DPA). I had gotten to know and to appreciate Prendergast when I worked as UN envoy to Colombia in 1999. Early on he had taken the view, which I shared, that the unilateral decision of the United States, the United Kingdom, and their allies to invade Iraq was a wrong and dangerous move that would undermine the order the UN stands on. Hans Blix, the UN's able chief arms inspector, and his team were not given time to prove or disprove the existence of possible weapons of mass destruction. We all knew very well that Saddam had had such weapons, and had used them even against civilians. As a Norwegian Red Cross official, I had seen the terrible wounds suffered by victims of Iraqi poison gas attacks (I helped organize hospital care for Iranian patients in Norway at the end of the 1980s). But Saddam had not used such arms for more than a decade, and with the arms inspectors in place it was hardly the time to start attacking Iraq. Moreover, the job was not finished in Afghanistan, where it was indeed proved that al-Qaeda and Osama bin Laden had established a safe haven.

Since late August, Kevin Kennedy has been in charge of the "stay-behind" team living and working next to the Canal Hotel ruins in Baghdad. At our daily morning meeting, usually chaired by Deputy Secretary-General Fréchette but at times even by Annan himself, Kevin gives his updates through a speakerphone in the middle of the meeting table. It is close to midnight in Baghdad when Kevin, in his succinct military style, says his daily "good morning DSG" to Ms. Fréchette and then provides a point-by-point update on how programs continue with Iraqi national staff; how extra security measures are being built one sandbag at a time; and how the U.S. military and Iraqi guards are providing extra security for the outer perimeter. Then, on September 22, Kevin reports that a suicide bomber in a car approaching the UN compound has just blown himself to pieces and killed or wounded several Iraqi guards at the outer perimeter of barbed wire and concrete barriers.

Prendergast has argued against an early return of UN staff to Iraq after the war. Prendergast's talented special assistant, Richard Hooper, whom I knew from his fine work in the Middle East, died in the August 19 blast. Prendergast feels it would be "reckless to the extreme" to stay on in Iraq after we have become targets of deadly attacks. It was Prendergast who had first called to sound me out on whether I might be available to return to the UN as undersecretary-general for humanitarian affairs. Now he is arguing that I "behave like an NGO activist."

In the wake of the first attack, most members of the Iraq Steering Group wanted to recommend leaving Baghdad with all international staff. Now, following this second attack on September 22, all members but me want a unanimous recommendation from the steering group to the secretary-general that the UN leave with all international staff immediately. I argue that by leaving now we are setting a dangerous precedent: we will prove to the terrorists that by attacking our headquarters in Iraq and elsewhere they can succeed in driving us out of an entire country, with the civilian population left to their plight of increasing chaos and violence. Twice in late August and September the secretary-general has decided that we will not leave entirely, but instead keep a minimum of staff with a maximum of security measures. This increases the pressure on me since some feel my dissenting voice is the fig leaf that gives Annan a chance to keep his staff in harm's way.

The pressure is nearly unbearable. Am I, an official safe in New York, reckless with the lives of colleagues? When I speak daily with Kevin on the phone he assures me that neither he nor his courageous colleagues in the new bunker-like compound next to the Canal Hotel want to pull the plug and leave. I understand, however, that given the constant danger we can only defend a continued presence if the actual benefit of our work and our presence is commensurate with the risk. Thus in early October, I convince a reluctant Annan to let me go to Baghdad to assess what the UN actually can and should be doing under the new and adverse circumstances.

The secretary-general and the heads of security in New York and Baghdad set down one condition: I must go with four UN bodyguards from New York and Cairo. These are American and Egyptian policemen with special forces training. My delegation consists only of two German colleagues: my chief of staff, Hansjoerg Strohmeyer, and our New York–based desk officer, Oliver Ulich. In Amman, Jordan, on October 18, we get a series of briefings into the night by the large UN community of staff who were evacuated from Iraq. Several hundred of them are crowded into Amman hotels, waiting to go back if and when conditions permit. Some feel it is important to find a way to go back as soon as possible, to finish the important humanitarian and developmental programs of the UN in Iraq. Others are still traumatized; they are unwilling and unable to return to a country where so many colleagues were killed and maimed.

Early the next morning, I fly to northern Iraq with Hansjoerg and the close protection team in a Belgian C-130 Hercules military plane that continuously ejects antimissile devices as we prepare for landing. On the plane my close protection unit converts from being easygoing blue-shirt UN guards to their new and impressive special forces incarnation with blue-black uniforms, automatic guns, and bulletproof vests. This is my third visit to Iraq in less than a year. I had visited Iraq as secretary-general of the Norwegian Red Cross the previous December during the intense military and political buildup to war, and then again in May, a month after the Saddam statue fell.

There are no other passengers on the plane. Looking through the small, round military-style windows at the long-tormented Kurdish areas of Iraq, I think back to my Red Cross mission to the country when the Saddam regime was firmly in control. I had never, except for in North Korea, seen and felt totalitarianism as complete as the Baathist regime's. Saddam images were everywhere, inside and outside, just as Kim Il Sung and his son were pictured everywhere when I traveled for the Red Cross in North Korea. No one, not even Iraqi Red Crescent colleagues, dared to speak about anything remotely political, even in private. Most families have seen relatives or colleagues detained, exiled, tortured, or killed.

But Iraq was also a complex, multicultural, and industrialized society where the extensive infrastructure and previously high standards of living were crumbling due to neglect by the regime, as well as from long-lasting, crude, failed sanctions. This is no poor third world country like those I normally work and travel in. It has a sizable, well-educated middle class, extensive highways, and a capital, Baghdad, that goes on and on with well-built public buildings and apartment blocks. But in December 2002, the decay was visible everywhere. In Basra in the Shia–dominated south, with a population of more than two million, we saw large, poor communities virtually floating on a sea of sewage and wastewater because of the failing facilities. There was nothing charming in what was once called "the Venice of the Middle East." When I returned to Oslo I wrote an article titled "A Chronicle of an Announced Disaster," in which I argued that a war could have disastrous consequences for the vulnerable civilian population in Iraq, a country rife with internal tension.

I came back to Baghdad in May for a meeting of the International Committee of the Red Cross (ICRC) and Red Crescent to plan humanitarian work. I then realized that we had exaggerated the immediate negative consequences of the invasion. It was clear that the U.S.-led bombing and ground offensives had caused limited destruction and little movement of people. There had been no breakdown in supplies to the civilian population. The struggling water and sewage facilities, vital for public health, had not been dramatically affected. The "shock and awe" campaign of thousands of cruise missiles and air attacks had caused relatively few casualties. To me it did indeed look like precision bombing as we drove by the destroyed bridges, military installations, telecommunications centers, ministries, and Saddam's palaces.

Our vast humanitarian preparedness in the neighboring countries was as unused and overstocked in early 2003 as it had been underprepared and wanting after the first Gulf War in 1991, when Saddam's Republican Guards attacked Kurds in the north and Shiites in the south and hundreds of thousands of civilians fled toward Turkey, Iran, and Jordan. The scandalously weak and chaotic international humanitarian response at that time had triggered the creation of a UN Department for Humanitarian Affairs, which was later renamed and became OCHA, as well as my new post as undersecretary general for humanitarian affairs and emergency relief coordinator. UN member states wanted to ensure that the UN could and would mobilize lifesaving support before, during, and after wars and natural disasters. In Iraq in May 2003, it looked as if the humanitarian community had mobilized too much and too early.

I was part of the "lessons learned" effort when I visited Iraq in 1991 as political adviser for the Norwegian foreign minister. We brought a planeload of fifty Norwegian relief workers and supplies for the Kurdish war victims in northern Iraq to help jump-start new and improved UN standby arrangements for humanitarian operations. The operation became a model for hundreds of future joint ventures involving UN agencies and resources from UN member states. The relief workers were soon deployed all over the northern Kurdish areas. However, I was grounded in Baghdad by the Iraqi regime because I was traveling on a diplomatic passport from one of the countries in the U.S.-led coalition that liberated Kuwait.

The possibility of building a new and better Iraq on the ruins of dictatorship dissipated before our eyes twelve years and one war later, in May 2003. The successful military campaign was followed by a vacuum of authority and order—an invitation to chaos, crime, and pillaging. These were the weeks when the U.S.-led coalition lost the advantage that it had won through a well-prepared war, because there was no plan for the day after Saddam fell.

I had not expected to be back only five weeks after the war, but our Red Cross delegates in Baghdad felt it was safe for internationals to visit. The Iraqis were generally relieved that Saddam was gone and welcomed our presence. People who even in private had not dared to speak their minds in December 2002 now welcomed the freedom to talk, to discuss and hope for real and positive change. The eerie, nightmarish feeling that Big Brother was watching was gone along with Saddam's images.

But the Iraqis had already started to feel that freedom was coming with an excessive price. Not only political prisoners but dangerous criminals had been set free. The streets were filled with the looters. We saw no police anywhere. The U.S. soldiers and Marines

patroling downtown streets stayed in their vehicles and made no attempt to perform police functions. High-ranking U.S. and British
occupation officials who briefed our international Red Cross delegations were surprisingly candid. Not even in our wildest fantasies
had they believed that Saddam's armies and regime would collapse
so fast and so completely after three weeks of fighting. They had
detailed plans for extended urban warfare and for large refugee
movements, but had neither capacity nor plans for taking over
all law and order functions and all administration so soon. Now,
they admitted, they were at risk of losing the peace after winning
the war.

The sense that something was fundamentally wrong sank in
when we visited water works and sewage stations that had survived
the invasion but were now shutting down because their instruments
and metal components had been looted. However, the most wrench-
ing sign of collapse came in a visit to the al-Rashad mental hospital
on the outskirts of Baghdad. The international and Norwegian Red
Cross organizations had helped rehabilitate this institution in recent
years since the Saddam regime did not want to care for the mentally
ill. By early 2003 it had become a model institution, with committed staff and new wards treating a thousand patients, many with serious mental illnesses. In May 2003 at the hospital, the few remaining
doctors and nurses told me that looters from the nearby Sadr City
neighborhood had gathered outside the walls in the days after Baghdad fell. They were unable to break into the hospital until U.S. Marines used tanks to smash through the western wall of the facility at
three different points. The American soldiers then stood by as the
mobs looted and burned hospital facilities, including laboratories
and pharmacies. All one thousand patients were let loose into the
streets of Baghdad, including, the hospital director said, 117 individuals who had been charged with serious crimes, including murder. "Why on earth would the U.S. Marines want to destroy a Red
Crescent hospital?" I asked incredulously as I walked through one

ward after another in which windows, beds, sinks, pipes, and equipment had been smashed or stolen. (Much of it had been funded
with Norwegian aid money.) "Well, it probably was some twenty-
five-year-old sergeant who thought he helped freedom-loving
Iraqis to free the prisoners of Saddam," a female psychiatrist answered. "There hasn't been much logic to anything the Americans
have done in the weeks after the dictatorship crumbled."

Five months later in Iraq, the atmosphere is very different. A
sense of freedom and optimism has given way to an intense and
growing fear among Iraqis. Erbil, in the Kurdish north, is still much
calmer than the central and southern parts of the country, but the
security measures are extreme. An entire neighborhood around the
UN offices has been cordoned off and a large contingent of Kurdish
security forces checks anyone entering or leaving the compound.
Still, we meet confident and optimistic Kurdish politicians who
command their own local army and look forward to governing
themselves after many years of fierce oppression by the Baath Party
and the tense, internationally assisted self-rule Saddam was forced
to accept for the Kurds after the 1991 Gulf War. We see some of
the half million internally displaced people who are living in miserable camps in Kurdish areas. Many are victims of the "Arabiza-
tion" campaigns that drove the Kurds out of cities and towns in the
northern areas, but tens of thousands are refugees from the internal
battles between the two main Kurdish political factions. Through
the evening we receive briefings from UN colleagues and nongovernmental organization (NGO) workers on their vast humanitarian
programs, which have operated since the 1991 refugee crisis.

A key reason why we have not seen any major humanitarian crisis in Iraq in recent years, and don't see one on this day in September 2003, is the effective assistance that UN agencies and NGOs,
working with Iraqi partners, have been able to deliver using resources from the controversial Oil-for-Food program and generous
donor support gained through broad humanitarian appeals in 2002

and 2003. Since April, some two billion dollars' worth of humanitarian assistance has been delivered. The local Iraqi UN employees are fearful of the plans to hand over Oil-for-Food, the largest assistance program in UN history, to Iraqi authorities and the Coalition Provisional Authority (CPA) at the end of November without knowing whether their expertise will be accepted. Thanks to the competence of the highly qualified Iraqi staff, most of the large public services programs have continued while only core international staff remains in Baghdad and Erbil after the attacks in August and September. Most impressive is that our support for the Public Distribution System has allowed the delivery of more than two million tons of food and other commodities since April. It is clear to us that the Americans we met in the CPA office in Erbil and in Baghdad do not understand how much this support has contributed to meeting basic needs and maintaining stability. "We are ready. Hand it over," they tell me. As the deadline for taking over approaches and the magnitude of the task becomes evident, the American and British officials in charge end up asking the UN World Food Programme and other UN agencies to extend most of their services beyond November.

The next morning we fly to Baghdad. A rapid downward spiral over the airport leads to a quick "combat-style" landing complete with flares to deflect missile attacks. It is already clear at the airport that no one travels with a sense of security. As we sit in the comfortable unused chairs from Saddam's palaces in the waiting room of U.S. forces at the Baghdad Airport, the soldiers tell us that the danger of attacks and improvised explosive devices (IEDs) starts just outside the airport gates. Recent weeks have seen a growing insurgency and an influx of foreign terrorists. My close protection officers order me never to leave the bulletproof car without their signal of two bangs on the roof. We will move as little and as fast as we can outside the airport, the CPA Green Zone headquarters, and the provisional UN compound next to the Canal Hotel. When we ar-

rive at Baghdad's Town Hall, I obediently wait for the signal while
our UN guards have their guns at ready. Immediately upon leaving
the car, I am ordered to dive back to my seat. After a few minutes
there are two knocks on the roof again. "I saw a movement on that
roof, but it turned out to be some workers. Sorry," the head of the
team says as we enter the office of the deputy mayor of Baghdad,
Faris Abdul al-Assam.

Al-Assam is a talented technocrat responsible for all public services in Baghdad. He was the respected head of the water and sewage networks under Saddam. He urges a return by the UN, with its
proven strengths in Iraq. "We need you here. We must work together
to build a new and better Iraq. We are struggling to get looting and
common crime under control locally. We will also work hard to
get the worsening national security situation reversed. For that to
happen we need to have the Americans stay in their barracks and
get more Iraqi security forces out into the streets. I myself go around
by foot in Baghdad without bodyguards. I want to be close to the
people I represent." One week later this good man is shot point-
blank in his own neighborhood. He is not the only one of our interlocutors who will lose his life in the coming months as security
worsens.

From Town Hall we go in our bulletproof black vehicles to the
infamous Green Zone where Saddam once reigned and where Iraq's
new rulers, the Coalition Provisional Authority, now resides. The
heavily fortified six-square-mile enclave is located on an elbow-
shaped bend in the Tigris River in the heart of Baghdad. Here Saddam built palaces, exclusive homes, ministries, offices, Baath Party
headquarters, the al-Rashid Hotel, and the gigantic Conference
Center, which later is to become the parliament. There are hundreds
of mainly American civilian and military planners busily running
around in the old ministries as they try to come to grips with the
chaotic situation. The whole area is sealed off with fortifications
guarded by American soldiers and private security personnel. A

group of Nepalese Gurkha soldiers are at the gates when we enter
the old Republican Palace of Saddam to meet with the CPA leadership. The chief administrator and presidential envoy, L. Paul Bremer,
is not in Baghdad, so we meet with his American and British deputies. Rank and file sit together behind rows of desks in the large and
crowded reception halls of the palace.

The Americans we encounter are stressed and edgy, but oddly
confident as we sit down in a smaller meeting room. There is surprisingly little awareness of the effects the security crisis is already
having on their ambitious plans to rebuild a new and democratic
Iraq outside the fortified Green Zone. And there is no sympathy for
the UN evacuations after the bombing. "It was wrong to evacuate.
We need a more activist engagement from the UN. There are many
places in the world with worse security even than central and western Iraq. Under these circumstances you should ask for volunteers.
You just don't leave. That is what we do in the U.S. services," Bremer's
chief of staff, Ambassador Patrick Kennedy, informs me. I find his
attitude wholly inappropriate. "I don't think you are right," I tell
him. "All U.S. diplomats have just been evacuated from Gaza because one car took one bullet. We lost twenty-two colleagues in a
place where we have not been asked, as you well know, to play any
central political role at the moment."

The British CPA staff have a more nuanced view of the UN di-
lemmas. They explain the importance of the first twenty billion dollars in reconstruction aid, which is on its way from the U.S. Congress
to the CPA. A multitude of ambitious programs are being drawn up
to answer to the challenges, from the production of electricity and
oil to restoring law and order by training a large Iraqi security force.
I ask whether the British representatives could get the CPA to con-
sult more broadly with national and international actors on what is
going on, and on what should happen in this crucial transition phase.
One British ambassador smiles. "Believe me, we are trying. But be
aware that in terms of who decides what, the 'coalition' is ninety-

five percent American, four percent British, and the remaining one percent is divided among the other one dozen partners."

When we arrive in the UN compound it is already late afternoon. Here, as in Erbil, one sees the revolting fact that international civil servants who have come to help must live behind numerous layers of concrete barriers, barbed wire, and sandbags. American soldiers and Iraqi police guard the outer security perimeters. They provide indispensable protection, given the threat against us, but it also makes us more vulnerable in the long term since we are not seen as impartial do-gooders, but rather as part of the invading coalition.

We first pay an emotional visit to the Canal Hotel ruins. Where Sergio's office was there is a gaping hole in the floor and in the wall facing the street, where the truck came through with its ton of explosives. It is worse than I had expected. Papers from the filing cabinets are spread all over the floors in the adjacent offices with smashed glass and pieces of furniture, walls, floors, and roofs. I look at a paper I have just stepped on. It is a thank-you letter to Sergio from a visitor, "for taking the time to give us such a good briefing." Next to it is part of a torn map where actual and planned UN programs are marked.

We then visit some twenty representatives from nongovernmental organizations doing humanitarian work in Iraq, many in partnership with the UN. They have arrived to see me in the compound. They do not hide the fact that they feel uncomfortable going through the massive security precautions and meeting me with armed guards outside. Many of them have worked in Iraq as UN agency staff have done for years. They all tell of growing problems and extreme risks in their work. I am particularly impressed by the analysis of the CARE representative, Irishwoman Margaret Hassan, who is married to an Iraqi engineer and has worked in Iraq for decades. She is highly critical of how the coalition forces and the CPA have mishandled things in the months after the fall of the regime, and she is pessimistic about the future. (Exactly one year later, in October 2004, Margaret Hassan will be kidnapped by armed men in Baghdad. The heroic relief worker who did so much good for so many vulnerable Iraqis is killed a month after that.)

That night we have a barbecue using an old oil barrel, next to the sandbag bunker to which we are supposed to run if there are mortar attacks from beyond the outer perimeter. It all resembles a bad Vietnam movie. The spirit, however, is surprisingly good among the small UN band of volunteers led by Humanitarian Coordinator Ramiro Lopes da Silva, who survived the August bombing and is back to oversee future UN action. They are all determined to keep "the UN flag flying," as Larry Hollingsworth, the white-bearded veteran of the UN refugee and Oil-for-Food programs, puts it. The Swiss head of the ICRC, Pierre Gassman, whom I know well from Colombia, has joined our evening picnic. The ICRC, which had a group of delegates in Baghdad through the recent war, has deliberately kept a much lower profile than the UN, and believes it can avoid being targeted like us. As in so many other armed conflicts, the committee relies on all armed groups to respect the Red Cross and Red Crescent emblems. Gassman privately tells me that he hopes to raise the number of international staff in Iraq from thirty-five to fifty in the near future.

We spend hours with Iraqi and international colleagues discussing what my recommendations to Secretary-General Annan should be on the future work and presence of UN agencies in Iraq. Again I am struck by how the UN programs are surviving in extreme conditions. Some four million gallons of water are being transported every day to deprived areas of Baghdad, Basra, Mosul, and Kirkuk. Fuel and chemicals are likewise being delivered to support water and sewage facilities, many of which we are helping to rehabilitate. An immunization campaign reached about one million children last month, and a campaign to support more than 1,100 primary health care centers started in late September. Other programs include employment generation, rehabilitation in the electricity sector, assistance to internally displaced people, and support to agriculture. The operations depend on the efforts of more than four thousand Iraqi staff who now often work from their homes rather than going to the UN offices. We also work with several dozen NGOs and the Iraqi private sector.

We sleep well in the sandbag-covered containers that were trucked to the Canal Hotel compound after the August bombing. Returning the following day to Amman, I outline to the heads of UN and nongovernmental organizations that I hope "we can continue our presence and programs in Iraq, but those who return cannot anymore represent their own organization alone. In the future we must work as 'clusters' of organizations focusing on broad common themes and programs where experts on health, logistics, nutrition, water and sanitation, or administration of funds would go on behalf of the whole humanitarian community. It was wrong that we rushed back into Iraq, where there is no humanitarian crisis, with hundreds of provocatively visible and mostly Western staff."

Strohmeyer, Ulich, da Silva, and I travel from Amman to Madrid, where on October 23 the first major donor conference for the "reconstruction" of Iraq is taking place on the initiative of the United States. Kofi Annan decides, after much internal discussion, to go to Madrid, too, as do a large number of ministers from countries supporting the invasion and from those who were against it. Few in Madrid want to dwell on the growing threats to the stability of Iraq that I have just witnessed. All delegations seem to want to leave the acrimonious divisions of the past behind, and even the French and the Germans agree to generous European Union pledges for a new and democratic Iraq. Altogether an incredible $4.5 billion is pledged for rehabilitation and reconstruction in Iraq. Europeans and Japanese tell me they are eager to spend a lot of money through the UN. We may get as much money for Iraq, with its still limited humanitarian needs, as we have for all African wars and disasters combined.

I remind the delegates that United Nations humanitarian assistance to the Iraqi people is more than two decades old, and that "this continued commitment to assist always has, and always will be independent of the political circumstances at the time." I pledge that the UN will try to "start a new and important phase in our humanitarian operations as we help build a bridge from emergency operations to reconstruction and development," but stress that the "security environment will remain the single most important factor that will determine our ability to initiate, monitor, and carry out new assistance programs."

The day after we return to New York, a large bomb goes off in front of the Baghdad headquarters of the ICRC in an attack similar to the one against the UN. Two Iraqi Red Crescent members are dead. If the early morning bomb had been detonated a short while later, it could have killed many international staff. Not even the most impartial and neutral of humanitarian agencies has managed to stay beyond the reach of this new kind of international terror, one that systematically pursues soft-skin targets that offer much publicity, paralyzes vital programs, and thereby adds to the chaos and despair that is its goal. The Americans in the CPA had said when I visited Baghdad that the bombing campaign "is a sign of desperation" among the armed opposition. This opinion is repeated again and again by high administration officials in Washington, D.C., in the coming months, but nothing could be more wrong. Instead the violence, the terror, and the internal strife worsen.

At the end of October, Secretary-General Annan decides to close down the Canal Hotel compound and withdraw all international staff from Iraq. The bombing of the ICRC was the final straw. Larry Hollingsworth sends desperate e-mails arguing that it will be hard to return if we leave now; "the flag must not be lowered." But I am no longer putting up a fight. If terrorists have decided to target international relief again and again inside Iraq, the work that our small remaining staff can do is of little consequence compared to the risks. We will also scale down our presence in Amman, since it is another potential target for terrorists. No new programs are started, but none of the ongoing humanitarian operations are closed down, thanks to the resilience of Iraqi national staff and private Iraqi contractors directed remotely from Jordan, Kuwait, and various agency headquarters.

With all our colleagues out of the country, there is increased attention to whether the August bombing could have been prevented. Sergio Vieira de Mello himself had last July addressed the Security Council about the risks to the organization and acknowledged that "the United Nations' presence in Iraq remains vulnerable to any who would seek to target our organization, as recent events in Mosul, described in the secretary-general's report, illustrate. Our security continues to rely significantly on the reputation of the United Nations, our ability to demonstrate meaningfully that we are in Iraq to assist its people, and our independence."

In reality, little has been done to undertake physical protective measures. In the angry aftermath of the bombing, many wanted to pin down "who was responsible for what." The UN staff association played an active and, in my view, unconstructive role when it noisily demanded that managers be held "accountable" for what had happened. The staff association at the New York headquarters is a trade union dominated by office workers with little or no field experience. Their frustration about other justifiable management-employee issues has spilled over into a call for punitive action against "those responsible" for not preventing the tragedy. The critics concentrate on why the UN decided to go in without proper security assessments in late April and why it apparently was "business as usual" in and by the UN even after the Jordanian embassy and other international targets had been attacked earlier that summer.

Annan meets the criticisms by setting up a commission of inquiry with external experts, led by the respected Finnish statesman and former UN envoy, Martti Ahtisaari. The report from the panel contains scathing criticism of the lack of action by the chain of command in Baghdad and by security officials at headquarters. The panel asks for an "individual audit" of who was responsible for what, including the lack of protective barriers and walls and the lack of bomb-blast film on the windows of the building. My humanitarian colleagues who know the operation well are, however, highly critical of the quality of the report. They find factual errors and little understanding of the actual realities in Baghdad.

When the decision is made to do the individual audit, and when investigators subsequently recommend firing, demoting, or reprimanding three UN officials in Baghdad and New York, there is full-scale rebellion among the humanitarian veterans from Iraq inside OCHA. The most senior colleagues who are singled out for punishment, Tun Myat and Ramiro Lopes da Silva, are veterans in humanitarian work but are now seen as scapegoats for a system that failed to interpret the early warnings adequately and take appropriate action. Angry staff in OCHA organize a petition to the secretary-general signed by hundreds in the humanitarian agencies. They ask, "When did witch hunts become the fashion in this organization and why does not the secretary-general and deputy secretary-general publicly acknowledge that the buck stops with them and key decisions were taken by them as for when, how, and with how many the UN would go to Iraq?"

I agree with much of the criticism. A bad process leads to individual colleagues paying the price. The system must learn from this. However, now we see managers so afraid of not being careful enough that they retreat into risk aversion in conflict situations where you cannot assist and protect civilians without some degree of risk. Retreating to bunkers, evacuating staff, and avoiding contact with the people in the crossfire is not the way we should work. In contrast, the ICRC stays on in Baghdad even after the bombing against them; they learn to live with the risk.

In the years that follow, all of the grim predictions from the visits in 2003 turn out to be true. The security situation continues to worsen and in October 2006, exactly three years after my last visit, humanitarian agencies still working in Iraq again ask me to go public on the carnage in the country. I give press briefings in Geneva and Washington, D.C. Among my statements: "The violence inside Iraq has dramatically worsened as armed sectarian militias and death squads murder an average of one hundred people every day. They are policemen and their recruits, judges, lawyers, journalists; and increasingly, they are women targeted for so-called honor killing. Revenge killings between Shiites and Sunni armed groups are also totally out of control." My report is based on information from our staff inside Iraq and in neighboring countries. It includes daily reports from morgues, hospitals, and displacement camps.

The briefing material I get from the small international staff we now have in the Green Zone in Baghdad is worse than I expected. In less than eight months in 2006, at least 315,000 people have fled their homes, driven by military operations or sectarian violence that escalated after the Shiite shrine in Samarra was bombed in February. By 2007 there were more than 2.2 million internally displaced persons within Iraq, as well as more than two million Iraqi refugees in neighboring countries. Iraq is experiencing a serious "brain drain," with reports that some universities and hospitals in Baghdad have lost up to 80 percent of their professional staff. In total, a third or more of Iraqi professionals are estimated to have left their country in recent years. Toward the end of 2007 there was a hopeful decline in violence due to local talks with insurgents, fewer arms flowing in from Iran, and a U.S. troop "surge."

I end the press conference in 2006 with the following: "Our appeal goes to everybody who can curb the violence. Religious leaders, ethnic leaders, and cultural leaders have to see that this has spiraled totally out of control—Sunnis being pressured out of Shiite areas, Shiites out of Sunni areas. Exchanges of people in the tens of thousands are happening. That means that those who remain as minorities in areas with such 'ethnic engineering,' as some call it, become increasingly vulnerable. And you have then an accelerating trend of mass movement of people. It has to stop and all of those who can influence it must do their utmost to stop it."

In 2006 and 2007 there is, finally, a willingness even in U.S. political and public opinion to see the reality in Iraq. In no other place on earth, Darfur and the Congo included, have so many lives been lost to violence as in Iraq after 2004. Moreover, it was glaringly clear as early as late 2003 that the American and British arguments for the war—to rid Saddam's Iraq of weapons of mass destruction and an al-Qaeda terrorist presence—were false. The chemical, biological, and nuclear weapons programs had already been either destroyed or shelved in the 1990s. And al-Qaeda got its first serious foothold in Iraq only *after* the invasion. It was equally clear in 2003 and 2004 that the invasion led to a nation-building process that failed as Iraq headed for horrific internal strife and widespread terror against innocent civilians. These bitter realities led to soul-searching by the United Kingdom and most other European coalition allies in 2003 and 2004. However, the trauma lingering in the United States from the September 11, 2001, terrorist attacks seemed to prevent the same openness to the facts.

In October 2006, an X-ray on a post-Saddam Iraq engulfed in violence was provided by experts at the Johns Hopkins Bloomberg School of Public Health working with al-Mustansiriya University in Baghdad. Two years earlier, a mortality study undertaken for March 2003–September 2004 found a staggering 100,000 excess deaths— beyond normal mortality levels—attributed to the war in Iraq. The massive new survey in May–July 2006 looked at 1,849 households with 12,800 individuals. Each family was interviewed and death certificates were studied. While a large survey done by the Iraqi Health Ministry and the WHO, published January 2008, concluded that an estimated 151,000 Iraqis had died in the first forty post-invasion months, the John Hopkins study concluded that an estimated

655,000 Iraqis died as a consequence of the war in the three years and four months that followed the 2003 invasion. The vast majority, 601,000, died from blunt violence. Gunfire was the most common cause of death, but deaths due to car bombings were on the increase.

I have absorbed many mortality studies through my years as global emergency relief coordinator. Three were particularly significant: from Darfur in 2004, from the Democratic Republic of Congo in 2003 and 2005, and Iraq in 2006. In Darfur, where an estimated 10,000 civilians, mostly children, died each month in the summer of 2004, our UN and Sudanese Health Ministry teams found that the majority died from preventable disease and acute malnutrition due to the conflict and the government-sponsored terror campaigns. In the Congo, the survey by the International Crisis Group found that as many as 1,200 died per day, again mostly due to preventable disease in a chaotic and brutal war. Both the Darfur and the Congo studies were accepted in Washington, D.C., without hesitation. The Darfur study was even an important premise when the Bush administration declared that the Sudanese government was responsible for genocide in the western provinces of the country, and started a massive relief operation in partnership with the UN. But the Iraq study, which is more representative, was belittled and ridiculed by the same American authorities. They refused to see the real extent of the violence that has torn Iraqi society apart since the U.S.-led invasion.

The story of Iraq—in all its multifaceted conflict, strife, hope, and tragedy—is partly one of impotent multilateralism, but it is first and foremost a damning verdict on the limits and pitfalls of unilateralism. Multilateral weapons inspectors were forced to withdraw before they could finish their inspections, so a unilateral invasion could prove that the bilateral intelligence that led to the war was wrong. The bitter lesson of Iraq is that the United Nations in general and the Security Council in particular cannot allow themselves to be paralyzed in the face of member states' noncompliance with international norms and regional peace and stability. There is an ob-

ligation inherent in being a Security Council nation to reach common ground and take collective action. Once massive military action
is unleashed by any nation or groups of nations it cannot be undone,
and the consequences of force may be very different than what was
expected. An invasion can end a dictatorship and crush old security
regimes, but building a new, democratic nation cannot and will not
be done from the Pentagon in Washington, D.C. Only coherent efforts from many Iraqi communities, from neighboring states, from
the UN and the U.S.-led coalition can in the end lead to the political reconciliation that the improved security situation has yet to
produce.

3.

No End to Violence in Colombia

I⊤ WAS an ordinary weekday evening in September 1975 in my childhood home in Stavanger, Norway. I had bicycled back from handball practice and eaten the usual evening meal, sandwiches and a half liter of milk, as I watched the evening news. A Catholic priest, Rafael García Herreros, was being interviewed on Norwegian television. The subject was social justice in one of the world's most violent societies, Colombia. I listened attentively. Latin America was my biggest fascination. I had written my essay in secondary school on the life and revolutionary struggle of Che Guevara in Cuba and Bolivia. In high school I had founded an Amnesty International group and now I was involved in campaigns for the release of political prisoners in Pinochet's Chile, and against torture in military-ruled Uruguay. García Herreros looked into the camera and said, "I would hereby like to invite Norwegian youth with a social conscience to come and help me here in Colombia."

This was the invitation I had been waiting for. It was as if the priest knew I was sitting in my comfortable middle-class home in peaceful Stavanger and awaiting a challenge. The next day I got the address of García Herreros's organization, El Minuto de Dios (God's Minute), and wrote a letter of thanks for the invitation. In my one year's worth of high school Spanish I described myself as an active seventeen-year-old campaigning for human rights who sang bass in a youth choir and loved sports. It ended with an appeal: "Take me. I graduate from high school next summer and I am more than ready for something very different from my overprotected Norwegian affluence. I will work as a volunteer with anything, anywhere in Colombia."

One month later I received an answer: "We would like to invite you to come to Bogota, where we will identify an appropriate project for you in the countryside." "This will change my life," I thought as I translated the letter I held with trembling hands. My parents knew how much it would mean to me to realize the dream of living with those who worked for social justice in one of the greatest dramas of Latin America. My mother was a housewife who had returned to university after her three children had grown up. My father was president of a district college and a social democratic politician who would, a few months later, join the Norwegian cabinet as minister of education. They had brought up my brother, my sister, and me in the belief that we should recognize how privileged we were in our peaceful welfare state. They backed my plan to travel and volunteer in a third world country even though they didn't know how dangerous the work in war-torn Colombia would be. (Now I know. Our two daughters will not have our support to do the same.)

The next summer I worked thirteen hours a day, seven days a week as a lifeguard and caretaker at a public outdoor pool in Stavanger. I earned enough to travel with three fellow graduates by air to Canada and then by Greyhound bus to Chicago, where we bought a big used station wagon for $1,200. We began an unforgettable three-month tour through the United States and Central America. Previously we had only driven at home in Stavanger, population eighty thousand, but here we were on the American highway going everywhere: to New York, Washington, D.C., Atlanta, New Orleans, through Texas to the Grand Canyon, Las Vegas, San Francisco, and down California's beautiful coastal road to Los Angeles and the Mexican border.

The U.S.-Mexican border is one of the few places where the industrialized North and the developing South meet. After a twenty-minute drive through Tijuana we were stopped by Mexican police who noticed our U.S. license plates. We had driven "irresponsibly" through a crossing, they said. We could either spend a few days waiting for our case to come up at a local court or instead pay a "direct fine" to the policemen then and there. We chose the latter option and hurried into the real Mexico beyond the border belt. Like the United States, Mexico had so much to offer that we spent a full month exploring.

We then traveled to tiny Belize on the Caribbean coast, where we nearly ruined our faithful station wagon by pushing through on a bad track to the as-yet-unexcavated ancient Mayan ruins of Tikal, in Guatemala. The Guatemalan president was a right-wing army general of Norwegian heritage, Kjell Laugerud. The country, even poorer than Mexico, was engulfed in civil war and had been struck recently by a devastating earthquake. The relief programs that Norwegian Church Aid initiated that year were the embryo of a peace process I would actively take part in many years later. Indeed, in 1996, exactly twenty years after we drove through Guatemala, I presided over the formal cease-fire ceremony between the government and Marxist guerrillas in the Oslo Town Hall, which marked the end to a generation of internal armed conflict.

We went on to El Salvador, Honduras, Nicaragua, and Costa Rica and reached the end of the international highway in Panama. We had covered nearly twenty thousand miles on the road. We had slept in the car, in a tent, and in cheap motels. Nearly everywhere, in both North America and Central America, we had been received with great friendliness. Only in Nicaragua, where the infamous U.S.-installed Somoza family ruled, were we and our American car cursed at as we drove through towns and villages.

Latin America appeared at the time a continent of conflict. On the one side were brutal right-wing and military-dominated dictatorships supported by a tiny economic elite and the United States. On the other side was a left-leaning popular resistance. Later I would meet enough Marxist guerrilla leaders and politicians to see that there are, as is nearly always the case in war, more shades of gray and black than there is black and white.

In Panama I parted with my high school friends, who turned around to drive all the way back to Los Angeles and sell what was left of our sturdy vehicle. There are no roads connecting Panama to South America over the wild Darien Gap, so I flew on to the El Dorado Airport in Bogota to start my year as a volunteer with El Minuto de Dios in Colombia. I had been looking forward to meeting Father García Herreros and his enthusiastic young followers.

In the midst of Colombia's conflict and misery this priest had become a national symbol of compassion. As the country's first televangelist he was using his popularity and moral authority to create social justice projects for the least privileged. Every year he persuaded the president and his wife and the rest of the social and economic elite to contribute handsomely to El Minuto's social work and appear at the annual banquet, where a glass of wine, a piece of bread, and a brief sermon "in memory of the life of Jesus and in solidarity with the poor" was served. I thought the handsome and charismatic man with curly, gray hair was the best in humankind. García Herreros was in turn fascinated by the young, blond Norwegian who had come all the way from the "North Pole" to volunteer on the basis of a one-sentence invitation in a television interview.

My first month was spent in a model borough on the outskirts of Bogota where García Herreros had funded hundreds of three-room apartments in small houses given to poor families from the slums. I stayed with five young Catholic "brothers" in one of the family units. We shared food, clothes, and books. Clean clothes returned from the neighborhood laundry were dropped in a box from which we took whatever fit. Whoever had money, mostly me, bought some food that we prepared together.

In December and January I worked in a peasant cooperative in Northern Santander province. Here, in the mountains north of the capital, I realized for the first time the extent and brutality of the civil wars that had raged for so long in Colombia; even then they were the biggest and longest-running conflicts in the Western Hemisphere. When we worked in the fields or visited the remotest small farms we heard again and again stories about the cruelties of the civil war in the 1950s, "La Violencia," and the successor guerrilla wars. La Violencia was triggered by the assassination of the Liberal presidential candidate Jorge Eliécer Gaitán on April 9, 1948.

Gaitán was hugely popular and a favorite to win the upcoming election. The day he was shot he was supposed to meet a Cuban student delegation led by the young Fidel Castro. Riots in Bogota later became nationwide terror campaigns between "conservatives" and "liberals" that lasted up until the year I was born, 1957. Every family I met in the Santander Mountains had had one or more family members killed in the strife. The war formally ended when the two dominant parties agreed to rotate the presidency between them every four years until 1974, two years before I came to Colombia. Nearly everyone I worked with in the fields had family or friends in the army and, just as frequently, in the two left-wing guerrilla movements, the FARC (the Revolutionary Armed Forces of Colombia) or the ELN (the National Liberation Army). Many years later I would be the first United Nations representative to meet two feared and legendary guerrilla leaders, FARC's Manuel Marulanda, alias "Tirofijo" (Sureshot), and ELN's Nicolás Rodríguez, alias "El Gabino" (the Kid).

For Christmas and New Year's I took the bus back to Bogota and my "brothers" in El Minuto de Dios. Every week I wrote to and received letters from my parents, who had moved to Oslo, where my father was serving in the cabinet. The day before Christmas a letter arrived with the sad news that my dear grandfather had died. I had never before felt as lonely and sad as I did that Christmas.

In late January, Father García Herreros asked whether I was ready for a new, big "challenge." "Yes," I answered, full of anticipation. "In that case," he said, "we leave next week to the Motilones, an Indian tribe who live by Catatumbo River in the jungles at our Venezuelan border. You can live with them for one month with a promising student of theology who needs to learn how to tackle tough challenges."

The expedition to the Motilone Indians was a journey to a different world and age. First, we took the express bus for a full day to García Herreros's city of birth, Cúcuta, in the tropical northeast. Bogota is about 8,500 feet above sea level and stays around 65 degrees Fahrenheit, whereas here, close to sea level, the heat was constant. We stayed overnight in the house of García Herreros's sister and continued on the next day with a smaller bus on bad roads to the small town of Tibú, where oil companies were organizing their exploration of the promising petroleum reserves in the rain forest. From Tibú a pickup truck took us for the last few hours along a crude road to a small trading village at the Catatumbo River. It looked like a settlement in a bad cowboy movie. The chaotic collection of huts sold everything from liquor and Coca-Cola to medicines, guns, and prostitutes.

It was already late afternoon when we went upstream in a rented canoe made from a single, large log with a single outboard engine at the rear. It was a remarkably beautiful journey deep inside the rain forest; the sun peeked from between the trees that were about sixty-five feet tall and surrounded by smaller trees, bushes, and flowers. We saw new small farms along the riverside where mestizos of mixed indigenous and European heritage were wearing sombreros against the blazing sun while working.

"We are soon there," García Herreros announced as the river took a wide turn. "I came here for the first time ten years ago as the first white man who wanted to help the beleaguered Indians. The foreign oil companies were buying the rain forest, building electric fences against the Motilones, and hiring men with guns to hunt down those who were shooting bows and arrows at the bulldozers that had entered their hunting grounds. We managed to stop some of the excesses. We bought some land and secured other areas for the Indians. But we made a tragic mistake. We did not know that we brought the common cold and other bacillus the Indians had no resistance against. In the group we are about to visit all the adults died. Only the children, who are now young adults with their own children, survived our diseases."

At the next bend in the river, I saw an open space in which stood a large collective hut with a roof and no walls and several smaller surrounding huts. The jungle had been cut and burned all along the river. In the last sunlight I saw corn, bananas, cocoa, and yucca roots growing in the ashes of the rain forest. There was a joyous reunion. The priest and the young Indians had not seen one another for two years. "I will unfortunately have to return tomorrow," father said, "but I would appreciate if you could give hospitality for one month to my student Guillermo and my young friend Jan who comes, as you will see, from the other side of the world."

That night we sat late around an open fire and ate from a big soup casserole into which had gone a couple of hens, some eggs, pieces of meat from various wild animals, cooking bananas, yucca roots, and some other stuff I didn't recognize and wouldn't want to know about. The next morning Father García Herreros returned down river and that same evening Guillermo made it clear that this life was too "primitive" for him. "I cannot live for a month in a place where you use any pair of bushes as a toilet, eat the same goulash every evening with illiterate Indians and drink dangerous and polluted water. I'll return to Bogotá at the first opportunity. You may stay if you want to." Two days later he got a ride down to the trading post to start the long journey back. I was all by myself among people who spoke limited Spanish, in one of Colombia's wildest jungle areas, with guerrilla warfare, cocaine production, and epidemic disease. If anyone fell ill it could take days to get to the nearest clinic. If guerrilla or paramilitary groups were to kidnap me for ransom, a frequent occurrence in the region, it would take even longer before anyone outside the forest would know. I realized that my childhood dream of living something very different was more than fulfilled.

Due to their frequent clashes with the Spanish colonial masters, pioneer farmers, oil explorers, and others who invaded their jungles, the Motilones had gotten a reputation as fierce and dangerous fighters. I found them to be in fact remarkably friendly and kind. They took me along when they hunted with bow and arrow or fished with spears. We worked most days clearing the rain forest with machete and ax. Agriculture here at the frontiers of human existence meant that the cleared jungle debris was left drying in the sun for some days and then burned. The corn and the banana and cocoa trees were planted in the ashes. Only two harvests of corn could be done before they had to let the jungle come back, because there was no fertilizer and the rain forest bed lacked minerals. If there had been fertilizer for the Indians, development projects, and law enforcement against the illegal coca production, the beautiful rain forest would have been saved.

After some days and evenings by the campfires I was slowly accepted as a friend. They appreciated that I worked with them in the sun with a long machete, ate their food, and slept next to them in my own hammock. When we had other food than the traditional all-you-have-in-the-casserole soup, we usually ate iguana reptile eggs we found in the sand along the river, fish from the river, or game from the forest. One evening an enormous rat–like animal was cooked. The entire head was served on my plate since I was "their guest of honor." It was the only time anywhere that I did not eat what I was served. I made up a lie that "in my family the tradition is that the guest should return the best food to the hunter." This was accepted as an honorable gesture and the strongest hunter ate the head with gusto.

After supper and on Sundays I provided "school" for the children and grown-ups with some notebooks and pencils I had found at the trading post. When we went down in their canoe to sell cocoa beans and bananas on Saturdays, I could see that the Indians were easily tricked into selling cheap. And they would fall for high prices and bad quality when they were the ones buying. So I encouraged them to guard their culture. The young adults spoke Motilon among themselves, but halting Spanish to their children. Having lost their parents to disease, they had not been taught to take pride in their heritage. I sang Norwegian and Swedish songs to them and asked in return that they sing their "Canto de las Flechas (Song of the Arrows)," which is part of the ritual when a boy is accepted as a man and given a secret name for life that only one selected friend can know. A fully grown male Indian would be about four foot three and dark-skinned, while I was six feet tall with light blond coloring. They had never seen anything as strange as me. One day they mustered enough courage to ask me if I was plagued with headaches "since I had to see the world through blue eyes."

It was an unforgettable and happy month with the Indians. But the day before my month was up and the canoe from the trading post was to come for me, I fell ill. It was as if my body understood that the challenge was soon to be over. I had slowly gotten stomach parasites and my digestion was totally gone; I feared another disease. I had followed some male government nurses on an antimalaria campaign up and down the river one day. Along the river many died every year, especially children and the elderly, because of this terrible blood parasite. I took my own tablets every week, but I saw how difficult it is to teach an illiterate local population that medicines should be taken preventively. It was only when people fell ill that they took the pills, and by then it was often too late.

As I bade an emotional farewell to my friends in the Motilone collective, I felt the fever coming on strong. I remember little from the journey by truck and bus back to Cúcuta and the house of García Herreros's sister. I could not see clearly when I collapsed in a real bed for the first time in five weeks. Three days later I woke up and the doctor could tell that the fever was gone. His medicines, including the strong but now prohibited drug Enterovioform, had done its job.

In April 1977 I left Bogota, Father García Herreros, and all my friends. The last night I was awakened in the middle of the night by a choir of friends from El Minuto de Dios singing in the street outside our open bedroom window. It was my plan to work my way back to Norway on merchant ships, but after the first leg on a small Colombian freighter to Aruba the problems started. When I left the ship the port police defined me as an immigrant worker and said I either had to produce a ticket to Europe that same day or I would go to jail. It took all the remaining wrinkled and dirty traveler's checks I had carried in a cloth bag on my chest for ten months to buy a ticket to Amsterdam and Oslo. I avoided prison in Aruba and was on my way to a new life as a student in Norway and then a year as a spokesman during my military service.

I have returned many times to beautiful, magical, tragic Colombia, where it always seems like there is more drama in twenty-four hours than there could be in twenty-four years in Norway. Colombia has the largest war, the biggest narcotics problem, the worst human rights abuses, and the greatest number of displaced persons in the Western Hemisphere. Yet to me it also has the most inspiring and intense people, the most wonderful natural features, the best-preserved Spanish colonial architecture, and the most beautiful beaches.

I went back for the first time to see my friends in El Minuto de Dios in 1981, when I was vice chair of Amnesty International's Executive Committee, which was responsible for growing the organization in the third world. I crisscrossed the country for a month connecting with Colombians who had contacted Amnesty to see whether it could and should set up a membership section in their strife-torn land. The guerrilla movements had strengthened since I had left, and not just FARC, the largest. ELN, now led by the Spanish priest Manuel Pérez, and the student and urban guerrilla group M-19 could both stage spectacular and violent operations nationwide. A few months before I returned, M-19 had occupied the Dominican Republic's embassy as it hosted a National Day reception in commemoration of that nation's 1844 independence from Haiti. M-19 seized over a hundred people as hostages, including ambassadors from the United States and other countries along with politicians and businessmen. Four years later the same group would garner world attention when it occupied the entire Supreme Court in downtown Bogota with some three hundred employees and visitors inside. Colombian armed forces stormed the building in an operation that led to the deaths of more than a hundred hostages, soldiers, and guerrillas.

Right-wing paramilitary groups had formed all over the country to fight the guerrillas. These groups were condoned or actively supported by landowners, businessmen, and elements in the armed forces. The day before I was to have a meeting in Bogota to inform the Colombian High Command of Amnesty's plans in Colombia, I received an urgent call from our headquarters in London: "Do not go to the meeting with the military tomorrow. We have gotten a tip that it may be dangerous. There are undisputed links between the army and the paramilitary groups and Amnesty is now issuing a report on that linkage!"

I carried long lists of students, academics, and human rights activists who wanted to start Amnesty groups in Colombia when I returned to London and Oslo in late 1981. But we were forced to conclude that it would be too dangerous to set up a visible Amnesty structure in the country while our international movement was campaigning against the atrocities committed by the army, guerrillas, and paramilitary groups. Trade unionists, peasant leaders, politicians, human rights activists, and indigenous leaders were killed or abducted every day in Colombia, which had become known as the most dangerous country in the world.

Some of my friends were killed. Héctor Abad Gómez, the president of the Human Rights Committee of Colombia's second city, Medellin, was perhaps the most impressive of my Amnesty contacts. We spent a long day and night together talking about how to better protect human rights in Colombia and in Medellin, the most violent city in the country. "We have to work together to protect freedom of expression and human rights in a place like this," Héctor Abad told me. "The counterforces are getting stronger and stronger; there are simply too many political extremists, too many drug barons, too few incorrupt police, and far too many guns." We kept in touch, until my friend was gunned down by men with machine pistols in the streets of Medellin in 1987.

In 1995 I returned once again to Colombia, this time as state secretary in the Norwegian Ministry for Foreign Affairs. I met President Ernesto Samper in the impressive Presidential Palace and his foreign minister, María Emma Mejía, in the beautiful Spanish colonial building. They both knew of my interest in Colombia and my roles in the ongoing, successful Guatemala peace process and in brokering the Oslo Accord between Israel and the Palestine Liberation Organization (PLO) in 1993. Their question was simple and direct: Would Norway be willing to help in possible future negotiations between the government and the FARC and ELN? M-19 had already demobilized along with parts of the FARC a few years earlier, but several hundred of those who had tried peaceful and democratic political work had been assassinated by the right-wing paramilitary "anticommunist" groups. I confirmed that Norway was indeed able and willing to undertake peace facilitation if both sides asked for it.

A few months later the Norwegian ambassador to Colombia was among the international "witnesses" when captured soldiers were released by the FARC inside a large area that Samper had ordered demilitarized. But it was evident that Samper was too weak to engage in a peace process with the guerrillas. He was embroiled in scandal when it was revealed that the large narcotics cartels in Medellin and Cali had given money to his presidential election campaign. Audiotapes allegedly documenting the transfer of drug money were sent to and later published by Samper's Conservative political opponent, Andrés Pastrana, who had barely lost the vote count in 1994. The United States had even denied a visa to Samper. I saw Pastrana over dinner in Bogota's old city during that visit. He had taken the job of director for the UN University's International Leadership Academy in Amman, Jordan, of which I was an advisory board member. Pastrana told me he might well be a presidential candidate again in 1998 and asked, as Samper had, if I could help peace efforts with the FARC and ELN.

Two years later, in October 1997, the social democratic government resigned from power in Norway and I left my position as state secretary after seven years in the Ministry of Foreign Affairs. I had hoped for a few weeks of relaxation before my next job, but had barely arrived at my cabin in the Norwegian mountains when I was asked to return to Oslo to meet the Colombian deputy planning minister, Arturo García. García had come to ask that I become a peace adviser and co-author of a series of studies called "La Paz es Rentable (Peace is Profitable)," which aimed to describe how a peace process might be organized and how a peaceful Colombia would prosper. "We realize that a peace process is unrealistic before Samper leaves next year, but we can at least prepare the ground for the next president," the affable deputy minister told me. "Why should Colombia remain the only country in Latin America locked in a vicious internal conflict when all other countries in our continent have escaped from their cold war conflicts?" One month later I traveled back to Colombia for the first of dozens of visits over four years.

In June 1998, Andrés Pastrana triumphed in his second attempt
to become president. During the campaign his friend and representative, the lawyer Victor G. Ricardo, met with FARC's leader Marulanda at an undisclosed venue in the Colombian countryside. The
meeting caused a sensation. It was organized by a former Conservative senator, and friend of the Pastrana family, who in one of Colombia's multiple paradoxes had maintained a trusted line of
communication with the Marxist group. When, a week before Election Day, Pastrana published photos of the meeting and issued a
statement that he would seek peace in direct talks with the FARC,
he built his first decisive lead over his Liberal opponent. Colombians were exhausted with a generation of war and grasped the hope
for peace. Indeed, the year before some ten million Colombians had
voted in favor of a peaceful settlement of the conflict in a referendum organized in municipal elections.

Just three days after Pastrana's victory I arrived in Bogota on one
of my trips for the "Peace is Profitable" studies. Pastrana asked to see
me immediately when I arrived at his festive election headquarters,
and so I bypassed the long lines of well-wishers and supporters waiting to congratulate the new head of state. The president-elect was
full of optimism, having received some six million votes, more than
any other candidate ever in a Colombia known for low participation in elections. I had from our first encounters taken a liking to
Pastrana. He was the son of a former Colombian president, and with
his boyish charm he always expressed new ideas with enthusiasm.
He had been a popular television journalist and won awards for programs on the country's powerful narcotics cartels. In 1988 he had
been kidnapped by groups associated with Latin America's foremost
drug lord, Pablo Escobar, and nearly lost his life when he was liberated in a dramatic police operation.

Pastrana had heard me lecture on "ten lessons from ten peace
processes" at the UN Academy in Amman when he was still its director. In his election headquarters he again affirmed that he wanted

cooperation: "Jan, it was my peace platform that gave me this victory. Now you must help me achieve peace in this war-torn country. The models for negotiations that you lectured about are needed in our talks with the FARC and later also with the ELN." Pastrana asked Ricardo and his election campaign leader and future minister for foreign affairs, Guillermo Fernández de Soto, to join us. He asked me to outline a scheme for the future peace efforts based on my experiences in Central America, the Middle East, and elsewhere.

"This will be an exceedingly difficult process. In such a violent and unpredictable climate and with so many counterforces you have to deliver some result while you still have election momentum," I concluded in my briefing. "You must waste no time in setting up an effective structure on both sides that can produce draft texts for approval at the negotiation table. It is equally important that you create a permanent but confidential back channel between yourself and Marulanda to manage the many coming crises and to prepare for and secure the implementation of confidence-building measures. Peace work is one percent vision and ninety-nine percent hard organizational labor." Pastrana agreed: "This is exactly what we need to do," he said. Fernández de Soto nodded. The only one who was not paying attention was the man who needed advice most. Ricardo excused himself repeatedly to answer his cell phone. When Ricardo was named high commissioner for peace, his reluctance to delegate and difficulty in organizing a full-scale peace process would hurt Pastrana's peace effort.

Pastrana asked me to report directly to him, the foreign minister, and the high commissioner for peace. Still based in Oslo, I started to work nearly full-time with the Colombia expert in the UN Development Programme (UNDP), James LeMoyne, a former correspondent in Latin America for the *New York Times*. In the coming weeks and months, at the request of Pastrana and de Soto, we produced a series of detailed proposals for how the peace process should be organized. In their first, and direct, encounter in July, Marulanda and Pastrana had decided to spend ninety days organizing the talks before negotiations would start. The deadline came and went, but neither side was ready to start real negotiations. High Commissioner Ricardo operated on his own with his cell phone and without a proper staff structure.

A series of deep controversies ensued over where and how the talks should be organized. Pastrana had agreed to the FARC request for a demilitarized zone consisting of sparsely populated grazing land and forests in southern Colombia, but they could not agree on the size of the zone and the degree of redeployment of the Colombian Armed Forces. In the end Pastrana realized that there would be no talks if he did not agree to withdraw all military and police from an area larger than Switzerland. For the FARC this was a "nonnegotiable" demand, based on its experience of assassinations of demobilized guerrillas and attacks on their representatives in previous talks. For the rank and file in the Colombian military it was, of course, equally unacceptable to "give away" a large piece of the candy to an illegal armed group that had not agreed to a cease-fire and thus could use the zone to rest, regroup, and organize criminal activity with guaranteed protection from all law enforcement agencies. In the end the army was ordered to leave the entire base of the Special Forces Battalion in the only town in the region, San Vicente. This was the final straw for several generals who protested publicly that the army was "humiliated" after having fought many bloody battles with the FARC in that region.

Since my first visits as a peace adviser in Colombia I had sought contact with the military high command. It is one of the basic lessons of Central America that the military can undermine any peace effort if it feels isolated and has no say in the process. For Pastrana these first confrontations with his own military were costly: many leading officials turned permanently hostile to the process. Several civil-military meetings were organized, some generals retired, and in December the battalion was withdrawn. We spent many nights in the old base as it was converted into a headquarters for the government representatives and for talking with the FARC in the zone.

A lot of time was lost in 1998 and 1999 because of the inflexible stands of the FARC, which had never compromised on anything, and because of poor organizational skills on the government side. On January 7, 1999, the demilitarized peace zone was ready to be officially opened in San Vicente. I was asked to participate along with LeMoyne and the corps of foreign diplomats in Bogota. The evening before we talked at length with Andrés Pastrana in the old officers' bar in the converted battalion base. Pastrana, who is a courageous man, had brought his young son and had left his security service in Bogota to demonstrate his confidence in the FARC's word of honor and in the peace process.

The next day we assembled in a blistering sun in the town square, where a tented platform had been erected and fitted with three white plastic tables—one in the middle with two chairs for Pastrana and Marulanda and one table on each side for the negotiation teams. Government ministers, ambassadors, the cultural elite of Colombia, and a hundred journalists were surrounded by heavily armed FARC fighters who were responsible for security. Less than an hour before the ceremony was to start, Pastrana was told by a FARC representative that Marulanda would not participate, "for security reasons." After some hesitation Pastrana decided that he would, but that Marulanda's empty chair was not to be removed. The president's speech was somber, eloquent, and forward-looking: "Let us put the war and the devastation behind us and look toward a new just and peaceful Colombia for all."

The FARC speech was another example of never losing an opportunity to lose an opportunity. For nearly an hour a commander read Marulanda's speech, which contained no details on what the guerrillas now wished to achieve, but lots of accusations against previous governments and groups in Colombia, including a detailed list of all the livestock the FARC had lost when its headquarters was attacked at the end of a peace effort in the 1980s. The next day the leading daily in the capital ran this headline: "FARC's main demand: Return the stolen chicken!"

After the national anthem was sung by the government and guerrilla sides alike, James LeMoyne and I approached one of the key guerrilla leaders, Raul Reyes, their external relations head. James, who had had previous contact with Reyes, asked without courtesies whether we could see him tonight since there was "much to discuss." The commander nodded slowly: "If you can fix transport we can meet at the ranch. I will stay overnight. Come at six P.M."

With one of Ricardo's cars and a driver we headed out of town that afternoon, riding through endless grazing land dotted by large trees and occasional herds of cattle. Just before we came to the white ranch house with a red tile roof, and surrounded by impressive trees, we were stopped by FARC sentries. "Wait by your car," a young guerrilla soldier ordered us as another entered the house to announce our presence. The FARC soldiers and commanders had their automatic guns at hand. Just before Reyes appeared, two civilians left the building. We recognized them as the Cuban diplomats who had taken part in the ceremony.

"Come. Let's sit down on the terrace. It is hot and may soon start to rain," Reyes said as he shook our hands with his rifle over his shoulder. "Why didn't Marulanda come today? It was a bad signal for the process to start with an empty chair," we queried. "The FARC Central Command had no choice. We had several sources swearing that paramilitaries would infiltrate the crowd and shoot our leader," Reyes responded.

It seemed surreal. The young head of state brings no bodyguards and his young son to a town that is totally in the hands of a large FARC force, and old Marulanda does not dare to leave his hideout. Only forty years on the run can explain this kind of paranoia.

For several hours that evening Reyes, James, and I sat on the terrace and discussed how the negotiations should be run and what the international community could do to facilitate them. I was struck by how vague the FARC demands for Colombia's future were. Reyes was one of FARC's few intellectuals and it was worrisome that he did not list any concrete measures the guerrillas wanted to see as part of a peace deal. After more than a generation of struggle it seemed unclear what they were fighting for. The survival of the movement, internal loyalties, revenge, and fear of enemies now appeared to be their priorities. Reyes did ask many questions about what the United Nations and the international community as a whole could offer Colombia, the FARC, and the peace process. Unlike the Guatemala guerrillas and the PLO, however, the FARC was clearly in no hurry to end the war. They wanted a long process that might lead to deals that were not yet clear to them.

All of 1999 was wasted on interminable discussions, on "talks about talks." The established demilitarized zone and a brief Christmas truce were the only visible outcomes of the process launched on January 7. With a growing number of allegations that the zone was used for drug trafficking, for planning attacks elsewhere, and even as a safe place to store people the FARC had kidnapped for ransom, the process started to be increasingly unpopular.

The new Colombian administration and its "Peace Diplomacy" were more successful elsewhere. Europe staunchly supported the talks and offered increased humanitarian funding. The Clinton administration, which had banned President Samper from visiting the United States, decided to invest in a major military and civilian support package for Colombia. The main purpose of this $1.6 billion "Plan Colombia" was to roll back the exploding narcotics trafficking through Colombia to North America. The Pastrana administration presented the new package as a kind of "Marshall Plan" that would invest in alternative development projects for communities that had been producing coca for cocaine and poppies for heroin. Left-leaning politicians, NGOs, and guerrillas saw a plan for a "gringo" military invasion—more U.S. military advisers, antinarcotics brigades, and Black Hawk helicopters.

In September 1999, Pastrana visited Secretary-General Kofi Annan in New York and proposed that I be appointed UN special envoy to Colombia to direct and coordinate UN assistance to the peace process and international assistance to Colombia. Annan agreed to the post on the undersecretary-general level and that I should be offered the position. The UN had for many years tried unsuccessfully to play a political role as both government and guerrillas ignored the organization. I was happy to accept since it was not easy to be a peace adviser when Colombia's High Commissioner Ricardo and his disorganized team made no use of any concrete proposals James LeMoyne and I offered.

Earlier that summer, Kofi Annan had called me on my cell phone as I was hiking near my family's mountain cabin in Norway. He had asked whether I would be available as his special representative and peace envoy to Cyprus. My friend, the U.S. presidential envoy for Cyprus, Richard Holbrooke, had put my name forward. But the support of the United States and Britain had made the Turkish-Cypriot government in the island's northern region nervous that I would be too proactive, and it vetoed my appointment. In Colombia I knew I would be received by the parties, but there was still a problem. Both Pastrana and the Clinton administration wanted me to promote the controversial Plan Colombia. I knew that any connection to the U.S.-Colombian effort, with its controversial aerial spraying of coca fields and its extensive military investment, would make it impossible for me to function as an independent and impartial UN envoy. Kofi Annan agreed. Plan Colombia was never part of my job description or my activities.

On my first visit to Bogota as UN envoy in December 1999 I told Pastrana that I had to establish direct and continuous contact with the leaderships of the FARC and the ELN if I were to be effective in my new job. "I will speak to Victor G," said Pastrana. "All

contact with the FARC is through him." In January 2000 I was back
with LeMoyne, who was now my UN deputy, and Andrés Salazar,
the young Spanish-American desk officer in the secretary-general's
Department of Political Affairs, which serves UN political envoys.

"I think you are on for a meeting with Marulanda tomorrow,"
Ricardo told us in his small peace secretariat in the Presidential Palace. "Meet me at the airport for small planes tomorrow at six A.M."

The next morning when we landed at the airstrip in the FARC
zone, Ricardo's four-wheel-drive vehicle was waiting. He was at the
wheel as we drove, without guards or support staff, for two hours to
the remote La Sombra (The Shadow) deep inside the zone. Ricardo
is no administrator, but like Pastrana he is a man of personal courage.
Political and personal fortitude is not hard to find in Colombia.

Apart from Ricardo, few people outside of the FARC had seen
the feared and legendary Manuel Marulanda. "You are in luck. He is
here. I can see his cars and personal security detail," Ricardo said as
we stopped at the guerrilla roadblock at the entrance to a hamlet of
about twenty-five houses. Marulanda greeted us by putting his
hands on our shoulders. He was accompanied by Raul Reyes and
one other commander, but when the FARC leader is present others
say little and nod a lot. "We can sit on the veranda of this house.
Would you want a whiskey?"

I had heard many stories about Manuel Marulanda since I came
to Colombia as a young volunteer, twenty-four years earlier. He is
one of the world's most powerful and longest-fighting guerrilla
leaders. He has been in hundreds of close encounters with death
and destruction, and he has many lives and kidnappings on his conscience. In real life he was somewhat of an anticlimax. The man we
sat next to on the small wooden veranda with plastic glasses of
Grant's whiskey looked and talked like an aging Colombian peasant.
He wore a brown, worn farmer's shirt, green military trousers, and
Wellington boots and had a small gray towel over his shoulder that
he frequently used to wipe the sweat from his forehead.

Marulanda was in his best mood. He told us how, as a young and poor peasant boy, he had joined the liberal militias of his area when civil war was raging in the 1950s. In 1964, strongly influenced by Marxist ideology, Marulanda was one of forty-eight comrades who founded what eventually became FARC. He got his nickname "Tirofijo" (Sureshot) because he was once an excellent marksman. By the time we sat there with him inside several circles of sentries and patrols, FARC had grown to a formidable countrywide peasant army of more than seventeen thousand soldiers. Nearly 40 percent of the force was female. We saw heavily armed women and girls in all units and functions whenever we met the guerrillas.

This army had some hundred "fronts" or battalions with decentralized powers to fight, kidnap for ransom, and skim profits from drug trafficking across the country. The Central Command could order any operational unit to undertake any operation, but it could not as easily demand that they stop unwanted activities. When, on behalf of desperate families, I brought up several cases of kidnapped civilians with Raul Reyes and other commanders, I remarked that local commanders were not willing to abstain from demanding ransom money or refrain from criminal activities that were the basis of their organizational and economic survival.

"You are the first representative of the United Nations I have seen during my forty years of continuous struggle," Marulanda told me. "And you," he said to LeMoyne, "are the first 'gringo' I have ever met." "You mean the first 'gringo' who still is alive?" James asked. "Yes, you may put it like that," the old man responded without a smile.

I described my mandate from Kofi Annan and the possible role of the international community in supporting and facilitating the peace process: "The whole world welcomes this attempt to end the war in Colombia. Our expectations are that you make speedy progress through negotiations so that the conflict and the suffering can end and we all can work together to build a new, socially just Colombia." Andrés Salazar was taking detailed notes. We continued the discussion through lunch: grilled chicken with rice and fried bananas.

Marulanda wanted to send conciliatory messages to Annan and UN member states. FARC wanted increased international assistance to Colombia with emphasis on the unemployed and the displaced. Of particular importance was investment in "alternative development for small farmers driven into the cultivation of drugs because of poverty," he declared. "We want to prove that social investment is more effective against coca and opium than Plan Colombia's Black Hawk helicopters. We therefore are willing to guarantee that the municipality of Cartagena de Chairá in south-central Colombia totally ends drug cultivation and trafficking if we get funding for alternative development and the government demilitarizes the municipality to enable our people to work in safety."

The proposal appeared to be part of an overall FARC game plan. The guerrillas were increasingly funding themselves through drug trafficking all over the country and they had many possibilities to demonstrate allegiance to alternative development with projects in the existing peace zone or elsewhere. I attempted to explain that we all welcomed the FARC as an ally against narcotics, but that proposals for a new free zone for the FARC would not be acceptable to the government and would lead to new delays in the process.

At the end of the meeting I brought up the most difficult issue: human rights abuse and violence against civilians. I told them, "We condemn the attacks against the civilian populations that all sides, including the FARC, are responsible for. It has to end. You have to do more to protect civilians, refrain from recruiting underage soldiers, respect that civilian communities want to be neutral in the struggle, and respect that the medical personnel and UN and other relief workers are protected persons." "Our expectations for FARC have grown dramatically as you are now a legitimate party to a peace negotiation," LeMoyne added. "Killing civilians, like the three U.S.

researchers on indigenous matters last month, is indefensible and devastating for your image in North America and elsewhere."

Marulanda and his commanders were not pleased. For perhaps the first time he was confronted with direct criticism of the FARC's abuse of a civilian population it claimed to represent. "Well, we have done much and will do more to shield the civilians in the war that still rages outside of this zone," he finally said. "We are sending a directive to all our fronts to protect noncombatants, but you must know that we are all the time accused of doing bad things that are really done by the army or the paramilitaries."

It was nearly 4 P.M. when Ricardo insisted that we return to the airstrip to take off before sunset. "We need more meetings soon to push the peace process forward," I said as we broke up. It had taken forty years for the UN and the FARC to meet officially for the first time. The next opportunity would be the following month when the government and the FARC negotiation teams planned to visit Scandinavia. I formally invited both sides to come to Oslo where I and my colleagues from the UN could brief them on how peace agreements could be negotiated and human rights secured.

Three weeks later an important chapter was written when Victor G. Ricardo and Raul Reyes and their delegations traveled to Sweden and Norway to learn from the "Scandinavian Social Model." It was a symbolically important visit as the Marxist guerrilla movement for the first time declared that their model for Colombia was the democratic welfare system of Scandinavia, with a market economy and a strong state, rather than the crumbling communist models. This gave reason for hope among the economists and businessmen in the government delegation, since economic issues were the first agenda item for the negotiations that were to start when they returned to Colombia.

I had only days to prepare a program in Oslo that included briefings on UN issues and on peaceful and democratic conflict resolution. Three of the six key commanders from the FARC leadership who checked in at the four-star hotel on a snow-covered hill over-looking Oslo had never before left the Colombian countryside. For them it was news that Europe had dramatically changed since the fall of the Berlin Wall in 1989, and that social exploitation was being fought through democratic channels. They visited a Norwegian military base where the officers explained to them that the army's main focus now was to participate in international peacekeeping operations.

In the Norwegian Parliament, members of the Conservative Party and the Socialist Left Party sat next to one another as they declared that, though they disagreed about a lot of things, they did agree that the only way to handle conflicts was through bargaining on the basis of election results. We viewed a documentary on how in less than a century Norway had gone from being Europe's poorest nation to one of the three richest countries in the world. Over supper the Colombians commented, "If Norway with its fierce climate and nature could become the richest in the world, Colombia should be able to do even better." "True," I responded, "but remember, the Norwegians have spent all their time working, trading, and investing, while you spend most of your time fighting, quarreling, and exploiting each other."

For two full days we highlighted the United Nations' potential to work for peace and development in Colombia. I explained that, at this same hotel in Oslo, with the mediation of the UN along with Mexico, Norway, Spain, Colombia, and the United States as a "Group of Friends," Guatemala's Marxist guerrillas and the country's government and army had negotiated human rights protections, refugee return, protection of indigenous rights, and a cease-fire.

The good news was that the FARC and other Colombians, liberals and conservatives alike, declared that the time had come for fundamental social change and a peaceful settlement of the long war. The bad news again was that the FARC side had demanded little that was concrete and the poorly organized government side had offered little, too. That everyone wished to see Scandinavian affluence and social welfare replicated in Colombia was not surprising. But what did the guerrillas think of the peace agreements that had finally been reached in El Salvador and Guatemala? The answer given by Simon Trinidad (who nearly four years later, on New Year's Eve of 2004, was extradited to the United States for drug trafficking and brought to trial there), to the question posed by one of our UN colleagues, was this: "We consider the peace deals in Central America treason against the revolutionary cause. The guerrillas there sold themselves cheaply!"

In spite of the many signals that there was little common ground beyond a common wish for peace, this "Eurotour," which also took the negotiating teams to Spain, France, Switzerland, and Italy, was probably the high point of the process. Both sides saw that Colombia had fallen hopelessly behind, with violent Marxist guerrillas and elites incapable of ending the deep sense of exclusion felt by so many in Colombian society.

For the last evening we had organized a sleigh ride to a restaurant in the woods. After dinner we sang Colombian and Latin American songs. At around midnight, government officials and guerrillas challenged one another to finish improvised verse lines to an old tune—a tradition in the province of Antioquia. The two most impressive participants were a prominent Conservative politician and one of the younger FARC commanders who together alternated in great tempo and always with an appropriate rhyme. That night we all saw how outdated and arbitrary the conflict for life or death is in today's Colombia. When we saw the Colombians off at the airport the next day, several of the negotiators on each side said they believed the impulse from Scandinavia would push the talks decisively forward. They would turn out to be wrong.

The optimism from the Eurotour was largely gone when we next saw our friends in Bogota and in the FARC zone. There was little left of the mutual trust that surfaced in Oslo, once back in Colombia, both parties had immediately become embroiled in mutual accusations in connection with new fighting, new massacres, and new allegations of abuse of the zone. Even toward LeMoyne and me there was a reserved attitude from the "Scandinavian" FARC commanders. Later we would hear why. In meetings with the rest of the Central Command, the returning FARC representatives were criticized for the conciliatory tone of the joint press statements and appearances in European media. They were ordered to burn all clothes, gifts, and purchases from Europe to eliminate any tracking devices that might have been placed in those items by government or U.S. agents. Marulanda and other hard-liners underscored that it was not from outside but from within that change would come.

All time lines were then ignored, since in the months to follow there were no real negotiations in the specially erected buildings at Los Pozos, inside the zone. Instead, a lot of time was spent on "events," such as public hearings on issues ranging from the environment and trade union rights to indigenous rights and alternative development. The hearings held valuable potential as a way for civil society to meet with and influence the FARC, but the clock was ticking and the process steadily lost credibility since it didn't produce any tangible results or decrease violence.

In March I gave three written proposals to the parties asking that they agree immediately to a nationwide cease-fire to enable the vaccination of millions of children in areas of conflict; that they establish how and where the two sides could cooperate in substituting drug cultivation with alternative development; and that a "group of friends" be created that would consist of countries willing and able to facilitate the peace process. Each of the proposals was carefully prepared to enable speedy implementation. Both sides welcomed the proposals, but neither invested any energy in furthering them.

With the FARC process stalled, there were some promising contacts in the spring of 2000 between the ELN leadership and a new high commissioner for peace, Camilo Gómez, Pastrana's former private secretary. Victor G. Ricardo had received a series of death threats from paramilitary leaders before, during, and after the Eurotour and had been sent to London as Colombian ambassador, where he made it clear that he missed the excitement of the FARC talks. In Oslo, Gómez had made it clear to me that he was skeptical about the real intentions of the FARC. Now he wanted me to join him on a mission in May to meet with the ELN leaders in the mountains close to the Magdalena River in northeastern Colombia. This is one of the most conflict-ridden areas of Colombia, a place where political and armed groups fight for money, employment, and influence over oil and lucrative agriculture. In 2000 it was a free-fire zone where the ELN, the FARC, the official armed forces, the right-wing paramilitary groups, and the drug cartels all fought for market share.

I had known that the ELN wanted to meet with me when I was named the first UN envoy to Colombia. One day in April my cell phone rang as I was walking in Bogota. An anonymous voice asked whether I would be willing to talk to ELN commander Francisco Galán, who was imprisoned in Medellin's biggest prison, Itagui, and "who had a message" for me. Though I was perplexed, I agreed. It was in my mandate to have contact with both guerrilla movements. I was then asked to call a number in Mainz, Germany. "Why Germany?" I asked. "Don't ask, just call," the voice said and the line went dead. The anonymous woman who answered in Germany did not sound surprised when I asked to talk to Galán. "Just one moment and I'll connect you to Paco," she said. A second later Galán greeted me like an old friend—from inside Itagui prison: "I am thrilled to speak to you finally. Please know that our leader, Nicolás Rodríguez, is waiting to see you in his hideout in the mountains at your convenience." Only in Colombia, I thought as I put my cell phone in my pocket and entered the Presidential Palace.

Because there was neither a zone nor a cease-fire with the ELN, our visits to this smaller of the two main guerrilla movements were both more cumbersome and dangerous than the visits to "FARC-landia." In May I flew with Camilo Gómez to the airport at Barranca, by the Magdalena River. Here we waited until a first set of coordinates were radioed by the ELN. We then took a small civilian helicopter into the forested mountains and when we reached the first target we received a second set of coordinates. At the second target area a brief message was received by the pilot. "Look for the smoke we are now sending from below and land at the field next to it." A jet of smoke suddenly appeared from a guerrilla unit that had stood ready with a fire and wet leaves.

We landed next to a humble farm and were greeted by some excited children, some frightened parents, and five ELN soldiers who came out from the woods to escort us to the meeting site. After a half-hour walk on a mountain trail we arrived at a tiny hamlet where Nicolás Rodríguez greeted us. Rodríguez was fourteen in 1964 when he joined the tiny armed group that later became the National Liberation Army, ELN, and received his alias, "Gabino" (the Kid). He offered warm cocoa milk but wasted no time in declaring that in his view the time had come for a historic compromise through peace negotiations that could bring the struggle to an end. The ELN Central Command had decided to request peace talks, but wanted it to be preceded by a "National Council" in which all their associated groups, units, and sympathizers could discuss the ELN positions before negotiations were opened. To achieve all of this, the ELN needed a free zone like the FARC's. The zone did not have to be as big as the demilitarized zone in the south, but it did have to be in the Middle Magdalena region.

It would clearly be even more difficult to get general acceptance for an ELN zone in this more populated and contested region in the heartland of Colombia than in the remote areas that the FARC had gotten in the south. I explained how difficult a peace process would be in these violent and complex surroundings, but also outlined a series of political, diplomatic, and economic measures the international community could offer if and when a real peace process started.

After a while Rodríguez asked whether he and I could talk alone. Camilo Gómez agreed and went away to smoke one of his Cuban cigars. "Can you ride?" Gabino asked. "Yes," I answered, "but give me a calm horse." Soon he was on horseback and I was on a mule, with ELN sentries before and after us on the trail. Discussing what agreements could bring, the ELN chief was more concrete in his questions and requests than any FARC leader had been: "In the event of a peace deal, do you think we can keep our arms for self-defense during a long transitional period? ... Can the UN and the government create special agricultural or developmental projects where our people could settle? ... Do you think we can keep funds that we have 'attained' through our revolutionary struggle to get started in a peaceful Colombia?"

The questions were encouraging, but the ELN was weaker than the FARC and less organized. We could not know if Rodríguez was speaking on behalf of the whole ELN leadership, and if they were strong enough to undertake a peace process separate from the FARC. I tried to avoid offering any illusions: "The paramilitary groups that are getting increasingly strong will fight against the zone and against any concession to you. The FARC may also not like any progress in a separate peace track with you. At the same time it will be impossible for the president to have negotiations with you if you continue with extortions and massive kidnappings for ransom of innocent civilians. You have to stop that altogether." "Well," he said, "if we cannot fund our existence through direct 'taxing' of the rich or drugs, can you help fund our five thousand fighters during months or years of talks, a national council, negotiations and integration?"

In the plane back to Bogota with Gómez, we discussed in detail how this peace process should be organized, and how the UN and a group of nations could become "friends of the process." We both saw valuable support coming to the process from the European Union, Spain, the Scandinavians, and Cuba, which maintains relations with both the ELN and the government and would be ideal to host initial talks. In meetings with Pastrana I supported the idea of an ELN zone and urged military action against three well-known paramilitary bases in Middle Magdalena that the army had allowed to thrive on drug trafficking and anti-guerrilla activity.

In the end it turned out that the enemies of peace had grown too strong in 1999 and 2000. Pastrana had invested all his prestige in creating the ELN zone, but a long series of violent road blockades and strikes in northern regions, orchestrated by the extreme right wing, were costly. "How do you distinguish between ELN fighters and paramilitary 'self-defense' groups?" I asked a courageous Franciscan father who walked those mountains. "It has become very easy. The ELN kids are skinny, dressed in torn uniforms and carrying old guns. The paras are well fed, wear Gucci sunglasses, and have the latest in uniforms and automatic weapons. The narcotics trade is very profitable."

In contrast to the quick meetings with the ELN in poor farm huts, in June 2000 we organized the first and the last international conference with the FARC in their zone. More than twenty diplomats from Europe, Latin America, Canada, Japan, and the UN held two days of meetings with the FARC leadership. I had several preparatory meetings with the diplomatic corps in Bogota before the conference. At these meetings, I urged them to participate and to send a blunt message to the commanders. The theme for the conference was drug substitution and alternative development, but the meeting also provided an opportunity to address the FARC's continued violence against civilians and their slow pace at the negotiation table.

Marulanda personally greeted us when the bus with the international guests arrived at the conference venue. A photo in which I am smiling as I greet the FARC leader, our hands on each other's shoulders, was published around the world. However, it did not reflect the tense atmosphere in the meeting. The FARC leadership's foreign representatives, who mostly met with left-wing groups, had reported that Europe and Latin America generally "sympathized" with their cause, and that criticism of their struggle mainly came from the United States and from human rights campaigners in the UN and elsewhere. However, the June meeting was a reality check. One ambassador after another condemned the attacks against civilians, the kidnappings, the extortions, the drug trafficking, and the lack of progress in the talks. Several ambassadors affirmed that "progress in your [FARC's] performance is a precondition for any future recognition."

Twice during 2000, the two sides exchanged written cease-fire proposals, but there were always procedural or substantive strings attached that prevented agreement on the how, when, and where. Since trust between the representatives of the two sides had dissipated, LeMoyne, young Salazar, and I always traveled without government officials to see the FARC. When we landed at the airstrip in San Vicente, a FARC car usually waited for us in the shadow of a tree, a mute soldier at the wheel. We had to move the guns in the backseat to make room. As we drove toward the seldom-used negotiation buildings in Los Pozos, the FARC radio was always on. The guerrilla programming consisted of propaganda about the great achievements of the movement, patriotic and popular music, and slogans for respecting the rights of women, protecting the rain forest and the environment, and promoting the revolutionary cause.

Marulanda, Reyes, and other FARC leaders were increasingly and understandably obsessed with the unchecked rise in paramilitary massacres of defenseless farmers who were suspected of guerrilla links. But they continued to propose events, meetings, or zones that would be unacceptable to the government and the international community and divert attention from the issues already on the table. Several times the FARC leaders exposed their brutality.

On one occasion we brought up reports of a FARC battalion that consisted mainly of child soldiers and had been decimated by an army ambush. Some of the government officers said it was their saddest victory. "Well, it is not easy to please the army," Marulanda observed. "Even the few times they beat us they complain."

There was also no progress in the ELN talks. Pastrana could not prevail against the forces that sabotaged the establishment of a zone in Middle Magdalena. The two sides did, however, agree to my proposal for a group of friends who started to accompany LeMoyne and me on visits to the ELN leadership. Spain and other members of the "friends" had agreed to deploy a group of observers to verify the existence and the good use of a zone should it be established. We tried to go in secret to the ELN meeting points, but it was impossible not to be noticed in our helicopter or four-wheel-drive vehicle. We heard that at least one of the hamlets that had hosted an ELN encounter was subsequently raided and burned to the ground. All our protests were in vain. Even the head of state seemed to be unable to make the military enforce the law and crack down on the drug-fueled, brutal paramilitary groups.

We stopped going to the ELN in the mountains and met with their representatives in Cuba, Venezuela, or Europe, or with Galán and his comrades in Medellin's notorious Itagui prison. The prison is a large community. Killers, common criminals, drug barons, and captured guerrilla soldiers are confined behind circles of barbed wire, watchtowers, armed guards, and dogs. Visiting for us meant being checked and controlled at the prison entrance when going into the maximum security wing and entering the ELN commanders' suite of four adjacent cells. "Heartily welcome. Do you want coffee and biscuits—or maybe tea?" the bearded Galán would say as we reached his personal cell. Notes, maps, documents, and radio equipment were spread all over. Galán had by then served ten years of a thirty-year prison sentence for "kidnapping, extortion, and terrorism." Each time there was dialogue between the ELN and the government, prison officials would come with telephones, radio, fax, and Internet links to his cell. Each time there was a break in contact, often due to mass kidnappings by ELN units, the officials would remove the equipment.

When, in late 2001, I was offered the position of secretary-general of the Norwegian Red Cross, both the FARC and ELN talks were stalemated and there were only a few months left in Andrés Pastrana's presidency. The FARC and the government specialized in accusing each other of provocations and atrocities. Paradoxically, the war had worsened while the peace dialogue took place. Nearly a quarter of a million Colombians were displaced every year by paramilitary groups, drug cartels, guerrillas, and army counterinsurgency operations. Massacres, kidnappings, and extortions became everyday events. The FARC's violence made banner headlines in the national press. We saw on live television how a woman had had a "collar bomb" fixed around her neck that apparently could not be defused. After a long day and night, and despite transmission of the woman's desperate pleas for help, the bomb was detonated by remote control and the woman was killed. The government blamed the incident on the FARC, and Pastrana once more had to suspend the talks. Police investigators later confirmed that elements in military intelligence working with drug-fueled paramilitary groups had orchestrated the cruel stunt to place blame on the FARC.

Realizing that we would not have the breakthrough that I had worked for during the last four years, I informed Kofi Annan that I had accepted the job in Oslo and started to hand over responsibilities as special adviser for the secretary-general to James LeMoyne. Our mission now became one of preventing a total collapse in the channel of communication before the next president could give the process a more effective shape and structure. The breakdown came sooner than we had imagined.

In July 2001, FARC guerrillas in Meta had kidnapped the department's former governor, Alan Jara, as he was traveling in a clearly marked United Nations vehicle. A FARC statement issued later accused Jara, wrongly, of paramilitary ties; criticized the UN for transporting him; and promised to submit the former governor to a "popular tribunal." The same week the FARC kidnapped three German development workers and demanded an end to fumigations of coca cultivations in the zone. Annan and I issued strong separate public protests on behalf of the United Nations and warned the FARC that patience from the international community would soon be gone.

When the FARC attempted to boost public confidence in the movement, their actions were usually undermined by parallel negative actions. In June 2001 they unilaterally released 242 captured soldiers and police agents not just as a sign of goodwill, but also as one of strength. At the same time their notorious military leader, Jorge Briceño threatened to start a massive campaign of kidnapping political leaders. That same week the guerrillas kidnapped the vice president in the Colombian Soccer Federation, an act that undermined Colombia's hosting of the Americas Cup.

October 2001 started with a joint declaration issued after a rare direct meeting between President Pastrana's envoys and the FARC leadership. The zone was given yet another extension until January 20 and the parties agreed to refocus on cease-fire negotiations. The FARC also pledged to stop its "miracles fishing," or the kidnapping of well-to-do travelers at roadblocks for ransom, and the government committed to strengthen its antiparamilitary efforts. The agreement was good on paper, but it seemed too late to change realities on the ground. Ten days later a U.S. State Department official testified to Congress that the FARC was "the most dangerous international terrorist group based in this hemisphere." Two days after that, Marulanda ordered his negotiators to refrain indefinitely from any contact with the government since it was allowing constant military overflights of the zone and, according to the FARC, had allowed military and paramilitary infiltration as well.

It was the deepest crisis of the fledgling peace process. I wanted desperately to keep the hope for peace alive so a new president could spur new momentum. The FARC had informed us it was "not safe to meet in the zone anymore" and that they were preparing to break all contact permanently unless there was an end to the overflights and strict controls were established over everyone and everything entering the zone. Through the Internet we managed to reestablish contact and win their consent for a discreet meeting in November, which they insisted take place "northwest" of the zone. The political and social climate was now so tense that it turned out to be nearly impossible to find anyone who would be willing to take us from the airport in the small southern city of Neiva and into the rural area where the FARC would pick us up.

In the end one of our loyal UN drivers volunteered to drive for ten hours from Bogota to Neiva and pick us up at the airport the next morning, along with some courageous pathfinders from the local Colombian Red Cross chapter. With a big Red Cross banner on the first vehicle and a blue UN flag on our car we drove without any guards or weapons for two hours. Twice we came across army roadblocks; the young lieutenants reluctantly let us pass when we said we were meeting with representatives of local communities in the conflict areas. At noon we reached the tiny hamlet along the track where the FARC had promised to collect us. As we stood waiting, I realized that this time we had been too reckless. We had gone into an active conflict zone on our own, on a mission to save a peace channel that many military and paramilitary groups did not want to succeed. I thought of my wife and our two daughters and regretted the whole thing. My mood was not exactly lifted when James LeMoyne said, "Jan, I had a bad dream last night. I saw us face-down on a country track like this. It resembled the photos after the assassination of the parliamentarian [Diego] Turbay and his family last December on the other side of the zone."

After fifteen minutes of waiting and a call from our satellite phone to our office in Bogota, an open FARC jeep appeared at full speed. "If you are the UN, jump in," a guerrilla said. Our UN driver had agreed to wait for us until sunset and then return with or without us to Neiva. The drive lasted longer than the one hour that had been indicated in our e-mail. "Wait and see" was the only message from our driver. When a heavy tropical shower started we put on some olive-green military-style ponchos he gave us. If we encountered military or paramilitary groups, that would not look good. Finally, at the top of a hill with a beautiful view of the rain forest, we stopped outside a ranch house. Raul Reyes and several other commanders came out and nodded approvingly. "We really didn't think you would have the guts to come," he said.

We had only a brief hour with the FARC leaders before we had to rush back; otherwise our UN car would leave us behind. "Make no mistake," we told them, "President Pastrana will become a popular man if he breaks off the whole peace process and goes to full war against you. Your next chance for real negotiations in a zone may not come in many years. The time for events, meetings, and smaller gestures is over. The one thing you now must do is agree on and realize a cease-fire." Reyes listened and took notes. It had always been our impression that he genuinely wanted a negotiated settlement. But his message on behalf of Marulanda and the Central Command was mixed: "We do want to do a final and serious attempt to negotiate and agree on an end to hostilities. But we have fought for forty years and we cannot and will not put down our arms quickly when we see the brutal paramilitary tool of the army and the elite is getting stronger and stronger. Tell Pastrana and the general public that we are willing to return to the table and resume talks on the existing proposals for a cease-fire. But it will take time. We accept no ultimatums!"

It was my last meeting with the FARC. When we landed at about 10 P.M. at the airport in Bogota, the press corps was waiting to hear my announcement that the talks would once again resume in the zone. We saw Camilo Gómez and Pastrana that night and the next morning. They both agreed, though without enthusiasm, to make another attempt.

In December I paid a good-bye visit as the first UN envoy for Colombia. The Catholic Church organized a farewell reception on behalf of the nongovernmental organizations and there were more than a hundred guests. I was deeply touched by the kind words from all who were there and in my speech I expressed regret that the joint peace efforts had not succeeded. The Colombian people deserved peace more than anyone, but it now looked as if there would be no end to the violence in the country. In my last meeting with Andrés Pastrana I told him how much I admired his political courage. He could have become popular again if he had followed the shift in public opinion and shut down the zone and the peace effort in 2000. His courage was not matched by an ability to find colleagues who could organize a sustained and systematic effort, and to find a counterpart who would accept a compromise. Pastrana looked sad when he gave me an embrace and announced that I would receive Colombia's highest order, the Great Cross of the Order of San Carlos.

In my final report to Secretary-General Annan I tried to sum up the peace process. He had agreed to appoint James LeMoyne as his representative.

Colombia took a long step in the right direction when the elected president and the FARC declared that there is no military solution to Colombia's social and political problems. But there was too little willingness in the FARC leadership to take concrete steps on the road toward peace, too little ability, and too much arrogance within the new government circles to organize an effective, coherent, and inclusive peace process, and too much room for the enemies of peace to systematically undermine the process. The latter was particularly apparent in the ELN talks where both sides demonstrated real interest in reaching agreements, but the paramili-

tary forces were allowed to sabotage the establishment of the zone in which real negotiations would have happened. We thus ended up with a large zone for the FARC, which misused the opportunity to negotiate, and no zone for the ELN, which probably would have been willing to end it all there and then.

My report ended with the following three scenarios:

The good scenario consists of continued and gradually successful negotiations under a new president for both of the two guerrilla movements with cease-fire, demobilization, and reintegration of the more than 20,000 guerrilla fighters and an equal number of paramilitary armed men. This scenario presupposes not only the positive ability of the guerrilla leadership to carry out such a momentous process of change, but the willingness of the Colombian elite to stop the social and political exclusion of others and an ability to protect the freedom of left-wing groups to participate in the democratic process.

The bad scenario is a continuation like now with continued massive violence against defenseless civilians, Indian communities, and Afro-Colombians. This second alternative is in practice a continuation of the present situation with continued contact between the parties, but no real agreements that can change the present hemorrhage of human life and human dignity.

There is also an ugly scenario with total breakdown in all lines of communication and total war where all groups use all of their forces and all of the fuel that the drug industry can provide. The bad scenario is unfortunately the most likely. The good scenario is regrettably the least probable.

In the following weeks, I watched from Oslo as James and diplomats from friendly countries and the Catholic Church fought to keep the peace effort alive. From day to day and hour to hour, James and other international representatives searched for a minimum of common ground between the parties to extend the FARC zone and the talks beyond the January 20, 2002, deadline. On that very day, with the army massing just outside the zone and the FARC packing their things, there was an agreement to resume cease-fire talks in accordance with a detailed schedule that would effect the cessation of hostilities by April 7 and extend the zone until April 10.

But the peace process had long been marked. In early February a new FARC offensive that consisted of sabotaging infrastructure and bombing urban areas led to many civilian casualties. On February 19 there was yet another exchange of cease-fire proposals. The government proposed maintaining the guerrilla fronts in small concentration areas separate from the armed forces. The next day, FARC, in one of its innumerable irrational and counterproductive moves, hijacked a commercial airliner and kidnapped a senator who was on board; he was the fifth member of the Colombian Congress to have been kidnapped and held captive since June 2001. That same day, February 20, 2002, Pastrana declared that he had had enough, that the peace process was over. Aerial bombing of FARC targets started at midnight and the zone was retaken. When a brave senator and presidential candidate, Ingrid Betancourt, traveled to the area three days later to advocate for the rights of the residents of the zone, she too was kidnapped by the FARC. She is still their prisoner.

Alvaro Uribe was elected president in June 2002 as a strongman who would use military power against the guerrillas. With his investment in and reorganization of the armed forces and the police, he managed to improve control of urban areas and reduce both kidnappings and new displacements. There was no political contact with the FARC, though there were continued talks in Cuba, and via Galán's cell in Itagui. (Galán was freed in January 2007 to boost the peace negotiations with the ELN in Cuba.)

For the first time there were also official talks with the paramilitary "self-defense" groups. Uribe and several others in his administration were accused by human rights groups and political opponents of collaborating with anti-guerrilla militias when Uribe was governor of Antioquia province. In the UN we always maintained, as had previous Colombian administrations, that the paramilitary groups were criminal gangs and did not merit political negotiations. Uribe, however, with the help of the Organization of American States, was able to demobilize and reintegrate thousands of former paramilitary fighters. At the same time many of those involved in horrific massacres and large-scale drug trafficking are still acting with impunity.

When I came back to Colombia once more, in late 2004 as UN undersecretary-general for humanitarian affairs, what I saw was a version of the "bad scenario" I had outlined for Kofi Annan. The urban middle class has seen improvement in security and that had made Uribe a very popular president. In the countryside the same strife and the same poverty were a sad reality. In the beautiful Spanish colonial city of Cartagena, the contrasts were strong. Within the city and its surroundings were the beautiful palaces and beaches that attract large numbers of tourists. In the outlying slums, on the other hand, I saw poverty as dramatic as in parts of Africa and I heard stories of drug gangs, paramilitary violence, and guerrilla activity. The leading Bogota daily published a front-page photo of my visit to these vast slums under the heading, "The dramatic face of Cartagena's poverty." For several of Colombia's remaining Indian tribes the situation is critical. Some will soon be extinct if there is no end to the violence and the illegal drug cultivation in their reservations.

In the Presidential Palace in Bogota that I knew so well, I asked Uribe to agree to UN contact with the FARC to bring relief to beleaguered communities in conflict areas. "I do not dispute your good intentions, but no, I will not have any contact, dialogue, or talks with the FARC before we have broken their offensive military capabilities. I can assure you that that will soon happen and there will then be talks about ending the war and the insurgency, but not before."

At the end of 2007, six years after the Pastrana process collapsed, the FARC is still fighting and not militarily broken. ELN is also fighting on and, like the FARC, funding itself by criminal means. Hundreds of kidnapped Colombians, including the French-Colombian politician Ingrid Betancourt, remain in cruel captivity somewhere in the rain forest. Some paramilitary groups are also reappearing. Criminality is again on the rise. Tens of thousands of armed men and women are at large and the civilian Colombian population is still waiting. They are also waiting for a North America and Europe that are completely focused on Iraq, Afghanistan, and the Middle East to wake up to the realities within their own hemisphere.

4.

Scorched Earth in Darfur

OUR VISIT to the small, run-down hospital in El Geneina, the main town in West Darfur, is unannounced. There are reports of wounded civilians and we need to see and speak to them without interruption. A frail, skinny woman, who looks older than her twenty-five years, sits quietly on a bed with a small girl in her lap. The girl can only breathe with great difficulty. She has a bandage around her neck and another around her leg. "They came in the morning," the mother says, looking disconsolately at her two-year-old daughter. "They were many and they had guns. We heard them break into neighboring huts and then they came for us. An Arab with a big gun came to the bed where I sat with my girl just like this," she says grabbing her daughter round the shoulder as the child starts to sob quietly. "The man yells at me that he will kill my child if I do not give him money. I cried to him that we are poor and have nothing. Then he shot my daughter through the neck and the leg. . . ."

It is Thursday, November 16, 2006, and I am on my fourth and final visit to Darfur in Western Sudan as UN emergency relief coordinator. It is by far the most depressing visit. On each previous trip there had been some progress, some hope to hold on to in the middle of this vast desert of suffering and systematic abuse of defenseless civilians. This time both the people and the aid workers are disillusioned and desperately anxious.

We arrive at the hospital in our convoy of jeeps with UN colleagues, bodyguards, and journalists. A local official wants us to wait to have our visit cleared from higher up, but the doctor in charge is only too pleased to usher us in and we walk toward the pediatric ward. We know that four days earlier in the small village of Sirba, northeast of El Geneina, three waves of attacks by government forces and Arab militia resulted in up to thirty civilians being killed and forty injured; the victims were mainly women and children. The hospital scene is only too familiar: sad and barren concrete walls and floors, a single lightbulb in the ceiling, and some metal military-style field beds with worn and dirty linen. Victims of the brutal attacks occupy several of the beds in the ward.

We are looking at a tiny speck of misery in the war of attrition mostly undertaken by Sudanese government forces and ruthless nomadic Arab militia, often called the Janjaweed, against the civilian African population of western Sudan. Hundreds of thousands have died since 2003, more of them by preventable disease than from direct violence.

The reason the little girl with the large, dark, and beautiful eyes miraculously survived is that the local chief managed to get her to the hospital, where the doctor standing next to me saved her life. The doctor and the nurses who are now helping mother and child recover are government employees who specialize in repairing what other branches of the same government destroy. My UN colleagues and several nongovernmental organizations are already providing medicines and equipment to the hospital. There and then we agree to do more. No one will die due to lack of supplies, but many more will die if the vulnerable communities do not get protection. Neither the government nor the African Union forces were able or willing to deploy in Sirba before the massacre, despite increasingly desperate warnings by villagers and aid workers of the impending attacks.

One has to have a heart of stone not to be outraged by these accounts of armed men abusing defenseless women and children. "How can you allow this to happen with total impunity?!" we ask ministers in Khartoum and governors in Darfur again and again.

"Large parts of Darfur are seeing a collapse of law and order, and you still object to a UN peacekeeping force that can take over from the small and ineffective African Union forces," I exclaimed in Khartoum a day earlier to Lam Akol, the Sudanese foreign minister, and Kosti Manibe, the humanitarian minister. These officials are always willing to meet, but they have little influence on events in Darfur since they both represent the South Sudanese (Sudan People's Liberation Movement/Army, or SPLM/A) side in the new Government of National Unity. Neither President Omar al-Bashir nor Vice President Ali Osman Taha is willing to see me this time. They know only too well that my message would be that the situation in Darfur is closer to the abyss than I have seen it since my first visit in 2004, and that they are largely responsible.

The displaced women's spokeswoman, whom I meet after the hospital visit on my first day in El Geneina, is articulate and beautiful, with the characteristic high cheekbones and large dark eyes of so many of her countrymen. She sits on the other side of the table in a dark blue robe among a dozen other black women. We are in one of the ugly UN office modules that have been imported in flat-packs at great cost and now form part of the growing number of international "compounds" that scar the barren Sahara landscape.

My UNHCR and OCHA colleagues have escorted the women from some distance to give me a briefing more important than any I have received by the male government representatives here in Darfur or in Khartoum, the capital. I have been to the large, overcrowded, and miserable camps the women come from, on previous

missions. I have seen too many of their ancient villages destroyed
in the Janjaweed's ruthless ethnic cleansing campaign—their huts
are burned down and their precious wells are contaminated and
destroyed.

Even the sultan of the Massalit tribe, whom we see the same afternoon in his impressive residence, is now angry with the government and frightened of what is to come. The Massalits have more
kinfolk among the ruthless aggressors than among the victims, and
the sultan has done little to protect the black African tribe members
who end up in the hospitals and camps for the displaced. But as he
and the nomadic leaders we meet later have learned through bitter
experience, it is easier to start a war than to stop one. "Tell your
leaders they are giving new arms to men who will only do more
harm," the sultan roars to a man with sunglasses at the door during
the extended meeting we have with the region's tribal elders. The
man turns out to be a national security police official who is moni-
toring our meeting and he is visibly upset by the scolding of a tribal
leader who has been a prominent government ally.

"Thank you for all your assistance," a displaced mother of three
says as she looks across the table at me and Manuel da Silva, our humanitarian coordinator in Sudan. Manuel, with his thousands of
hardworking, courageous colleagues, can take credit for having organized, against all odds, one of the most effective relief operations
ever. She tells him, "We have received food, water, health care, and
even primary school for our youngest children. Thanks to that we
are alive, but you must know that we have no life. We live every
night and every day in fear. If we, the women, leave our crowded
camps to collect grass or firewood we are raped and beaten. If our
sons leave to try to get work they are killed or kidnapped. Even inside our camps, inside our huts, they come to beat and humiliate us.
It is getting worse and worse. We just spent our Islamic holiday Eid
crying every day and every night. You have to help us!"

It is impossible to find words of comfort. The blunt truth is that we, the international community, have utterly failed these defenseless women as they face ruthless armed men and a government that has supported the abusers rather than the victims. The one thing the women beg of me—protection and security—is the only thing we cannot as UN humanitarian workers give them. In the awkward silence that follows, before I can muster a meaningful answer, three of the women, one with an infant at her breast, rise to give me some baskets made by hand from local straw. "The Arabs have stolen everything that we black people had," says the woman in the blue robe, who must remain nameless for fear of reprisals. "You are rich and have everything. But you listened to us and we wanted to welcome you to our land with the little we still can make. It took a lot of work and a lot of risk to get straw to make these baskets."

Six days later I am in New York City, a world away, to report to the UN what I have seen in Darfur. It is 10:25 A.M., Wednesday, November 22, 2006, and the Peruvian ambassador, who this month holds the presidency of the Security Council, is nearly half an hour late in calling the meeting to order in the large and prestigious Security Council plenary chambers. Carefully reading out notes from the UN Secretariat he asks, in Spanish, "for permission of the council to invite Mr. Egeland, the undersecretary-general for humanitarian affairs, to join the proceedings and brief the council on the situation in Darfur." In accordance with the rules of the world's most powerful international body, only then can I rise from one of the red chairs in the gallery reserved for UN staff and diplomats who are not members of the council and walk to one of the old and increasingly shabby blue chairs at the end of the horseshoe table that Norway donated fifty years ago.

I look at the large, dramatic mural symbolizing the struggle for human rights and justice that my countryman Per Krohg was commissioned to paint across the wall behind the president when Norway furnished these new chambers in the 1950s. I have spent many long hours at meetings on Darfur gazing at the mural's phoenix rising from the ashes of the Second World War while, in another corner of the painting, a measure of grain is being weighed for distribution to people of all colors as a symbol of equality.

The meeting is well attended by the "permanent representatives," as the blue-blooded ambassadors to the UN are called. The always helpful envoys from the United Kingdom, France, Denmark, and Japan are fortunately present. Japan's seat has thankfully been occupied since 2005 by my UN predecessor, Kenzo Oshima. In the gallery are many friends from the nongovernmental organizations who share our outrage over the continuing carnage in Darfur and have lobbied for the strongest possible statement. I fix my eyes on the Peruvian ambassador, draw my breath, and fulfil my promise to the women from the camps around El Geneina to convey their uncensored message to world leaders:

Mr. President, I have just concluded my fourth and final mission as emergency relief coordinator to Darfur. I return with a plea from beleaguered Darfurians for immediate action finally to stop the atrocities against them. For more than a thousand days and a thousand nights, the defenseless civilians of Darfur have been living in fear of their lives, and those of their children. The government's failure to protect its own citizens, even in areas where there are no rebels, has been shameful, and continues. So does our own failure more than a year after world leaders in this very building pledged their own responsibility to protect civilians where the government manifestly fails to do so.

It is a strong statement, perhaps the toughest of the ten briefings I have given to the Security Council since my first on April 2, 2004. Most of the ten-page manuscript has been drafted by Oliver Ulich, a young and talented German lawyer, who now sits behind me. Oliver left a promising career at one of the big New York law firms to join us at OCHA for less pay but more meaningful challenges. He also wrote the important first briefing, in which I accused the Sudanese regime of "ethnic cleansing" in Darfur. That finally got the exposure in the international media that we had been looking for when Darfur remained a forgotten emergency.

Next to Oliver sits, as always, Hansjoerg Strohmeyer, my chief of staff, and behind him David del Conte, an impressive young American who served for nearly two years as head of the Nyala field office in South Darfur, one of the toughest postings in the UN. David had spent months planning my November 2006 Darfur mission in minute detail. He still looks disappointed as I tell the council that most of this important trip that was cleared with the Sudanese Foreign Ministry had been blocked after my arrival in Khartoum by Salah Gosh, the powerful head of the Sudanese Agency for National Security.

The National Security people had called in Ramesh Rajasingham of Sri Lanka, who heads our excellent OCHA Sudan operation, and told him two days before my arrival that our journey beyond El Geneina was "too dangerous" to undertake as planned. I had intended to visit the Jebel Marra mountains to send a firm message to the strongest rebel group in Darfur, the Sudan Liberation Movement/Army (SLM/A), urging an immediate halt to hostilities and for them to support the cease-fire. I had also hoped to visit Tawilla in North Darfur to highlight a rare case of successful local security provision by the African Union forces, and to go east of El Geneina to see the powerful Musa Hilal, the presumed leader of the Arab Janjaweed, to protest the horrendous attacks against the civilian populations. All of these visits had been blocked. Instead the government suggested that I go to the quieter main town in North Darfur, El Fasher. I refused and went straight to Khartoum after El Geneina.

It was the third time that I was either blocked from entering Sudan altogether or had had my program sabotaged in mid-journey during more than three years of confrontations with Khartoum. The first time was the spring of 2004, when President Bashir wrote a five-page letter to Kofi Annan complaining that I was biased and should not lead the secretary-general's first mission to Darfur.

"Why don't we just ignore the security police and go to these places where people are waiting for us?" I had asked. "We have our own plane." "Because," answered a senior colleague, "when we have a formal warning like this, we can be shot down by anyone and the government can just say we had been warned."

In El Geneina I found more frustration. For the first time since I had come in June 2004 with Secretary-General Annan I could not visit the huge camps with hundreds of thousands of refugees. The reluctant but unanimous recommendation from our local aid workers was that it would be too dangerous for the displaced, for my colleagues, and for me to visit. The local government, installed in West Darfur by the Khartoum regime, allowed the brutal militias to operate freely outside and even inside the camps. A visit by me, along with journalists, advisers, and security officials, to the increasingly politicized camps—to which some three-quarters of a million had fled in West Darfur alone—would almost certainly result in fresh confrontations. We wanted to avoid what happened half a year earlier, in May 2006, when an interpreter was killed in antigovernment riots that followed my visit to Kalma camp in South Darfur, where some hundred thousand angry members of the Fur, one of the region's largest tribes, had sought refuge.

Paradoxically, the atmosphere was particularly charged at the beginning of May 2006 because the hard-won Darfur Peace Agreement had been signed between the government and one of the largest factions within the SLM/A. The deal had been brokered by the African Union in Abuja, Nigeria, with the United States, United Kingdom, and United Nations acting as midwives. Following the party line, I publicly welcomed the agreement as a step on the road to a negotiated settlement. However, we knew that only Minni Minnawi, the main commander from the Zaghawa tribe, had signed, while several of the other rebel groups within the SLM/A remained opposed to the deal.

Assembled under a huge tent, more than thirty sheiks and elders in Kalma first thanked me and my large delegation of local aid workers for the extensive humanitarian assistance to the camp by the UN, NGOs, and the Norwegian Refugee Council, the latter recently banned as camp coordinator by the governor of South Darfur. In 2004 Kalma was a symbol of hunger, disease, and child mortality beyond belief. Since 2005, more than twenty NGOs and UN agencies, generously funded by North American and European donors, had managed to provide a nutritional, medical, and educational standard among the population that was probably better than anything the displaced had experienced in their barren lands. All the same, the violence, abuse, and humiliation that drove them from their homes and villages and that they continued to confront outside the perimeters of their camps was the focus of their polite but trenchant criticism of me as a representative of the international community. Leaving the assembly tent escorted by their elders, I saw that the same tribal leaders had organized a less cordial demonstration: some ten thousand of the displaced were closing in around us, chanting antigovernment slogans and calling for an immediate "UN/U.S. protection force."

As we reached our convoy of vehicles, a local staff member from Oxfam explained to his British colleague that one of the slogans "is against the government and the Janjaweed militias." Someone in the crowd heard the word *Janjaweed* and started screaming abuse at the local relief worker, who was immediately attacked with fists and knives. Desperately the man dove into the nearest car, which happened to be the one into which CNN reporter Nick Robertson and his cameraman had already jumped. The dramatic images of knives flying through the air, windows being smashed, and Robertson yelling to the driver, "Go! Go! Go!" were repeated for days by

CNN. The news agencies reported, incorrectly, "UN official is forced to flee refugee camp." I was already on my way out of the area when the violence broke out.

During a meeting later with the African Union forces in Nyala, the main town of South Darfur, we received reports of a dangerously deteriorating situation. The Nigerian head of the African Union mission confirmed that a riot that started in another corner of Kalma after we had left ended with a mob overrunning the African Union's camp office. They looted everything and killed a local interpreter. Senseless violence had again taken the life of one who had come to Darfur to help.

The May journey had originally been planned for six weeks earlier. The carefully designed mission had been agreed to by the ministries of foreign affairs and humanitarian affairs. It was to have taken me on a ten-day journey to South Sudan, Khartoum, Darfur, and the increasing turmoil in eastern Chad, which was both suffering from and contributing to the conflict in Darfur. I had arrived in Juba, South Sudan, from meetings with the German government in Berlin. I spent a deeply emotional night and day on a barge going down the White Nile with jubilant Dinka refugees returning after more than fifteen years of displacement. The sun was dipping out of a purple sky as our helicopter landed in the savannah where we had boarded our barge.

As we jumped out of the helicopter, a hundred naked herdsmen rushed toward us with excited cries and waving sticks and spears. It was as if we had traveled back in time. "Are they friendly?" I asked Dawn Blalock, the UN's local public information officer, an American. "How would I know? We'll soon see," she replied. The herdsmen were only wearing white cow dung ashes smeared over their black bodies as protection against mosquitoes. Though they surrounded us with raised spears, they turned out to be very friendly. As we walked toward the barge they wanted to touch my hands and hair; others pointed toward the first aircraft they had ever seen up close.

Some four hundred women and children were already on the old Nile freight barge, sitting quietly as if waiting for Sunday school to start. "My heart is flying with joy," said one woman. "I was nine when I fled the war and our cattle farm in Bor with my parents. Now I am twenty-seven and am returning to Bor with my own four children. I will be home at last after eighteen years spent far away. My husband is walking across southern Sudan with our cattle. He will join us in one month and then we will start our new life in peace!"

The positive story we wanted to project internationally from the barge was the successful undertaking by the UN and the International Organization for Migration to help return the displaced to their homelands. It was a sign that peace was finally breaking out in South Sudan. Once again, however, the Sudanese government managed to shoot itself in the foot and eclipse any hope of the good news slipping out: it announced that it was blocking my trip onward to Khartoum, Darfur, and Chad. The next morning, after four hours of sleep, I awoke to the fabulous sound of psalms being sung by the Dinkas, as BBC World Service announced: "UN envoy again denied access to Darfur."

It turned out to be a long day in the blistering sun as the barge moved slowly downriver toward Bor. We passed many colorful camps with herdsmen who were rich in cattle but not in clothing. Sharing two toilets among four hundred people and conducting more than twenty media interviews by satellite phone turned what might have been a pleasantly lazy cruise into a fairly fraught experience. I had to explain that the only reason I could find for the government's refusal to allow me to travel farther was that it did not "want me to see how bad it has become."

Meanwhile, the government was telling anyone who asked,

"Egeland is welcome later, but not now," as it closed airports where I had been due to land in South Darfur and West Darfur indefinitely—for "repairs." In another sign of uncoordinated action between government ministries and the ruling party, a group of banner-waving demonstrators, summoned to picket the airports in the intense midday heat to protest against my mission, were never told that I had already been blocked from traveling, that the airport had been closed to make travel impossible. Even our request for an overflight to Chad was denied. Annan, the U.S. State Department, the European Union aid commissioner, the U.K. Foreign Office, and the Security Council president were among those who protested the denial of access. Before long, the Sudanese government yielded and I was back in Sudan the following month.

This relentless tug-of-war where we made progress providing emergency relief to millions of people, but failed in protecting civilians and in pressing through to a political solution, was part of my life from my third month on the job. I did believe—naïvely, it now appears—back in 2003 and early 2004 that the growing and forgotten Darfur crisis would get better if we managed to bring it to the attention of world leaders. This was, after all, not a natural disaster. The violence and ethnic cleansing were entirely man-made.

The extreme brutality was the result of the government decision to start arming the renegade Janjaweed, an amalgam of Chadian and Darfurian Arab militias bent on controlling the borderlands, in order to give its own troops support against two rebel movements in the Darfur region. In February 2003, as government police and troops began to suffer serious setbacks in the region, Khartoum decided to unleash the militias—an undisciplined and ruthless collection of heavily armed thugs—against rebel forces in the SLM/A and the Justice and Equality Movement. Both groups had roots in black African tribes and felt that Darfur was discriminated against and marginalized by the central government in Khartoum. Faced with humiliating losses in Darfur, not that far from the capital Khartoum, the government allowed the Janjaweed free rein to rape, pillage, and murder their way through any of the towns and villages whose mainly African-origin inhabitants could be deemed to support the rebels.

From September to December 2003, at the start of my involvement in the area, our UN humanitarian envoy, Tom Vraalsen, a former colleague from the Ministry of Foreign Affairs of Norway, had undertaken a number of initiatives to encourage peace talks, gain access for relief workers, and raise $23 million for a "Greater Darfur Initiative." In November the situation had deteriorated sharply and on December 5, 2003, I gave a press conference saying that Darfur "has quickly become one of the worst humanitarian crises in the world." Four days later we drafted an equally strong statement that was issued in the name of the secretary-general. There were already a million people in need of assistance, including some six hundred thousand who were either refugees in Chad or had been displaced inside Darfur.

Incredibly, nobody seemed interested in our cries for attention. When I went to the representatives of the United States, United Kingdom, and Norway, who together constituted the troika facilitating the North-South peace talks in Sudan, I was politely told to not "rock the boat." They did not want attention to wander from an "imminent" agreement between Khartoum and the Sudan People's Liberation Army, a separate rebel organization operating in South Sudan. The parties eventually signed a power-sharing agreement in 2003 that ended twenty years of brutal civil war.

In February 2004, I was invited by U.S. Ambassador John Negroponte for lunch in the formal UN Delegates Dining Room. Negroponte was, as always, cordial and accommodating, in glaring contrast to the abrasive John Bolton who followed. Over lunch I explained how hundreds of Darfurian villages were ablaze and tens of thousands had become victims of the scorched-earth methods of the regime. I asked to invite myself to the Security Council to brief it on what was going on in Darfur. "Why not?" said Negroponte, nodding. "No, probably not," one of his deputies interrupted, frowning. "We already checked with OCHA. Washington believes, like the U.K. and Norway, that it is better to wait until after a breakthrough in the Naivasha talks [held in Kenya] on peace in the South." Five months later, Secretary of State Colin Powell would declare that "genocide" had taken place in Darfur.

By March 2004, wait-and-see had become an unsustainable policy in Western capitals. Just before he left the post, our humanitarian coordinator in Sudan, Mukesh Kapila, had publicly likened Darfur to the pregenocide period in Rwanda ten years earlier. But because Pakistan, an ally of Sudan's, was president of the Security Council, Darfur stayed off the agenda. Two days into the German presidency of the Security Council in April, I was finally allowed to speak. Shortly before, Kapila had managed to arrange for a dozen humanitarian experts from OCHA to get into Darfur, which was virtually sealed off at the time. Their horrific reports were the basis for my wake-up call to the council. "Last month alone, there were reports of fifty-nine violent attacks with 212 civilians killed, of which 166 deaths were attributed to the Janjaweed, or troops associated with the government," I said. This was merely the "tip of an iceberg" involving the "ethnic cleansing of hundreds of thousands ... in one of the world's worst, and most neglected, humanitarian crises."

Chinese, Pakistani, and Algerian diplomats, however, ensured that the German permanent representative could only issue a bland statement after my address. The foreign correspondents who assembled for the daily noon briefing had a field day: Why, they would ask in their wire stories, does the Security Council only express "concern" and ask both parties to refrain from violence, when the emergency relief coordinator, who briefed the council on behalf of the secretary-general, said he could document "ethnic cleansing" and a "scorched-earth campaign with forced depopulation of entire areas" undertaken by the government-sponsored militias?

We finally had the media attention we needed, but world leaders still did not provide the political pressure or the physical protection that could stop the atrocities. Our only positive development was that donor nations responded generously with funding, enabling emergency relief to get to Darfur. The achievements of close to fourteen thousand Sudanese and international aid workers in the world's largest humanitarian operation have been nothing less than heroic. Since the end of 2004, my colleagues in Darfur have been able to deliver lifesaving relief every month to most of the people affected.

A comprehensive survey undertaken by UN and NGO experts showed in August 2006 that malnutrition levels had been reduced by half since we first gained access for our large international operation in mid-2004. Mortality rates had fallen to a fifth of what they were when we did our first survey in June 2004, and 70 percent of Darfurians had gained access to safe drinking water. Over a half-million tons of food was delivered in 2006 alone.

Nevertheless, my final visit to El Geneina in November 2006 proves once again how precarious are our efforts to alleviate problems in such areas. On the 17th I am told by the UN, nongovernmental, and Red Cross colleagues who gather to see me in the courtyard outside the OCHA office that our efforts in the region are "under massive attack." It is early morning and the winter desert wind is ice-cold. Even I, a Norwegian, am freezing. Some of our African women colleagues in sleeveless robes are longing for the intense Saharan heat.

The precise and always impressive briefings from French, American, British, Scandinavian, and other relief groups coincide with that of our UN colleagues; the spokesman for these groups tells me, "Militia attacks and banditry have rendered more than ninety-five percent of all roads in West Darfur no-go areas for humanitarian operations. As a result, an increasing number of camps are cut off from adequate and reliable assistance: in some instances, all basic humanitarian services have had to be shut down."

As if the local militias and authorities wanted to prove the local aid workers right, three hours after I leave El Geneina, a town with no antigovernment rebels, a UN vehicle with two volunteers is robbed at gunpoint by men in military camouflage just outside the town. "Most probably it was one of the nomadic leaders you met in El Geneina and lectured about protection of civilians, that ordered the carjacking," a colleague remarks when we hear the news in Khartoum. "They have reacted the same way as before when they did not like the message or the visitor."

Back in the Security Council on November 22, 2006, in my final Darfur briefing, I warn the world's most powerful nations in great detail about the gravity of the security situation. Few outside Sudan understand the risks humanitarian workers take as they are harassed, attacked, and even killed. Just three days before my arrival, a World Food Programme driver died from injuries sustained in one such gun attack. Looking at the ambassadors who have blocked sanctions against Sudanese leaders, I say, "Large new militias are being armed as we speak while none are being disarmed despite the demands and measures put in place by this council in 2004 and 2005. As the women from the displaced camps told me in El Geneina, the youngest and most reckless now receive new weapons and are recruited into militias. New displacement is also fueled by cross-border raids of armed groups who receive arms and safe havens on both sides of the Chad-Sudan border, thereby rapidly pushing the conflict toward a regional escalation."

There is neither a military nor a humanitarian solution to the freefall of humanity in Darfur. There is only a political solution in which both sides in the conflict agree to an immediate stop to all attacks, a cessation of hostilities, and respect for the cease-fire. But the belief in a military solution remains high both in government and in some rebel circles, even after several years of violence. When I left Sudan on November 20, two massive military operations started in the Jebel Marra and Birmaza areas of North Darfur. A dozen villages were attacked and looted, driving more than eight thousand men, women, and children from their homes and leaving many dead and injured. In the Birmaza area, huge amounts of livestock were stolen and houses burned; the attackers deliberately deprived the population of its means of survival. In the Jebel Marra Mountains, where the nights are freezing at that time of year, the attackers looted food, clothing, and blankets. This meant that babies and small children who survived the attacks might freeze to death. "Let us be clear," I tell the Security Council, "these acts are crimes of the most despicable kind. They are an affront to humanity."

Far more needs to be done to enable humanitarian lifesaving efforts to continue in the absence of a negotiated solution to the bitter conflict. Again, we have seen regression. I spent a long night, July 2–3, 2004, with the foreign minister of Sudan negotiating the first breakthrough agreement on access for humanitarian organizations to Darfur. President Bashir and Secretary-General Kofi Annan announced the so-called Moratorium on Restrictions at the end of our first visit. It meant an opening for what was to be one of the largest humanitarian operations ever.

Since then a new wall of administrative resistance to our operations has slowly been rebuilt both in Khartoum and Darfur. A maze of endless bureaucratic barriers consumes most of the time of humanitarian relief managers. Some NGOs have seen half their staff paralyzed due to the lack of travel, work, or residence permits, among many other obstacles. While all agencies and nationalities suffer from this, the NGOs in general, and U.S. aid workers in particular, have been affected disproportionately. The United States has been by far the largest donor to the humanitarian operations in Darfur.

When I visited Sudan in November 2006, twenty-six of forty

American NGO workers had been blocked from doing their work in Darfur. Relief workers of all nationalities have to be granted full access. The same is true for journalists who report back to the donor community on our activities. Two American journalists were prevented from traveling with me to Darfur. This is part of a broad effort by the government to restrict access and reporting on Darfur. Journalists have been detained, threatened with expulsion, and harassed by a multitude of government authorities, particularly National Security officials.

The Norwegian Refugee Council (NRC) was, when I visited, not only suspended from working in Kalma camp, but also received several letters confirming its expulsion from South Darfur. One letter demanded that NRC immediately hand over its assets to the government. This would have amounted to a confiscation of international property and was fortunately averted. NRC provided important services for several hundred thousand displaced people in South Darfur. The Security Council had to speak out in favor of the NRC on at least one previous occasion when the group had been suspended by the government.

I leave Khartoum for the last time, headed to Jordan and London and then on to New York, utterly disillusioned. My gloomy mood only deteriorates when we are delayed for hours in both stops. At London's Heathrow I miss my plane for New York. It gives me plenty of time to reflect. If the trend I have witnessed continues and the world's largest humanitarian operation falters, if the lifeline for millions of civilians collapses, the situation in Darfur will spiral out of control and we may have a new Rwanda and many new Srebrenicas. We will see another dramatic escalation of human suffering and loss of life beyond anything we have witnessed so far.

These thoughts were very much the backdrop of that last briefing I gave in the Security Council. Toward the end of my speech, I saw behind me, on one of the red chairs for diplomatic observers, a Sudanese diplomat. I looked at him as I concluded my briefing: "Each time I have traveled to Sudan, I have hoped to see a fundamental change in the attitude of the government, an attitude that has been characterized by denial, neglect, and the blaming of others. Yet again, this time, I saw no such change last week, but rather a further entrenching of this attitude. Senior government officials deny the killings, the displacements, and the rape of women." The Sudanese diplomat listened impassively.

In 2007 the Security Council finally agrees to deploy a 26,000-strong and well-equipped joint United Nations–African Union peacekeeping force to replace the small and demoralized AU units. That same autumn the ineffective international mediation efforts also intensified as the able Swedish diplomat Jan Eliasson is named UN envoy to the peace efforts. In August peace talks were organized in Tanzania by the AU and UN with many of the increasing number of armed groups involved in the Darfur conflict.

But, by early 2008, after fifteen hundred days and nights of fear and misery among Darfur's civilians, the outlook is again bleak. The Sudanese government is slowing down deployment of the new force, objecting to, among other things, the Norwegian-Swedish engineering battalion, as they would prefer, it seems, a friendlier Egyptian contribution. But UN member states are also slow in committing important air and other assets needed for the force. It is hoped the force will make its mark on the ground in 2008, but real protection for thousands of vulnerable communities will not be achieved without a political settlement of the conflict.

The greatest worry is therefore the stalled peace talks. A meeting, curiously called by the AU and UN in Libya at the end of 2007, was boycotted by the main rebel factions. Since then the mediators have had to shuttle between the government and the various rebel movements to seek scarce common ground. A more potent international coalition has to be mobilized to press not only the government, but also the rebel movements to realize the urgency of the situation. While men procrastinate in their government offices in Khartoum or in their rebel quarters in Paris, Chad, Eritrea, or Darfur, women and children continue to die in Darfur. This international coalition should be led by China, India, Arab nations, and Sudan's African neighbors, rather than the Western powers that have so far, with little effect, taken the lead.

5.

Tsunami!

MY CELL phone is where I left it, in the living room. But it rings loud enough to wake me and my whole family, including my eighty-three-year-old mother visiting us in New York from Norway, this early Sunday morning, December 26, 2004. It is the second day of Christmas and I have been looking forward to some quiet time, since the crises in Iraq, Darfur, the Congo, and elsewhere had kept us going at full steam right up to Christmas Eve. But I have a strong sense that it is not good news as I tear around searching for the phone in our rented apartment.

On the same day last Christmastime, Rashid Khalikov of our Geneva office had called with news of a devastating earthquake that had leveled the ancient city of Bam in southern Iran. Tens of thousands were dead or missing. I had taken an end-of-the-year leave to stay with my family in Norway, but I ended up working nonstop on the phone with colleagues in Tehran, Bam, Geneva, and New York. A few days later, I went to Iran to see the stricken areas, launch a global fund-raising appeal, and meet with Iranian president Mohammad Khatami and humanitarian colleagues in Tehran.

Bam was a horrific sight. The beautiful thousand-year-old city of mud and bricks had collapsed on its citizens while most were still asleep. The final count showed that twenty-six thousand people lost their lives within minutes, nearly all in a concentrated area in the old city. The Iranians and we internationals provided tents, food, and medical relief in a large and efficient operation, but the people were devastated by the loss of so many family members.

"It is Yvette. Sorry to wake you up, but a large tsunami has struck countries all around the Indian Ocean!" A tsunami? In the Indian Ocean? Questions race through my head. "Are you sure it is not the Pacific Ocean?" I ask. *Tsunami* is a Japanese word and giant earth-quake-triggered waves typically hit Japan, Hawaii, and other Pacific islands. My colleagues in Geneva are six hours ahead of us in New York. Yvette Stevens, who is West African and is the new director of OCHA Geneva, and Rashid Khalikov, her deputy, have just con-cluded a series of meetings by a hastily put together task force. "No, it is definitely in the Indian Ocean. We have multiple confirmations of devastation all over the map," they answer, and give a succinct overview of a horrific, intercontinental tsunami disaster. Informa-tion is still scant, but Indonesia, Thailand, India, the Maldives, and Sri Lanka are among the stricken nations. The governments in Sri Lanka and the Maldives have already requested international assistance.

Colleagues in Geneva usually call several times a week to pro-vide early warnings or confirmation of floods, hurricanes, mud-slides, earthquakes, and other catastrophic events. But this is clearly something different. It sounds uniquely frightening since it has si-multaneously affected large regions far apart from one another.

As was the case one year ago, our standby duty officer this night is an extremely experienced disaster response colleague, Arjun Katoch, who was an Indian army colonel. Arjun had been alerted at around 2 A.M. Geneva time, minutes after the seismic monitor-ing centers to which we are linked registered a huge earthquake: 7:58 A.M. local time west of the northern tip of the huge Indonesian island of Sumatra. Arjun had awakened a number of colleagues and the system had clanked into action. Some started to piece together a first situation report; others began alerting our standby personnel for immediate deployment to the field; still others started to answer press inquiries, draft the first press statement, and telephone the diplomatic missions of the affected countries in Geneva, the world's humanitarian capital, to offer UN support and expertise. "The first team is already on its way to Sri Lanka," Yvette reports. "We have offered all the affected nations UN assistance and coordination. We expect more than the Maldives and Sri Lanka to ask for help."

It is just after 6 A.M. in New York. I am grateful that our response system has lost no time. I give a green light to Geneva to step up the use of all our time-tested standby arrangements for seed money, personnel, disaster relief equipment, and coordination with both UN and non-UN relief agencies. Many have an image of the UN as slow and bureaucratic, but once again my office, OCHA, is ahead of governments, other multilateral institutions, and even the NGOs.

I barely manage to get dressed before Margareta Wahlström, my deputy, calls with an update: "In addition to the operations center working now for some time in Geneva, we also have a cell active here in New York. From both cities we are linking up to our UN country teams in the affected countries, but nearly all of the UN resident coordinators and humanitarian coordinators are on home leave over New Year's. Detailed information is nearly nonexistent at this stage. The huge, destructive wave has taken everybody by complete surprise, according to what we have heard from Sri Lanka, the Maldives, India, and Thailand."

Margareta is expert in responding to disasters. Before joining the UN and serving as humanitarian coordinator in Afghanistan, she was for many years head of operations in the International Federation of Red Cross and Red Crescent Societies, the world's biggest responder to natural disasters. She was among those called several hours earlier by Arjun Katoch. Arjun had confirmed that the earthquake close to Sumatra was of magnitude 9, one of the strongest earthquakes ever registered and thus more than powerful enough to trigger a very big tsunami. I tell him, "It is good the system is up and running and the first people are leaving for Sri Lanka as we speak on an early Christmas Sunday. We need to start calling our people back from vacations again, including the UN resident and humanitarian coordinators as we did for Iran last year. But if the epicenter is so close to western Sumatra, why are there no reports of what destruction it has caused there?" "I don't know. It is all very odd," Margareta responds. "I will draft instructions from you and the administrator of the UN Development Programme to all of the UN teams in the affected countries."

From that moment it is nonstop action, day and night, weekdays and weekends, for many weeks. No one in the UN or in the affected countries had been prepared for a huge tsunami hitting the heavily populated Indian Ocean shores. In the Pacific Ocean there are good warning systems and therefore normally few casualties compared to onshore earthquakes such as the one in Bam. The last large tsunami in the Indian Ocean was decades ago and there had never been an intercontinental catastrophe in modern times. It was the least likely of a long series of possible disasters listed by the governments in the region. As I eat breakfast with my wife, Anne Kristin, my daughters, Ane and Heidi, and my mother, Margot, I speak to the UN diplomats from the stricken countries that I can get on the phone. Most of the delegations to the UN have nobody reachable and the few I get on bad cell phone connections have heard nothing from their own countries.

Bad news trickles in from more countries via my UN colleagues throughout that first Sunday. The tsunami had traveled at over 300 miles per hour. It had reached Indonesian Sumatra in twenty minutes, and had taken about one and a half hours to reach Sri Lanka and Thailand, a couple of hours to reach India, three to get to the Maldives, and several hours to reach as far as the eastern coast of Africa. No organized warning or evacuation seems to have occurred anywhere. There is complete confusion in all of the affected countries. It is impossible for the governments even to formulate what kind of assistance they would need us to provide.

The first situation report, e-mailed to my BlackBerry, lists the countries hit from East Africa to Malaysia, but states that only fifty people have been confirmed dead. This is the first of hundreds of updates describing destruction, grief, and relief efforts. Thinking of how eleven thousand were killed by Hurricane Mitch in Central America in 1998, and how the combined death toll by floods and monsoons in Bangladesh in the last decades has been hundreds of thousands, I look at the figure of fifty dead and wonder how many zeroes we will add in coming weeks. As always in the first forty-eight hours of a major natural disaster, it is utterly frustrating that we have so little solid information on which to plan our relief operations.

I give the first interviews on the phone that afternoon as we have a Christmas dinner with Norwegian relatives in Connecticut. I tell CNN International and ABC radio and television that every hour gives us more information confirming destruction beyond belief along vast coastlines in a dozen countries, and that a huge international relief operation is needed. I can see on my BlackBerry that by 4:15 P.M., explicit directives drafted by Margareta have been e-mailed to the top UN representatives in all the affected countries in the name of Mark Malloch Brown, administrator of the United Nations Development Programme, and myself as emergency relief coordinator:

We do trust that you have already convened crisis meetings with your UN Country Team (UNCT), or are in the process of doing so. We depend on you to be fully updated on the situation in your respective country, on the action of the UNCT, on how you are mobilizing the existing resources of the UNCT, and what resources are required to immediately enable you to provide assistance to the governments. You are requested to continue the contacts established during today, Sunday, with OCHA to discuss further assistance that may be required from OCHA. This information, as well as any request for additional support from the respective agencies, should be relayed to the respective headquarters as soon as possible. In addition, the ERC is mobilizing reinforcements to all Country Teams through the deployment of relief personnel. Contact with each office will be established for this purpose.

The next day we assemble early in my office to assess the information that has come overnight from Geneva and the affected countries. The skeleton staff on duty between Christmas and New Year's has been strengthened by colleagues who have been ordered back for duty or have come in spontaneously to help. Our first team of coordinators has arrived in Sri Lanka. Geneva has managed to get an impressive twenty-two experts on their way to Sri Lanka, the Maldives, Indonesia, and Thailand in the first twenty-four hours. More are on their way today from European and Asian nations with which we have standby arrangements. We still have no detailed reports from the Aceh province in northern Sumatra, which is closest to the epicenter.

I call Kofi Annan, who is taking a few well-deserved days of rest on the Wyoming ranch of his friend James Wolfensohn, president of the World Bank. After another tough year of international crises and growing criticism of the "Oil-for-Food" program in Iraq, Annan needed some quiet but had fallen and injured his shoulder on Christmas Eve. He has just spoken with President Susilo Bambang Yudhoyono of Indonesia, who had assumed office only two months earlier. "The president confirmed that Aceh has been badly hit, but was thankful that he had reports of few casualties. He obviously has not gotten the real picture yet," the secretary-general says. "Yes, he is in for a very bad series of news," I say. "You cannot be next to the epicenter of such a tremendous earthquake and tsunami without immediate and terrible devastation. The president has the same problem we have. There is hardly anybody able to report on the actual devastation and who can assess the needs because everyone has been stricken. Those who have survived scramble to save themselves and their families. We have locally employed UN colleagues among the dead and the missing."

My staff has previously scheduled an end-of-year press conference for noon on Monday, December 27. The year 2004 was difficult for humanitarian work, with growing need in Africa and too little money to fund even basic lifesaving around the globe. It will now be a very different briefing. I grab the latest situation reports, a map of the Indian Ocean, a list of the actions taken and what we plan to do in the next hours and days, and take the elevator down thirty-four floors to the second-floor press briefing room and its familiar blue curtain with UN symbols.

There is no end-of-year quiet here. There is a remarkable turnout in addition to the usual group of accredited UN correspondents from wire services, major international newspapers, and the UN-based TV networks. The thicket of additional television cameras and reporters at the back of the room makes me realize for the first time that the tsunami is a huge international story and that I will be the first to give an international press conference on the subject anywhere in the world. My pulse starts racing. This press conference might be one of the most important ever for the humanitarian side of the United Nations. Thus I am relieved to see Fred Eckhart, the very experienced spokesman for the secretary-general, waiting for me at the podium. I traveled with Fred during two difficult months when the war-stricken Balkans were unraveling in 1993 and we were assisting Thorvald Stoltenberg and Lord David Owen, the UN and EU co-chairmen of the international mediation efforts.

Feeling in my gut that what we know of the tsunami disaster is the tip of the iceberg, I plunge into my first attempt to describe the intercontinental catastrophe: "The tsunami which struck several

104   JAN EGELAND

Asian countries over the weekend may be the worst natural disaster in recorded history. It has devastated heavily populated areas in Sri Lanka, Indonesia, India, Malaysia, and Bangladesh and inundated large parts of the Maldives. So far, there are 5,700 confirmed deaths in India, 4,900 in Sri Lanka, and 4,500 in Indonesia. Sri Lanka and Indonesia are, however, even more devastated than India. There are many communities in Indonesia that are among the closest to the epicenter where the number of affected are still unknown."

I go on to say that while the full effects of the tsunami will only be known weeks from now, the United Nations is getting reports from country teams on an hourly basis. But many areas and communities are still inaccessible and we have not been able to contact local staff in Aceh and elsewhere. I appeal to donors to respond generously because "the cost of the devastation will be in the billions of dollars, hundreds of thousands of livelihoods are gone, and the human costs to the poor societies and communities that have been wiped out cannot be fathomed."

After my fifteen-minute briefing there is a stream of questions that Fred Eckhart lets go on for a full hour. He is relieved to finally have an international press conference in the UN without a single question focusing on the Iraqi "Oil-for-Food" scandal, sexual exploitation by peacekeepers, or the various corruption charges against the UN and even the son of Secretary-General Annan. I also feel it is going well. My twenty-five years of experience in humanitarian and human rights work allows me to visualize the huge needs as well as to describe the relief effort that is under way: the first search-and-rescue phase, and the "second wave of needs" especially in terms of water, sanitation, shelter, and health care. After a while the questions concentrate on whether the disaster could have been prevented, and on the lack of a warning system in the Indian Ocean. Toward the end I get a question on whether "dealing with the tsunami may undercut funding for relief efforts elsewhere in the world, such as Sudan."

My answer relates to the purpose of the scheduled end-of-year briefing on the severe underfunding of many relief operations: "I think an unprecedented disaster like this one should lead to unprecedented generosity from countries providing new and additional funds, because I wouldn't want to see many of our friends, the donor countries, depleting their natural disaster coffers the first two weeks of January and have nothing more when we come to other disasters . . . I'm afraid for the coming year because there are several donors who are actually less generous than before in a growing world economy . . . We were more generous when we were less rich, many of the rich countries . . . Christmastime should remind many Western countries at least how rich we have become. And if actually the foreign assistance of many countries now is 0.1 or 0.2 percent of their gross national income, I think that is stingy, really. I don't think that is very generous."

On my way out, several of the reporters come forward to urge me to do daily news conferences through the holiday season since "the story is huge and growing and you're the only one with a real overview." I agree to come back the next day at noon and so without realizing it start a marathon series of briefings that I will conduct virtually every day in New York, Geneva, or Tokyo for the next thirty days. I rush back to my office and a series of video and phone conferences on the emerging operations. A meeting had been held this morning with all the relief agencies in Geneva. I would now have one with all the executive heads we can get hold of within the Inter-Agency Standing Committee, which I chair regularly in my capacity as emergency relief coordinator, as mandated by a General Assembly resolution. In this meeting of United Nations agencies, the International Federation of Red Cross and Red Crescent Societies, and various nongovernmental umbrella organizations, all agree to stay in close touch, to coordinate response, and to design a global needs-based common appeal for funds. The Red Cross and Red Crescent movement will as always launch an independent appeal document, but most of the nongovernmental relief groups want to join the UN consolidated appeal.

I then meet with the ambassadors of the affected countries in New York and inform them about the fund-raising effort, the relief teams that have already been sent, and the flights and shipments with relief goods that are on their way. I urge national authorities to work closely with the United Nations to help coordinate the response. It is important that there be one ministry clearly in charge of and accountable for the disaster response and that there be clear lines of command as relief starts to arrive. I also ask for full and unimpeded access for international relief workers, including nongovernmental organizations, to all affected areas.

The tsunami has hit three active conflict zones: Aceh in Indonesia, the Tamil areas in northern Sri Lanka, and Somalia, where various armed militias and warlords fight one another. The diplomats have less information about the effect of the tsunami on their countries than I do, and they are grateful for the immediate and forceful UN response. But I have to warn them that international relief is still being organized and is nearly nonexistent on the disaster-stricken beaches. "It is your own people through local communities, authorities, and civil society that are doing all the lifesaving for the time being," I tell them.

Some thirteen hours after leaving my apartment, I am back to a late meal with my family and mother. The news in North America and Europe is dominated by the stories of missing and dead tourists; the worst-hit coastline in Thailand is a major tourist hub at this time of the year. From my native Scandinavia hundreds are reported missing in the tsunami zone and authorities and public opinion in both Sweden and Norway seem as overwhelmed with these limited numbers of tourists as the affected countries are with their utter devastation. It is later confirmed that Sweden is fifth and Germany sixth on the sad list of countries with dead and missing nationals.

Excerpts of my own press conference are run repeatedly by the major American and international television networks, which concentrate on the huge relief operation that is on its way, and on the scale of the disaster. A typical line comes from Colum Lynch of the *Washington Post:* "The huge underwater earthquake that drove a tsunami across the Indian Ocean is shaping up to be one of the most expensive and destructive natural disasters on record, requiring several billion dollars in international assistance, the top U.N. relief official said Monday."

That evening we fax my first report to the UN secretary-general to give an overview of the destruction and the needs. Logistical problems will clearly be our greatest difficulty, we conclude. Where we need the roads, the harbors, and the airstrips most, they are all gone in a wide strip along the coast. Rapid, flexible, and high-level coordination will be another critical necessity in places where the UN has the leading role. It is more prophetic than we expect when we write on this second day of the disaster that the "outpouring of overwhelming public support, dispatching of rescue and medical teams, provision of humanitarian goods, and arrival of humanitarian personnel are likely to create unforeseen bottlenecks, particularly in Indonesia. It is imperative that national and international relief efforts are carried out in a coherent and coordinated manner, so as to pave the way for the critical recovery and rehabilitation efforts on a regional scale."

To this end, I recommend the immediate appointment of a special humanitarian envoy of the secretary-general for Southeast Asia. I propose that in the short term Margareta Wahlström be appointed. Margareta, a good soldier, leaves for the field the next evening and will travel constantly between the disaster-stricken countries to advise and direct the UN resident coordinators, whom I have also nominated as humanitarian coordinators in each of the most affected countries. The role of a roving special coordinator is well received by national and international actors. When Margareta is back in New York after five weeks, I ask her to leave for the field again after only three days at headquarters.

In the late evening of this second day of disaster, Brian Grogan, our young and talented assistant press officer, calls to say that the CNN online edition has taken an unexpected angle: "U.S., rich countries stingy, says UN official." Brian was on vacation several hours north of New York City and had spent the whole previous afternoon and evening driving back with his wife and their infant on snowy roads as a winter storm hit the Northeast. The CNN article was worrisome in linking my well-known stand on the over-all "stinginess" of rich countries with the modest initial pledge by the United States of $4 million (later in the evening increased to $15 million) to the tsunami-stricken countries.

I understand immediately that this may be explosive. I had been careful not to single out any country, and especially not for a tsunami response that was yet to come. I didn't even know what the Americans were planning to give when I held my press conference. Washington is generally among the quickest and biggest donors in large disasters. And in emergency relief the United States is, overall, our biggest donor. It is the American development assistance that is so small; the United States is among the least generous of countries in the Organization for Economic Co-operation and Development, giving only a modest 0.15 percent of Gross National Income (GNI) in foreign assistance, below the global average of donors and well below the UN target of 0.7 percent of GNI. Brian offers to call CNN. There the desk agrees, after some review, that the story is based on a misunderstanding since my remark did not refer to American tsunami relief. An hour later the story is off the Internet.

But the damage is already done. The next morning, when I arrive at my office I receive a printout from Brian of a front-page article by Bill Sammon in the conservative *Washington Times* headlined "U.N. official slams U.S. as 'stingy' over aid." The lead: "The Bush administration yesterday pledged $15 million to Asian nations hit by a tsunami that has killed more than 22,500 people, although the United Nations' humanitarian-aid chief called the donation 'stingy.'" Sammon, who had not been at the press conference, had taken several of my quotes on the rich world's lack of generosity from the UN transcripts of the press conference, and contrasted those with U.S. pledges to help in the tsunami. He had also gotten White House deputy press secretary Trent Duffy to "respond" to my comments by pointing out that the United States is "the largest contributor to international relief and aid efforts, not only through the government, but through charitable organizations. The American people are very giving."

The article is not unnoticed in Washington. When Secretary of State Colin Powell makes the rounds on the morning television shows to counter the appearance of initial Christmas inaction in the administration and announce the U.S. intent to step up civilian and military relief efforts, he is confronted with my apparent criticism of "stingy" America. The secretary was not amused. He became angrier in each interview when asked how it felt to be "stingy." Later in the day on CNN's *Lou Dobbs Tonight*, guest anchor Kitty Pilgrim says, "a United Nations official implies the United States is not giving its fair share of aid to the flood-ravaged areas." CNN anchor Tony Harris reports that "many countries have pledged money and emergency supplies. The United States is one of the first to step forward with an initial offering of $15 million. But an official with the United Nations called that amount 'stingy.'" Soon it looks like a second tsunami in U.S. news media: radio talk shows, television networks, newspapers, and bloggers all seem to be on my case. Led by Fox News, the *Washington Times* (Sammon works for both), and the New York tabloids the *Post* and the *Sun*, conservative outlets start an aggressive campaign that goes on and on. I am all bad things at one and the same time: UN bureaucrat, European, socialist, and anti-American.

With my small team in New York I try to get the real story through. I again explain in interviews ranging from the morning TV shows to the networks' evening news that the U.S. response to the tsunami was laudable since it grew from $4 million to $15 million to $35 million in the first days. But I do not yield an inch in my criticism of the mostly pitiful levels of generosity from the world's wealthy amid child hunger and preventable disease.

In the evening, I am back in the CNN studio close to Columbus Circle for a live interview with Anderson Cooper. After a helpful exchange on the need to assist, and on our emerging international relief operations, Cooper asks, "Earlier at your press conference you said it's going to cost billions of dollars. You said rich nations—you didn't point out anyone in particular—are being, I think, *stingy* was the word you used. You don't think rich nations are paying their fair share?"

"No, I don't think so," I answer. "I have been in relief work now in nongovernmental organizations and the Red Cross and the UN for many years. It bothers me that we, the rich nations, are not becoming more generous the richer we become. The average rich nation pays 0.2 percent of its national income in international solidarity, in international assistance. We keep 99.8 percent to ourselves, on average. I don't think that is very generous."

As I leave the CNN studios for the cold winter street, I check my BlackBerry. I am surprised to see more than a hundred new e-mails have arrived in the last ninety minutes. Most messages are strong personal attacks from "patriotic Americans" who demand that I "leave America immediately," that I "publicly apologize to the American people," that I publicly admit that the United States is "by far the most generous in the world," that when I "go away in shame" I take "the corrupt and useless UN" with me, that I must realize that I am "a parasite on the American taxpayer," etc., etc. The e-mails just keep coming in as I scroll down the screen. I feel tired, cold, and old. I jump into one of New York's abundant yellow cabs and call the office on my way home. "Hi! You were lucky to get through," my enormously helpful Irish personal assistant, Marianne Moran, says. "All of America seems to be calling to yell at you." The right wing Web sites have started their assault. My phone numbers and e-mail have been posted with a call for the troops to attack. That night I "Google" myself and get thousands of hits. Web pages such as "Kerry Haters" come up:

> *After calling Americans "stingy" because our government is giving so "little" aid to the tsunami victims, we should remind Jan Egeland at the United Nations that we are a charitable people and give our aid through private organizations. This exemplifies how the world misunderstands us AND charity; governments should not rob people of more money through taxes to give aid! Jan Egeland can be reached at . . . his direct fax number is . . . We should let him know his comments are not appreciated—especially since the UN is doing nothing for Iraq, and last time I checked Saddam murdered over a million people. The people in SE Asia who are weeping because the "sea ate their children" could really use the $23,000,000,000 lost in the Oil-for-Food scam. I could just spit.*

Fortunately there is no time for self-pity. Every few minutes new telephone conferences, briefings, and meetings give a clearer picture of the magnitude of the crisis and the rapidly building relief operation. The estimates of dead and missing climb to 50,000 and then 77,000 on days three and four. Overall, there is an overwhelmingly positive response to our advocacy and our proactive deployment of relief workers and supplies to the field. I welcome and encourage the use of military and civil defense assets since they can arrive in strength faster than our civilian assets, and this is especially true for regional powers such as Australia and India, and superpower the United States. Fund-raising is setting new records each day. Individuals and governments not only see the suffering around the clock through the graphic images on their television screens, but they hear

again and again from the UN, the Red Cross, and the nongovernmental relief groups that we can and will be able to help if they give
us the resources. We have a hard time recording the rapid increase in
relief funds; initially modest contributions turn into double- and
triple-digit million-dollar pledges.

"I have spoken with spokesman Duffy at the White House,"
Brian tells me in the morning of December 29. "He has seen your
clarifications and after hearing my account of what was said in the
original press conference he has told the press that you have indeed
been misrepresented." "Thank God," I say. "That should be all behind us now and we can concentrate all energies on getting helicopters and emergency relief in. If the U.S. administration has
understood I am not worried about some right-wing extremists on
the Internet."

But it is not behind us. Duffy has not been able to talk to his
boss, President George W. Bush, who interrupts his Texas ranch vacation to give his first press conference on the tsunami. The first vol-
ley from the White House press corps seeks his comments on "the
UN official" who criticized U.S. response to the tsunami as "stingy."
Bush was clearly prepared for the question: "Well, I felt like the person who made that statement was very misguided and ill-informed.
We're a very generous, kindhearted nation, and, you know, what
you're beginning to see is a typical response from America." He
noted that the United States provided $2.4 billion "in food, in cash,
in humanitarian relief to cover the disasters for last year...That's
forty percent of all the relief aid given in the world last year."

I hear about the Bush press conference while I am teleconfer-
encing with our team that is setting up camp in the utter devastation of Banda Aceh, the main town on northern Sumatra. I am
bewildered. In all my jobs in governmental and nongovernmental
life, I have benefited from fair and positive media attention. Now I
learn what it feels like to be misunderstood and attacked, yet powerless to set the record straight. I have criticized the rich world for

being tight-fisted hundreds of times. It is part of my job description: to impatiently ask for more for the world's unfortunate. Nevertheless, I have clearly touched a raw nerve and have given ammunition to both sides in an ongoing American debate about the role and place of the United States in the world community. Some colleagues are scared about the degree to which our work is now scrutinized and criticized; others are thrilled that my initial remarks have inadvertently helped increase U.S. pledges from the initial $15 million to $35 million and later to $350 million, and that I have started a debate on relative levels of generosity, not only in the United States, but also in oil-rich Persian Gulf countries and several European nations that are lagging in international assistance.

President Bush promises huge military resources, including transport aircrafts, Marine expeditionary units, and the aircraft carrier *Abraham Lincoln* with lots of helicopters. He also makes a potentially worrying announcement: "The United States has established a regional core group with India, Japan, and Australia to help coordinate relief efforts. I'm confident more nations will join this core group in short order." The rest of the day we try to find out what this odd group would actually do, given the fact that the United States and the other "core" countries had already given the UN and my office the mandate to coordinate relief efforts. We speak to contacts in Washington and with diplomats from Japan, Australia, and India, none of whom understand the rationale behind such a group. On the contrary, all the diplomats, including the Americans, are highly appreciative of the rapid UN deployment to the field, our briefings to diplomats, agencies, and affected countries, and our continuous advocacy for a coherent international response coordinated with local and national governments. This is also the clear message I get after calling Marc Grossman, one of Secretary Powell's deputies, whom I know well from my days as the UN envoy to Colombia, a State Department priority country. Grossman assures me the "core" group will do nothing but help the UN be overall coordinator of the effort. He also said that, in spite of the president's comments, the United States was "way beyond" any unhappiness with my initial remarks. "We know you were misunderstood and appreciate your clarification," Marc tells me.

Secretary-General Annan has cut short his vacation in Wyoming and arrives in New York on the evening of Wednesday the 29th. I brief him on the progress of our work and about all the meetings scheduled for tomorrow. We will have an important videoconference with Colin Powell in Washington, at which the United States is supposed to invite the UN to participate in the new core group. "Clearly somebody in the White House has improvised the idea of the U.S. 'leading' the global relief effort with a select group of allies to get a better spin on the tsunami challenge after a growing chorus of congressional Democrats and other national and international critics have said the U.S. response was slow and inadequate," I conclude.

The next morning several senior UN officials greet me as I come for the morning meeting with Annan and his deputies. Several are full of praise for my performance on behalf of the UN in the news media, and for my having engaged the U.S. president, who by now is on the defensive. I do not like it. Even in my own workplace I am struggling to set the record straight: "Our work has just started. The jury will be out for a long time while deciding on whether we succeed or flunk in helping the millions that had their lives destroyed by the devastation. And I never asked for a fight with Washington. Their tsunami help is just fine. It is the overall aid from the rich world and the U.S. which is stingy." "Well," one of them responds, "the discussion is on and it is great for getting a debate on aid and generosity. Did you see today's *New York Times* editorial?" "No, I have been meeting our logistics experts about the plane that hit a cow and closed down the only airport we can use for relief flights close to Aceh," I answer, and grab the paper.

Under the title "Are We Stingy? Yes," the editorial goes on to say:

In the worst act of terror against the UN ever, a bomb killed twenty-two of our colleagues in Baghdad on August 19, 2003. The explosion left a gaping hole in the wall of the old Canal Hotel, where Sergio de Mello and our OCHA office were located. (Sabah Arar/AFP/Getty Images)

My first meeting as chair of the executive Inter-Agency Standing Committee (IASC) was held in Geneva in the wake of the Baghdad bombing. Kofi Annan and I held a press briefing, where we pledged to try to stay on in Iraq. (UNDPI)

As a nineteen-year-old volunteer with the Catholic El Minuto de Dios I worked with the Motilone Indians in the Colombian jungle. The Motilones were hunting less and farming more, and had to cut and burn the rain forest to plant their corn and yucca. (Courtesy of the author)

Meeting the FARC guerrilla commanders in southern Colombia for peace talks. Raul Reyes (*far right*) and supreme leader Manuel Marulanda wear pistols and machetes as presidential peace commissioner Camilo Gómez and I talk with them. (Colombian Presidency)

In June/July 2004, I accompanied Kofi Annan on our first mission to Darfur. From our helicopter, we see thousands of refugees lined up to meet us in a refugee camp in the desert of eastern Chad. (UNDPI)

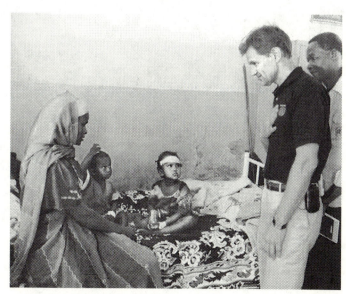

On my fourth and last visit to Darfur in November 2006, a woman with two wounded children tells a harrowing story of how Janjaweed militias attacked the defenseless Sirba village and shot her two-year-old daughter as she held her in her arms. (Eric Miller)

On the morning of December 26, 2004, a tsunami struck the town of Banda Aceh with overwhelming force and killed tens of thousands in seconds. The destruction was so total that we did not get detailed reports of the devastation for two days. When I arrived in October 2005, I heard reports of effective emergency relief. (Aftenposten/Scanpix/Sipa Press)

President Clinton embarked on his mission as Special Envoy for tsunami recovery with lots of energy in April 2005. Here we attend the global consortium for tsunami assistance, which I initiated as Emergency Relief Coordinator and which Clinton took over after he was named Special Envoy. (UN OCHA)

Inspecting the sad ruins of our local OCHA office in Guiglo, western Ivory Coast, in February 2006 with Besida Tonwe, head of OCHA there. The government-sponsored Jeune Patriots were allowed to destroy all international aid bases in the town. (Ky Chung, UNOCI)

I met thousands of desperate, displaced Burkinabe victims of the government-supported violence outside Guiglo. The refugees quietly asked: "Now that you in the international community have fled, who will now defend us against the armed gangs?" (Ky Chung, UNOCI)

Uri Savir (*seated, right*) and Abu Ala (*left*) initialed the Oslo Accord during the secret late-night event on August 19–20, 1993. Foreign Minister Johan Holst is seated at center; I am behind him, with Mona Juul and Terje Rød-Larsen to my left. (Norwegian Security Police)

Just after the fierce Israeli bombing of the Shiite southern suburbs of Beirut on July 23, 2006, we toured the rubble. At this improvised press briefing, I called the bombing of the heavily populated residential area "disproportionate" and a "violation of international law." (© Mohamed Messara/epa/Corbis)

At the end of my meeting with the leadership of the Lord's Resistance Army, I showed them our detailed statistics of all their atrocities. Top commander Joseph Kony is at left; his deputy Vincent Otti is in the middle. (Eric Miller)

Each year, just before the high-level segment of the General Debate of the UN, the Secretary-General and the U.S. President meet, with four advisers each, in a small windowless room behind the great General Assembly Hall. (UNDPI)

We can save a lot of time using helicopters on missions in war or disaster zones, where distances are great, roads poor or nonexistent, and security bad. Here I am guarded by SPLA soldiers as we are to meet the LRA leadership in South Sudan on the border with Congo. (Eric Miller)

*President Bush finally roused himself yesterday from his vacation in
Crawford, Tex., to telephone his sympathy to the leaders of India, Sri
Lanka, Thailand and Indonesia, and to speak publicly about the devastation of Sunday's tsunamis in Asia. He also hurried to put as much
distance as possible between himself and America's initial measly aid
offer of $15 million, and he took issue with an earlier statement by the
United Nations' emergency relief coordinator, Jan Egeland, who had
called the overall aid efforts by rich Western nations "stingy." "The person who made that statement was very misguided and ill informed," the
president said. We beg to differ. Mr. Egeland was right on target. We hope
Secretary of State Colin Powell was privately embarrassed when, two
days into a catastrophic disaster that hit 12 of the world's poorer countries and will cost billions of dollars to meliorate, he held a press conference to say that America, the world's richest nation, would contribute
$15 million. That's less than half of what Republicans plan to spend on
the Bush inaugural festivities. The American aid figure for the current
disaster is now $35 million, and we applaud Mr. Bush's turnaround.
But $35 million remains a miserly drop in the bucket, and is in keeping
with the pitiful amount of the United States budget that we allocate for
nonmilitary foreign aid. According to a poll, most Americans believe the
United States spends 24 percent of its budget on aid to poor countries; it
actually spends well under a quarter of 1 percent.*

As I am reading the editorial, the secretary-general comes from
his office into the adjacent meeting room. We rise as the old-style
form of the thirty-eighth floor dictates, and Annan greets us with
his sore shoulder and kind words to we who have had no rest since
the 26th. I am asked to give an overview of the situation and start by
giving the latest figures: "at least one hundred and fifteen thousand
are dead in the region; half a million injured; one million displaced;
and at least five million in need of immediate assistance. We have
had the best response ever to our appeals. As of today a total of half a
billion dollars' worth of assistance has been pledged or received.

More than thirty countries have stepped forward to help, as have millions of individuals from around the world."

I then list the logistical nightmares that prevent most of the non-military international aid from arriving to the actual beneficiaries, especially in Aceh in Indonesia and in some of Sri Lanka's eastern and southern shores. Aid workers we are sending in have to be totally self-contained, bringing with them tents, food, water, sanitation, and transport, because there is "nothing left in Banda Aceh and the coastal towns along the Sumatra coast. The epicenter was so close to the Aceh coast of Sumatra that it in some places reached twenty meters high as it crashed into the shoreline."

The string of meetings that follow the 9 A.M. morning one go well. At 9:30 we meet the key UN and non-UN humanitarian agencies, and the secretary-general reaffirms our OCHA appeals for strong coordination of the waves of relief and relief workers on their way to Indonesia and Sri Lanka. Annan also explains that Secretary Powell yesterday had confirmed that the core group consisting of Australia, India, Japan, and the United States would not compete with, but rather support UN global coordination. This is indeed reconfirmed in the videoconference we have at 10:30 with Powell and his team in Washington. With Marc Grossman at the secretary's side there is agreement that I will join, on behalf of the UN, the daily telephone conferences that Grossman will organize every evening.

Then, at 11 A.M., we see the ambassadors of the twelve Asian and African countries affected. At noon Annan and I go to the press briefing, where again a record number of reporters are assembled. My hardworking OCHA colleagues, many working now for the fourth straight day from eight in the morning until midnight, have prepared an introduction for the secretary-general that concludes: "As the death toll mounts, and we continue to search for the missing, we should also not forget the survivors, especially the poor, and the many millions of vulnerable in that region. This is an unprecedented, global catastrophe and it requires an unprecedented, global response. Over the past few days, it has registered deeply in the consciousness and conscience of the world, as we seek to grasp the speed, the force, and magnitude with which it happened."

I am grateful that Annan, who himself worked for several years for the UN High Commissioner for Refugees, again underlines that "coordination of the response is now absolutely essential. How well the international community and the affected countries work together now will determine how well we will deal with all aspects of the disaster—both in the immediate and the longer term." Later it will be more than evident that we should have been stronger in warning against the flood of do-gooders from hundreds of more or less well-prepared Western groups that are now mobilizing to descend on the stricken populations.

That evening at 10 P.M. we have our first "core group" meeting. It is early morning in India and late morning in Australia and Japan, but Jan Berteling, the humanitarian director of the Dutch Ministry for Foreign Affairs, has to get up at 4 A.M. to participate. It is unclear why the Dutch as well as the Canadians are added to the exclusive group, since Powell and Grossman have rejected Annan's proposal to add regional powers such as China, Malaysia, and Singapore because it would, the Americans feel, make it "more bureaucratic." Again I see an invisible political hand from the White House. After welcoming all the participants, most of them on an impressive deputy foreign minister level, Marc Grossman turns to me for an "operational update."

I tell them that the first fifty trucks of relief supplies have arrived in Banda Aceh and that tomorrow there are eight airplanes arriving. Tomorrow, we will also set up a self-contained camp for ninety relief workers from the UN as well as for nongovernmental organizations, to jump-start relief work and avoid the foreigners putting an additional burden on the people already there. All in all more than a hundred people from some twenty countries have been sent to strengthen the work of UN teams on the ground. The Red Cross and the NGOs are sending more people. Then I start to list what we need from the "core countries": heavy-duty transport planes, airport offloading equipment, small vessels to help load and transport relief along the coasts, machinery to repair the airport in Medan and possibly the airstrip in Banda Aceh, and an air-freight handling center in Medan. The ministers carefully note these and other requests I have received from our UN logistics experts in Rome, Geneva, and Jakarta and promise to report back the next night, New Year's Eve.

December 31 is the first day that I truly feel our humanitarian system is working and producing as it should. We have now established good systems for information sharing and handling. In the daily briefings that I receive from the UN Joint Logistics Center in Rome, the OCHA logistical service in Geneva, and the military-civilian liaison unit connected to the U.S. military center in Bangkok, it is evident that the UN has become a clearinghouse for "what is needed by whom where and for what." We are also completing a long series of assessments on the needs of the local populations that will be the basis of an important hundred-page appeal that Annan will present at an international conference hosted by the Indonesian president in Jakarta on January 6.

Colleagues in Geneva who will work on producing a coherent book of projects and programs in the next seventy-two hours say that it will be our most ambitious flash appeal ever. They ask for nearly $1 billion for the next six months. It will also probably be the most immediately funded appeal ever. The military-civilian cooperation is also producing results. "They are worth their weight in gold!" exclaims the front page of one of the same New York tabloids that had angrily attacked my "stingy" remark. It is a quote from me in yesterday's press conference on the fifty helicopters of the USS *Abraham Lincoln* that have helped jump-start airborne relief to Aceh and have enabled our colleagues in the World Health Organization and UNICEF to send medical assessment teams to inaccessible areas all along Sumatra. In the elevators and hallways, UN staff that I do not know tell me they have seen many interviews and are now "proud once more to serve with the UN."

The attacks by phone, e-mail, and fax continue but are increasingly driven by fringe groups on the political right. Stephanie Bunker, my press spokesperson, handles the radio talk shows. One epic battle takes place when an initially polite caller asks if she works for Undersecretary-General Egeland. As she confirms that fact, the caller yells, "You're on the air, asshole!" Stephanie was born and raised in Peru, Indiana, and is not easily scared. The caller ends up regretting he had called. At the noon briefing, I admit that the "donations are so large and coming in so fast that we really have to confirm that we heard right, that the number of zeroes is right." Donors have raised or are in the process of raising their pledges to hundreds of millions of dollars, with Japan's $500 million, Australia's more than $400 million, and Germany's and the EU's 500 million euros (600 million dollars) the largest.

In the evening my family has Norwegian and American friends over for New Year's Eve in our apartment. The mood is somber. The number of missing Norwegian tourists in Thailand is still, due to chaotic registration work by Norwegian authorities, more than 460, and by some estimates even much higher. Later it would turn out that eighty-four of my countrymen lost their lives—a terrible tragedy for a small country. The chaos in Norway, Sweden, and many other Western countries bears witness to how affluent societies are not able to cope with unexpected disasters. At 10 P.M., I brief the "core countries" in the regular teleconference. I have a new wishlist, including additional heavy-duty machinery for airports and harbors in Indonesia and Sri Lanka, but I can also give an overview of the massive military, civil defense, and civilian humanitarian resources being deployed from the stricken societies themselves and from more than thirty nations currently providing assistance in the field. "If there are no more comments I think we can take comfort in

Jan's statement that we have more reason for optimism today than yesterday. Happy New Year, colleagues," Marc Grossman concludes one hour before his boss, Colin Powell, will help drop the New Year's Eve ball in Times Square, some seven blocks west from where we are in Manhattan.

In the following days we try to build the widest possible coalition for tsunami relief and early recovery efforts. The several hundred projects that we manage to detail in the "flash appeal" that Kofi Annan launches in Jakarta on January 6 include forty partner organizations asking for $977 million for the next six months. Within a week after the appeal is launched, it is nearly fully funded as part of the incredible $4 billion that has been pledged by corporations, governments, and private individuals. The Jakarta conference has been hastily convened by President Susilo Bambang Yudhoyono in cooperation with Sri Lanka, Thailand, and the other hard-hit countries. Among those attending are Secretary Powell, Japanese prime minister Junichiro Koizumi, Chinese premier Wen Jiabao, and other leaders from Asia and Europe. The main donor nations and executives of the large aid organizations agree that it is indeed the countries themselves that will be in charge of their own recovery.

I watch the outcome of the Jakarta conference from New York, where we have a dozen daily meetings, conferences, and videoconferences with humanitarian partners in the affected regions. Perhaps the clearest sign that we have proved that the UN can provide the needed leadership in crisis is that the "core group" announces that it has dissolved itself after only eight days "to fold into the overall coordination of the United Nations." The conference reaffirms that the UN will be firmly in charge of international relief coordination.

As logistical bottlenecks are overcome, political problems surface. Muslim groups in Aceh are campaigning to impose deadlines for the Western military and civilian presence, and the government agrees that the foreign military forces should only stay a few weeks and hints that it may limit the number of Western organizations and expatriate relief workers. The first notion, I reject publicly as a bad idea. This is not the time to do anything but welcome the military contributions that bring crucial water purification plants, field hospitals, helicopters, landing crafts, and airport handling crews. The idea of limiting the number of aid groups is something we understand they want to discuss, but we warn that it is not easy to block some groups and allow others to start work.

Nearly all of the approximately two hundred international relief organizations coming to Aceh are bringing in generous funding, but perhaps too many amateurs are setting up shop in a field of action where the distance from high- and low-quality action is measured in human lives. In many live phone-in shows with BBC World Radio and TV, and other major outlets, we in the large UN agencies are often contrasted with the small, "unbureaucratic" nongovernmental aid groups that "without administrative overhead and red tape can go straight to the needy with their relief." Journalists instinctively love small groups and idealists, and are skeptical of large agencies and organizations. I choose to praise the undisputed idealism and speed of action of the smaller NGOs, but try to warn of the effects of hundreds of organizations not being coordinated with one another or with the national authorities as they chase worthy emergency projects. I should, in retrospect, have taken the unpopular view that all groups that had no previous contact with Sri Lanka or Indonesia should have stayed home and sent their money to those organizations that have a track record of providing humanitarian assistance in these areas.

Another disturbing development is the resurgence of old political and military divides in Sri Lanka. Sri Lanka does not have anti-Western lobbies, as does Indonesia, but its political leaders lack the Indonesian government's ability to view the national tragedy as an opportunity for peace with the armed opposition. Whereas in Indonesia, peace talks with the Acehnese armed opposition group GAM intensify and lead to a cease-fire and ultimately a successful peace agreement, in Sri Lanka the initial signs of cooperation between the army and the Tamil Tigers in assisting casualties and retrieving and exchanging wounded and diseased persons are soon overtaken by old political antipathies.

The first sign that Sri Lankan president Chandrika Kumaratunga is neither able nor willing to seize the opportunity for peace comes when a visiting Kofi Annan is not allowed to tour the Tamil Tiger–held areas of northern Sri Lanka, where the tsunami devastation is as bad as on the government-controlled eastern and southern shores. Not even a personal appeal from Annan himself, when he arrives in Colombo after visits to Jakarta and Aceh, can deter Kumaratunga. "We concluded it was not worth it for the world's topmost diplomat to go. The talks with the Tamil Tigers would be embarrassing for the government," she tells Annan in her presidential palace. Thus a great opportunity for bridge building is lost. The tsunami triggers successful peace talks for Aceh, but not here. Margareta Wahlström can visit as special coordinator for tsunami relief, as can other relief officials and relief consignments, but the peace process is not advanced, and Sri Lanka will pay a great price for the government's intransigence.

Two weeks after the tsunami I chair a large international donors' conference in Geneva. With my acting chief of staff, Sudanese Amjad Abbashar, and Geneva colleagues I finalize our main Power-Point presentation on the next six months' needs and plans just five minutes before going to the podium to open the event, which has drawn 250 high-ranking delegates from nearly one hundred nations. I propose a minute of silence in respect for the staggering number of 156,000 dead and missing. To outsiders we look like a well-functioning machine that has organized and coordinated an incredible amount of international activity in only two hectic weeks. But inside we are barely coping with what is really a chaotic shoestring operation in which small groups of overworked and exhausted people in the field and at headquarters constantly improvise to meet the unexpected problems and challenges of an extreme interconti- nental catastrophe.

Reporters from around the world cover the Geneva pledging. The *People's Daily* in Beijing point to China's new role as an impor- tant donor and tell their readers, "More than sixty nations from around the globe have pledged extraordinary levels of money, and provided in-kind assistance, manpower, and much-needed equip- ment for the relief efforts." It is indeed remarkable. Nigeria has al- ready transferred $1 million. Macedonia is in the process of giving. East Timor is giving. Trinidad and Tobago has given $2.5 million.

The unprecedented generosity leads, naturally, to unprece- dented levels of accountability for us who receive the money. When, among the hundreds of businesses and corporations offering to help, the international auditing firm PricewaterhouseCoopers offers its services pro bono, we leap at the chance to enhance our public tracking system of money received and money spent. OCHA al- ready has a public, Web-based financial tracking system, but it is too slow and has too little updated detail on where the money really goes. All money flowing through the UN is of course externally and internally accounted for and audited, but in the new age it is not enough to report extensively to member states. We also need new levels of openness toward the general public.

On the second Friday in January we establish initial contact with the international auditing firm. That weekend we work with them in New York, and on Monday they travel to Geneva to continue work on an enhanced Internet-based financial tracking system. In addition, the firm offers thousands of hours' worth of free risk anal- ysis and on-the-spot fraud protection advice or investigations to all UN agencies in the field and at headquarters. It takes a lot of con- vincing to get all UN agencies on board in this new joint venture,

but soon there is a growing enthusiasm for using the external advisers with their new software and procedures that can track and control the flows of money in real time.

Announcing our additional help from PricewaterhouseCoopers,
we declare, "The system should make it possible for my aunt to see
where her money is and how we have spent it." Our system is indeed enhanced. Much more information is available on the Internet
on how the money has been pledged, received, allocated, and spent.
The risk analysis capacity of the UN agencies is enhanced and control mechanisms are able to detect potential problems earlier. The
Financial Times, however, testing our Internet-based tracking system,
concludes, "Your aunt must be very good and very eager to be able
to track her money through the system—because we weren't."

As the full scale of the disaster is understood, the question again
and again surfaces: Could the effects of the tsunami have been prevented? A rare opportunity for answers is provided at the World
Conference on Disaster Reduction in Kobe, Japan, that I will open
on January 18, less than four weeks after the tsunami. By then the
number of dead or missing is 160,000. When I close the conference
on January 22 it is 220,000, close to the staggering final count of
227,000 made in mid-April. We had, through the secretariat of the
International Strategy for Disaster Reduction in Geneva, prepared
for the world conference for more than a year, but the shock of the
tsunami had suddenly made the otherwise unspectacular, although
important, congress an event of global importance. It is the biggest
gathering ever to discuss and commit to disaster reduction: almost
four thousand participants from sixty-eight countries, 240 organizations and, astonishingly, 562 journalists from all over the world.

Yes, the experts in Kobe answer, very many lives and livelihoods
could have been spared through early warning systems, disaster-
proof housing and public buildings, and education on the risk of
disasters and what to do and where to build. The conference has

been called to seek global agreement on a road map for future action to reduce risk and build resilient communities. As I arrive in Kobe, after sixteen hours of travel from New York, I am told that the emperor and empress of Japan will be present at the opening ceremony, and will grant the head of the organizing team, Salvano Briceño, and myself an audience before we start. The protocol is surprisingly light when we see the imperial majesties. I have read books about the fall of the shogun and samurai culture when the emperor was still regarded as a descendant of the gods and one had to lie on one's stomach when addressing him. Now I am struck by the grace and cordiality of the modern-day emperor and empress, who ask about how disasters can be prevented and how the bitter lessons of the earthquake in Kobe exactly ten years ago can help people prepare for natural disasters elsewhere.

In spite of the enormous size of the conference, important progress is made by the delegates in the shadow of the Indian Ocean disaster. We reach agreement on a declaration, taking the name of the surrounding Hyogo prefecture as well as a framework for action for the next decade, 2005–2015. I contribute little to the negotiations because I fall ill just after my opening address and the departure of the emperor and empress. For forty-eight hours with a growing fever, I alternate between bed and the meetings and press conferences that I cannot cancel. I can do little to help UN and NGO colleagues who fight to have industrialized countries agree on risk reduction being a "shared responsibility" with low-income but disaster-prone countries. The fact of the matter is that natural disasters are spread evenly all over the world, but nearly all lives lost are in poor third world societies. Too many of the recommendations concentrate on what developing countries should do and give little attention to what assistance they need to protect their own people. As much as the tsunami highlighted a need for risk reduction, the public focus is overwhelmingly on tsunami early-warning systems in the Indian Ocean. The United States and other climate skeptics prevent references to the effects of climate change—namely more hurricanes, floods, and droughts.

My fever is high when I stumble from my bed to deliver the closing speech in the huge plenary room where Japanese prime minister Junichiro Koizumi has taken the emperor's place. In spite of the familiar problems to move the United States and other large nations to formally take on new global commitments, I conclude that we have made historic progress in the arena of disaster prevention through the agreement by all delegations on the *Hyogo Framework for Action 2005–2015,* subtitled "Building the Resilience of Nations and Communities":

> *An ambitious agenda is set out in this framework. We have promised to substantially reduce the losses in lives and social, economic, and environmental assets of communities and countries. It is my personal conviction that through the faithful implementation of this action plan in the next ten years, the number of deaths caused by natural disasters should be halved compared to those of the last decade. Hundreds of thousands of lives and many millions of livelihoods will be protected. It is also realistic to have all new schools and all new hospitals and clinics in all disaster-prone areas made disaster proof. We shall in the course of the coming years have national disaster reduction platforms in all the 168 states that have come here to Kobe this week. While the decisions at this conference are not legally binding, they carry a strong commitment by states and organizations to guide our policies and actions in the next ten years. All country delegates I have met with have pledged commitment to invest in the follow-up, and make sure we act. We must not fail in its implementation.*

My colleagues from Geneva and our Japanese hosts are thrilled that their hard work for development and prevention of disasters has, for the first time ever, gotten worldwide attention. More than five hundred journalists file stories on our concluding press conference, which I barely manage to get through. I am obsessed to get on a plane by late afternoon that could get me to New York by Sunday morning and a possibility of recovering from the fever in my own bed and in the care of my family. A month's marathon is nearing its end. I doze through the more than twelve hours of flight until the captain comes with bad news. Snowstorms on the U.S. East Coast have worsened, all airports in and around New York are closed, and we have to land in Chicago. I spend thirty-six hours in endless lines at Chicago's O'Hare Airport before I finally make it back to New York on late Monday night, one month after the tsunami struck.

In the next weeks and months, the emergency phase slowly gives way to recovery work. Fishermen are getting boats and nets, primary schools open, local medical clinics reopen, and slowly the homeless are getting better tents or even prefabricated temporary housing. However, the problems we had signaled since day one—large numbers of uncoordinated international aid groups with lots of money—are becoming more acute as the emergency phase is coming to an end. To provide on-the-spot leadership in Aceh in January, I had sent the director of our Response Coordination Branch in Geneva, Joel Boutroue, to Banda Aceh. In his handover note to his successor in mid-February, Joel concluded, "We need to constantly remind ourselves that we are here to lend our full support to the authorities and help them set up mechanisms that will be able to absorb the massive emergency, recovery, and development aid in the pipeline. For such a set-up to be viable and sustainable, it must be under the full control of civilian authorities at provincial, district, and sub-district levels. . . . We were so far fairly successful in ensuring a stable dialogue and exchange of information between the UN, NGOs, authorities—generally from Jakarta—in charge of the operations and the Indonesian Military. . . . During the transition period it will be crucial to ensure that most of the key actors adhere to broad sector strategies. Failure to achieve this could result in substantial waste of money, duplication, and unsustainable level of assistance."

I will see for myself nine months later that Joel's hope for strong partnership and coordination between internationals in support of local and national authorities will not be fulfilled.

The clearest sign that my role as tsunami emergency relief coordinator is coming to an end is Secretary-General Annan's announcement in February that former president Bill Clinton will be special envoy for tsunami recovery. We had begun looking for such a high-profile personality for the longer haul already in late January. In the end it is Mark Malloch Brown, just named the secretary-general's new chief of staff, who came up with the idea of asking President Clinton. Clinton had already embarked on a joint fund-raising effort with his predecessor, President George H. W. Bush, to raise funds in the United States for the tsunami victims and it took until April for Clinton to take on the special envoy function.

A visibly pleased Annan introduced his special envoy in our UN press briefing room on April 13, saying rightly that "no one could possibly be better qualified. It's vitally important that we have someone capable of sustaining international interest in the fate of the survivors and their communities—and someone with vision and commitment to ensure that this time the international community really does follow through and support the transition from immediate relief to longer-term recovery and reconstruction." Clinton generously started by saying that "Jan Egeland, Margareta Wahlström, and all their colleagues have been terrific," and then declared, "My job is to ensure first of all that the money which has been committed by the donor countries be invested, and that we assure the donors that it is spent effectively, responsibly, and in a transparent manner."

I have a series of meetings with Clinton to brief him on the work done so far, to plan joint work on early warning and disaster prevention issues, and to hand over to his leadership the global coalition of international actors that I initiated for tsunami recovery work in February, consisting of humanitarian and reconstruction actors such as the World Bank and the Asian Development Bank. In our first encounters Clinton looks frail, since he has just recovered from surgery to remove scar tissue after a heart operation, but he is fully engaged and interested to learn, to read, and to discuss—and always willing to stay longer than his schedule permits. This leads to a challenge in having a former U.S. president as your UN colleague. His ambitious staff of young advisers, some as keen as rottweilers and others seemingly unaware that the time in the White House is over, insist on presidential-style protocol and time spent on detailed planning of schedules and meetings—which are then routinely broken as Clinton himself spends relaxed time discussing and meeting new colleagues, and even greeting the long lines of female admirers that always show up in the UN and other places.

It is nearly ten months before I am able to visit the tsunami-stricken communities in Sri Lanka and Aceh, Indonesia. Margareta Wahlström, as initial special coordinator in the Indian Ocean region, and then Special Envoy Clinton and his deputies, Erskine Bowles and Eric Schwartz, have covered well the need for visits in the affected regions. It is to learn what went right and what went wrong that I want to see for myself.

And there are indeed many lessons to be drawn. I am pleased to hear, time and again from Sri Lankans and Indonesians alike, that they appreciated the strong initial response from the UN, the early relief and the teams of relief workers, and our strong advocacy for action, funds, and coordination. I am disappointed to see, in October 2005, so many people especially in Aceh, still sitting passively in the same tents they were provided with in the first weeks after the tsunami struck. In Sri Lanka more than fifty thousand prefabricated temporary housing units have been produced, but here too the process is too slow to provide permanent housing to the hundreds of thousands of homeless, in part due to the government's slow allocation of land where new and safe housing can be built.

Leaving the airport in Banda Aceh on October 17, I meet the

local press and cannot hide my disappointment that reconstruction in Aceh province is moving too slowly. I urge aid groups to work more closely together to get survivors out of tents and into permanent housing. On the first anniversary of the tsunami, tens of thousands are still in tents and without any livelihood. At the second anniversary nearly all have solid roofs and are helped into old or new livelihoods.

My own observations are very much in line with the conclusions in a huge set of evaluation reports undertaken by independent experts and published under the name of the Tsunami Evaluation Coalition. OCHA, along with forty donor governments and UN and non-UN organizations, helped initiate and coordinate the thousands of pages of lessons learned. The evaluation confirmed that "generous relief provided affected populations with the security they needed to begin planning what to do next. Large amounts of funding allowed rapid initial recovery activities . . . Within a few months there was palpable evidence of recovery. In all countries, children were back in school quickly and health facilities and services were partly restored and, in some cases, much improved. . . ." Sadly, the evaluators find that in key areas the colossal tsunami effort was a "missed opportunity." They sum it all up in four key recommendations:

1. The international humanitarian community needs a fundamental reorientation from supplying aid to supporting and facilitating communities' own relief and recovery priorities.
2. All actors should strive to increase their disaster response capacities and to improve the linkages and coherence between themselves and other actors in the international disaster response system, including those from the affected countries themselves.
3. The international relief system should establish an accredita-

tion and certification system to distinguish agencies that work
to a professional standard in a particular sector.

4. All actors need to make the current funding system impartial,
as well as more efficient, flexible, transparent, and better
aligned with principles of good donorship.

The evaluators conclude that the international response was
most effective when enabling, facilitating and supporting local and
national actors, and when accountable to them. Overall, international relief personnel were less successful in their recovery and risk
reduction activities than they were in the relief phase.

The tsunami brought the most rapidly and generously funded
disaster response in history. The global total of $13.5 billion repre-
sents an astonishing $7,100 for every affected person, as opposed to
only three dollars per head actually spent on someone affected by
floods in Bangladesh in 2004. We saw nature at its worst and humanity at our best during and after the tsunami. I hoped in January
2005 that we had set a new standard for how humanity would help
one another in the new millennium. I was wrong. Even after we
proved that there are tools like never before to eliminate misery,
still, more often than not, we continue to underfund even lifesaving
relief.

6.

More Dead Children than Soldiers in the Middle East

I_T HAS_ been a mission like no other. As we take off from Ben-Gurion Airport outside Tel Aviv on Thursday, July 27, 2006, it is time to take stock. We have been through three exploding war zones in five long days and nights. I have witnessed firsthand how once again civilian populations are suffering in the crossfire more than soldiers or militiamen, this time in Lebanon, in northern Israel, and in Gaza. The destruction, the number of casualties, the terror is greater than I had expected. It was intolerable when I arrived last Saturday. Every day it has gotten worse.

The war started two weeks ago, when Lebanon-based Hezbollah militants attacked an army post in northern Israel, killing eight soldiers and taking two hostages somewhere into Lebanon. Israel retaliated with massive air strikes and last Saturday sent troops, tanks, and bulldozers across the border. The rest of the world, and even the parties themselves, are shocked by the uncontrolled escalation. Hezbollah has launched hundreds of rockets from Lebanon at civilians in northern Israel. Israel has used its sledgehammer left and right on the Lebanese infrastructure, as well as on residential areas that might harbor Hezbollah and its missiles. I feel in my gut that neither Hezbollah nor the Israeli political or military leaders understand the consequences of what they are doing to their populations and to future generations of haters in this part of the world. I have seen too many examples in Beirut, in the Lebanese interior, and in Haifa in northern Israel.

It is just as bad in the Palestinian areas. In Gaza, the day before yesterday, I could scarcely believe my eyes. Six huge transformers had been surgically bombed beyond repair. It is not the degree of the destruction that fuels my anger; I have just seen worse in South Beirut. No one was killed at the power plant attack less than a month ago, but this is madness. The newly elected Israeli government ordered the destruction of the only large Palestinian power plant that serves the impoverished Gazan civilian population; it is co-owned by American companies.

I was among the many Palestinians, Israelis, Americans, and Europeans who, over a decade of peace efforts, had planned, raised funds, and worked to make it possible for the Palestinian population to produce their own electricity, and not rely on donor charity or on buying electricity from the Israelis. Now, after thirteen years of development efforts, the government in Jerusalem has bombed one of the few symbols of hope and positive change in Gaza. Israel has angered its neighbors as well as the Western donors, and has fueled more terrorism. Has everyone gone mad in this region? How can ancient and illustrious Jewish and Arab civilizations have become so embroiled in violence and so far removed from diplomacy and discussion as a way of solving differences? In the years before we succeeded in setting up the Norwegian channel that led to the Oslo Accord, we would say of the PLO that it never lost an opportunity to lose an opportunity. It now seems that all sides in this endless conflict are following suit.

Tomorrow, I will brief the UN Security Council in an open session on what I have seen and what must now be done. To maximize flexibility and access I have traveled this week with only my chief of staff, Hansjoerg Strohmeyer, who knows Lebanon well from his recent assignment to the UN investigator of the assassination of former prime minister Rafik Hariri. As soon as we take off, I start to draft my report to Secretary-General Kofi Annan:

Tens of thousands flee every day from Southern Lebanon. Hundreds are wounded and dozens die every day. Lebanese and international humanitarian organizations are trying to come to the relief of as many as possible. Today another ten-truck UN convoy is painstakingly making its way on some of the roads that are still usable from Beirut to Tyre on the coast in the South. What used to be a 1½-hour drive has now become a six-hour ordeal, on totally clogged roads. We have managed to establish humanitarian corridors for emergency relief supplies by land from Syria at the northern border and by sea from Cyprus to Beirut. We also now have a notification system agreed with the High Command of the Israeli Defense Forces (IDF). This should ensure safe passage for our increasing number of convoys from our hubs in Beirut, going down south and inland where the situation is increasingly dramatic for hundreds of thousands.

Through these corridors, which I called for in letters to the Israeli and Lebanese governments last week, our UN logisticians tell me we may be able to provide more than ten thousand tons of relief supplies in the next month. That is, provided there are no attacks at any of our convoys. But this is first and foremost a crisis of protection for defenseless civilians. We need an immediate cessation of hostilities, followed by a cease-fire agreement, a security force, and the political settlement of the conflict as already proposed by you as secretary-general.

It is only seven days since Deputy Secretary-General Mark Malloch Brown called me from his office in the UN Secretariat building as I sat by my desk two floors below: "Jan, I just spoke to the secretary-general. He feels it is now time that you go to Lebanon, Israel, and the Palestinian areas. The political mission of ours has not yet found any middle ground among the parties; it is clearly going to get worse and the UN is seen by many as not engaged. You should witness what is happening on the ground, set up the humanitarian operation, and report back to the secretary-general and the Security Council." It was the green light that I had been asking for since the beginning of the week. Kofi Annan had felt that the political mission led by his adviser, the Indian diplomat Vijay Nambiar, should complete its visit to the region before I left. For several days criticism had been building within the Middle East and in international media that the UN was "silent" and "absent" from the escalating conflict.

Ten minutes after Malloch Brown's call, I assembled a task force of OCHA colleagues in my office to prepare the ground for the mission. Two hours later it was confirmed that we could leave the following evening via London to Cyprus. From the British base on the eastern coast we would be flown into Beirut by a British military Chinook helicopter.

As so often happens in times of war, it is not the expected problems caused by blockade or armed actors that delays our arrival in Beirut, but rather something more mundane—a broken airplane leaving too late. We lose our direct Cyprus Air flight from London and so we get to Cyprus seven hours late by way of Athens. It is already dark, too late to go on to Lebanon. The British military base near Larnaca is, however, willing to fly us there at dawn, and after less than three hours of sleep we are in a dark green Chinook just above sea level on our way to Beirut. At 9 A.M. on Sunday, July 23, we are welcomed by Mona Hammam, our Egyptian UN resident coordinator, and Jaime McGoldrick, the Scotsman sent from OCHA Geneva to set up the first humanitarian coordination team.

Driving towards the posh Mövenpick Hotel, where the UN has lodged its incoming teams, we see how a precision-guided missile has blown the lamp in the top of the harbor lighthouse to pieces.

Normally bustling Beirut looks like a ghost town, but we see no damage in the central, western, and northern areas. The civilian death toll in Lebanon, however, already stands at nearly six hundred, according to the minister of health; the majority are women and children. A ferocious bombing was taking place in the southern Shiia suburbs that morning. We had planned to visit this area, but Hammam, who is the designated official for security, says we can only go if we have assurance of a bombing pause from the Israeli side. One hour later Kevin Kennedy, our OCHA veteran and former U.S. Marines colonel who is the new UN humanitarian coordinator for the Palestinians in Jerusalem, calls to say that he has received guarantees from the IDF of a three-hour minimum window of no bombing in South Beirut. As we jump into the waiting cars, our OCHA colleagues warn that Hezbollah commanders in South Beirut say they cannot guarantee our security. "The clock is ticking," I say. "Let's go and talk to the commanders when we arrive."

Less than an hour later, our convoy of UN vehicles is briefly stopped, redirected, and then allowed passage by Hezbollah militiamen with Kalashnikov rifles. We enter the epicenter of the bombing campaign, South Beirut's Dahiyeh suburb, a Hezbollah political stronghold. Six- to ten-story apartment buildings have been leveled, block by block. The rubble is covered with schoolbooks, children's clothing, photographs, and other personal belongings.

We are unprepared for the extent of the destruction. Smoke and dust are still thick in the air from this morning's massive bombardment. In our time wars are usually waged in the countryside, where small arms are used in so-called low-intensity warfare, more often than not against defenseless peasant populations. In Sudan, the Congo, Colombia, and elsewhere I have seen burned-down hamlets many times. Here, now, hundreds of tons of explosives have destroyed large urban residential structures. It resembles what I saw in

Grozny, Chechnya, in 2003; in Vukovar, Croatia, after the Serb-Croat war in 1993; and in Beirut itself along the so-called Green Line that divided the city during the Lebanese Civil War from 1975 to 1990.

In addition to angry Hezbollah militiamen and a few shell-shocked Dahiyeh residents looking for anything familiar in the rubble of their homes, national and international journalists are arriving, running toward us with cameras and microphones. An improvised, chaotic press conference follows with journalists literally tripping over one another as they try to balance their way through the rubble. "It is a terrible war," I say. "We see lots of children dead and wounded; we see thousands of homeless and endless suffering. This is a war where civilians pay a disproportionate price in Lebanon and in northern Israel."

"Time is up. It is not safe here anymore. We need to leave," the UN security officers declare. Two bodyguards take my arms firmly and steer me through an increasingly agitated crowd of homeless residents, militiamen, and reporters. The three-hour pause in the bombing that the Israelis had guaranteed is about to come to an end. Equally worrying to the UN security officers is the growing anger of Hezbollah militiamen and destitute local residents. One man tries to drag me over to a pile of rubble he says had been his home. "It cost me $120,000. All my money, all my savings. Who will repay me? Will Israel, will the UN, will America? I had nothing to do with Hezbollah. I need to know who will compensate me!" he screams in my face. Israel, the United States, and the United Nations have yet another family who see us as enemies.

"Is this a violation of humanitarian law?" the BBC's Beirut correspondent shouts as we struggle to get out of the debris and back to the vehicles. My bodyguards try to push them away as I answer over my shoulder, "This seems to be a disproportionate response to me. Of course I don't know whether there were any military targets here, but a disproportionate response by Israel is a violation of international humanitarian law." The exchange takes less than twenty seconds, but it is enough for the BBC. For the next twenty-four hours they have their story: "The UN's Jan Egeland has condemned the devastation caused by Israeli air strikes in Beirut, saying it is a violation of humanitarian law." The story continues: "Mr. Egeland arrived in southern Beirut on Sunday just hours after Israeli strikes on the Hezbollah stronghold. A visibly moved Mr. Egeland expressed shock that 'block after block' of buildings had been levelled." The quotes are widely picked up by commentators across the world. Many are pleased that finally someone is "speaking the truth from the UN side." The Israeli government cancels a meeting planned for me two days later with Prime Minister Ehud Olmert in Jerusalem.

From South Beirut we go straight to the government buildings in downtown Beirut to see the High Relief Council, headed by Prime Minister Fouad Siniora. We are led directly to the cabinet meeting room. Several ministers are present from this odd and strained coalition government that includes Christian, Sunni, and Shiia ministers. Two of them represent the political wing of Hezbollah, the movement that triggered this latest sorry cycle of violence. When the prime minister arrives, we sit down with him at the head of the table and five ministers across from us, including the outspoken minister of finance. With me are Mona Hammam and the recently arrived World Food Programme representative, Jordanian Amer Daoudi. I know how angry the Lebanese are and I say, "I will protest the indiscriminate and disproportionate use of force the day after tomorrow in Israel, but the rain of rockets from Lebanese territory into Israel must also stop immediately." I glance at the Hezbollah ministers, who are motionless.

Prime Minister Siniora is a cultured, articulate man who has done miracles in holding together one of the most complex political situations in the world. He looks pale, tired, and depressed. "I hope we can join forces," he says. "We are committed to the humanitarian corridors that you have proposed. But we are also concerned that Israel may use them as an argument that they can continue with their campaign to destroy all of Lebanon. The speed with which relief is provided is most important. You should not plan for a perfect operation. Use domestic Lebanese transportation. The patient may be dying before he comes to the operating room. We have discussed corridors for a few days, but too little is happening. And in the meantime our population is dying."

I explain that tomorrow I will launch a flash appeal for massive emergency relief to Lebanon with a video link to New York and Geneva. It is true that the UN development teams in Lebanon had not been able to respond as speedily as they should, but this is changing with the arrival of effective emergency managers such as Daoudi. "We have already ordered several dozen new trucks from abroad," Daoudi explains. "But since that will take time, we need your help in getting enough trucks to start up with convoys from Beirut immediately. We also need enough drivers willing to go in spite of the bombing and we need to find fuel in spite of the Israeli boycott."

Several of the ministers, including these from Hezbollah, speak out. They are angry with the Israeli destruction of civilian lives and property, and angry with the UN, the U.S., the EU, and the Arab world for standing by passively in their hour of greatest need. None mention Hezbollah's missiles, or the Israeli soldiers held captive in Lebanon.

"We can give you trucks and find drivers if you get the Israelis to provide security guarantees for the convoys and allow fuel and other vital supplies into the country," Siniora says. A top adviser who has just entered interjects, "There are agency reports out this hour saying that Israel has agreed to the corridors by sea from Cyprus to Beirut and also by air, but we can only use helicopters since they bombed the airport."

"So, where do we go from here?" Siniora asks.

"We will work to have not only the corridors from outside to Beirut firmly established, but also a system of notification to the IDF for inland forward transport," I reply. "We will use our own civilian trucks and drivers and can include Lebanese civil society supplies. But we need to inspect and be accountable for the content of all items in convoys under our flag. You need to establish on your side one focal point for the provision of emergency relief. We cannot deal with a collective. I will appoint a humanitarian coordinator assisted by a team sent in from OCHA. We will in the next days and weeks step up our international relief operation dramatically, but, as I will also say in Israel, only a political settlement will end the suffering that we now try to alleviate."

As we rise to shake hands, Siniora adds a final request: "Remember our blood is as precious as Israeli blood." "I know," I say. We leave for a meeting with more than thirty Lebanese and international nongovernmental organizations.

The next morning, from our comfortable hotel terrace we see and hear new massive air raids and naval bombardments from Israeli warships against an already devastated South Beirut. There is also news of Hezbollah rockets falling on northern Israel. Our hopes to go down to the besieged southern Lebanese towns and villages are ended when the main road is rendered unusable and the IDF is unwilling to guarantee a bombing pause.

We decide to go east, inland from Beirut, to visit the numerous improvised camps for the internally displaced in the Metn region, a Druze area. After a two-hour drive we are among several hundred refugees from southern Lebanon, 85 percent of them women, children, and infants, crowded into a school with six toilets. Each small classroom is occupied by twenty people. They have few belongings and face skyrocketing prices for basic goods. This small district is host to more than 250,000 displaced; 67,000 are sheltered in schools, hospitals, or community centers.

We walk from classroom to classroom. I meet some of the survivors from the village of Srifa in South Lebanon, where twenty people died during Israeli air strikes on July 19. The women end their stories with desperate appeals and tears running down their cheeks:

"We lost everything when the bombs rained," one older woman says, her head covered with a green scarf. "We could not even recover the bodies of my husband, my daughter, and other family members. They are still there under the rubble of our homes. We cannot sleep at night. We have heard that the dogs are eating their bodies. You must help us!"

Two days later, I raise the request of the women of Srifa with the Israeli ministers for foreign affairs and defense: assistance in the recovery and burial of bodies in accordance with Islamic tradition. A few days after this, the International Committee of the Red Cross accompanies some of the villagers back to retrieve the bodies.

Lebanese of all religions and cultures have opened their homes, their schools, and community buildings to the Shiia population. The Israeli air strikes were aimed at destroying and isolating Hezbollah, but by destroying civilian infrastructure all over Lebanon—a futile attempt to prevent missiles being brought into the country—the Israelis have united the Lebanese. Christians, Druze, and Sunnis were as enraged as the Shiia and the Hezbollah.

From the school we drive on to the Mdeirij Bridge, the highest in the Middle East, on the highway that connects Beirut and Damascus, Syria. The bridge was the culmination of a four-year joint development venture with Italy and is a symbol of national pride as well as vital to economic revival. It has been rendered unusable by air raids, just as was done to highway from Beirut to the south. The same afternoon another air raid destroys it. The damage to Lebanese infrastructure is estimated at billions of dollars.

In the early afternoon, with video link to an auditorium of ambassadors in New York, and with the Lebanese and international press crew present in the UN's Beirut building, I launch our UN flash appeal for the Lebanon crisis. I ask for $150 million. We agree to allocate $4.5 million from our new Central Emergency Response Fund, primarily to ensure an immediate start-up for the convoys of relief trucks; a telecommunications system for relief workers from

UN and non-UN aid organizations; and water and sanitation equipment for the overcrowded schools and community centers where tens of thousands of displaced persons are assembling. With the country team of UN agencies we flesh out the details of an ambitious operation, in which the World Food Programme would coordinate logistics by sea, air, and land across the border and deep into southern Lebanon.

The number of displaced, primarily from southern Lebanon and the southern suburbs of Beirut, is approaching a staggering 700,000 after only two weeks of fighting. An estimated 100,000 people are blocked by siege of their homes, towns, and villages. Some 210,000 have fled Lebanon to neighboring Syria and Cyprus—among them 115,000 third-country nationals who do not have the financial means to get home.

Arriving at Larnaca, Cyprus, airport in early evening, courtesy of British military helicopter, we are met by the UN representative at Cyprus, Michael Möller, who has organized yet another press conference. An Associated Press reporter asks what I think about Hezbollah's apparent success in fighting the mighty IDF. It is a cue I had waited for after questions about disproportionate Israeli use of force.

"Consistently, from the Hezbollah heartland, my message was that their fighters must stop this cowardly blending into the civilian population among women and children," I reply. "I heard they were proud because they lost very few fighters. I don't think anyone should be proud of having many more children and women dead than armed men." As I later enjoy a rare nice meal at a Greek fish restaurant, I am unaware that the young AP female reporter has put out her scoop. Forty-eight hours later Google registers tens of thousands of hits for the "cowardly blending into the civilian population" quote. Suddenly the situation is turned upside down: the Israeli government is happy with my statement and the radical Arab press is angry.

At 11 P.M. we land at Ben-Gurion Airport outside Tel Aviv, Israel, and are met by Kevin Kennedy and David Shearer, the veteran head of the OCHA office for the Occupied Palestinian Territories. They brief me on the latest changes to the program as we drive toward my favorite hotel in the Middle East, the old American Colony in East Jerusalem.

Early next morning we arrive at the eerily quiet Erez border crossing at the northern tip of Gaza. The forgotten conflict in Gaza rages behind closed borders. Short-range and homemade Qassam rockets are being fired by Palestinian terrorist groups from within Gaza and striking Israeli territory across the border. Thousands of Israeli shells and grenades are raining in retaliation on the Palestinian towns and villages close to where the extremists have fired the Qassams. The once-flourishing daily trade and cross-border migration of Palestinian day laborers is gone. Only our small group is allowed to cross into the crowded strip of land this morning.

Soon we see a UN school that had been badly damaged by Israeli tanks in recent days, and bedrooms, kitchens, and living rooms in Palestinian refugee camps destroyed by Israeli artillery shells. Our colleagues from UN Relief and Works Agency and other humanitarian groups are disillusioned.

At the end of the sad Gaza tour, as I look at the destroyed transformers at the power plant, I reflect gloomily on how it could ever have gone so wrong in the thirteen years since the historic Oslo Accord between Israel and the PLO. My UN colleagues bring me back to reality: the thirty journalists who have trailed us this morning have placed more than ten microphones in front of a blackened transformer that was sent to Gaza from Sweden. "What do you want to say?" David Shearer asks. "I don't know," I reply. "I was not prepared for a press conference here." I see cameramen from the major Western and Arab media. "This is very clearly disproportional use of force. Civilian infrastructure is protected. The law is very clear. The

Gaza power plant supplied seventy percent of the power to the 1.4 million residents here. This plant is more important for hospitals, for sewage, and for water to civilians than for any Hamas man or Islamic Jihad man with a missile on his shoulder. He doesn't need electricity, such as a mother trying to care for her child needs it."

Today's visit to Gaza is the most depressing in my twenty-five years of coming to Israel and the Occupied Territories. The bitterness among Palestinians is greater than anything I can recall. As I leave Gaza in the UN convoy of white Land Rovers, I reflect on how differently it has ended for ordinary Palestinians compared to the high hopes we held during happier visits after the Oslo Accord. Occupied, miserable Gaza should become the "Singapore of the Middle East," Shimon Peres, then foreign minister of Israel, had said. Massive investments in joint Israeli-Palestinian industrial parks were planned; one was partially built here at Erez, but was closed down in April 2004. How could it go so wrong in just one decade? As we drive to Ramallah in the West Bank to see Palestinian president Mahmoud Abbas (Abu Mazen), I think about what I will say in the Security Council in New York later that week:

> When visiting Gaza, I was deeply saddened to find the great visions that we had in Oslo for a peaceful and prosperous Palestine, coexisting in safety and security with a recognized Israel, shattered. These hopes have been replaced by a deep sense of despair and disillusionment. The destruction of vital civilian infrastructure such as bridges, roads, and the only electrical power plant in Gaza, the ongoing closure of most border crossings into and out of Gaza, and frequent roadblocks are suffocating any attempt at building a viable economic and social infrastructure in Gaza. As a result, anger and the readiness to resort to militant violence seem to be growing, particularly among young people.

I had been at the presidential compound in Ramallah as a representative of Norway and of the Red Cross when Yasser Arafat was still alive. The meetings were never easy. Arafat was not a good listener. He preferred to spend time listing real and imagined reasons for the ongoing crises. Abu Mazen is much easier to engage. He listens and responds and asks questions, but he is even more powerless, one might say, than his predecessor. His political opponents in Hamas won a clear majority in the Palestinian legislature in January and have since controlled the cabinet and the ministries of the Palestinian Authority. Because of Hamas's history as a sponsor of terrorism committed to the destruction of Israel, the democratically elected government is boycotted by the European Union and the United States. As a result, the administration built by Arafat's and Abu Mazen's PLO, and by donors, is crumbling.

Many years ago I had chaired, on behalf of Norway, the international donor forum for the Palestinians. Many great things were achieved because the donors were united, creative, and proactive. Today most of the Western donors seem to stick their heads in the sand to avoid the fact that their boycott is hurting average Palestinians more than it is the Hamas politicians. Doctors, nurses, teachers, administrators, and policemen are not being paid and there is increasing chaos. I feel sad for the paralyzed president. I accompany his adviser, Saeb Erekat, who was always there in Arafat's days, to appeal for more money for the Palestinians through the international media who are waiting at the entrance.

On the way back to Jerusalem we stop to look at the barrier the Israelis are building inside the Occupied Territory to keep terrorists out. Like a growing snake it encircles more and more Palestinian communities, separating them from their roads, their arable lands, and their schools and clinics. In the UN the name of the new structure has become a political issue. The Arabs want it to be called "the wall" and the Israelis like "the fence." Kofi Annan settles for "the barrier." What I see with my own eyes is a massive structure that is taller than the Berlin Wall and built with concrete, too.

It is nearly midnight when the long day ends at the peaceful American Colony Hotel in East Jerusalem. The last portion of the program is a series of live television interviews from the busy Jerusalem studios of the increasing number of foreign news organizations. I had hoped to go straight to bed but more bad news is waiting. The UN special representative for the Middle East, Alvaro de Soto, has come to the hotel to hand me a copy of a hastily prepared statement just issued by Kofi Annan. It expresses uncharacteristic anger.

"I am shocked and deeply distressed by the apparently deliberate targeting by Israeli Defense Forces of a UN Observer post in southern Lebanon that has killed two UN military observers, with two more feared dead. This coordinated artillery and aerial attack on a long established and clearly marked UN post at Khiyam occurred despite personal assurances given to me by Prime Minister Ehud Olmert that UN positions would be spared Israeli fire. Furthermore, General Alain Pellegrini, the UN Force Commander in south Lebanon, had been in repeated contact with Israeli officers throughout the day on Tuesday, stressing the need to protect that particular UN position from attack. I call on the Government of Israel to conduct a full investigation into this very disturbing incident and demand that any further attack on UN positions and personnel must stop."

I cannot believe it. Are we being targeted by the Israelis? Are we gambling with the lives of our colleagues as they are placed in the crossfire to provide humanitarian aid and observe? "Why does Annan say 'apparently deliberate targeting'? The Israelis would have no interest in targeting us!" I say.

"I don't know why they used the term," de Soto says. "It was drafted in Rome where the SG is attending the international crisis meeting on Lebanon. What I know for sure is that the Israelis will be mad as hell because of this statement, which is out this evening, and that your meetings tomorrow with Foreign Minister [Tzipi] Livni and Defense Minister [Amir] Peretz will be the first encounters between the UN and the Israeli government since these killings. Therefore we will organize a briefing for you at 6:30 A.M. with officials from the UN military observer force here in Jerusalem who can give you the latest."

It is my fourth night with less than four hours of sleep. The UN military officers who come to the American Colony in the early morning confirm that all four colleagues—from Austria, Canada, China, and Finland—are confirmed dead. Why an Israeli fighter jet would send a precision guided missile into the middle of the observer post is inexplicable. "That is why you must insist that the UN be part of the Israeli investigation. We need to know the truth and ensure there is no whitewash," I am told.

We gulp down some coffee and drive north toward Haifa. It is important that the United Nations witness that the impact of the conflicts is in no way confined to Lebanon and the Palestinian territories. Hundreds of thousands of Israeli civilians suffer as well. Daily Hezbollah rocket attacks are spreading constant fear and terror in the northern part of the country. In Haifa, we are escorted by police cars with blinking blue lights to a residential area where I see the damage done by one of the eighty Katyusha rocket attacks Haifa has sustained, this one to a three-story family home. The Israeli Ministry of Foreign Affairs has announced my arrival and a large crowd of Israeli and international media is waiting with Foreign Minister Tzipi Livni and Haifa's mayor, Yona Yahav. The journalists surround our cars and in the chaos it is hard to open the doors.

Livni has only been on the job two months. She is under enormous pressure along with her colleagues in the new government, which is led by the young Kadima party. Under Prime Minister Olmert's leadership it wants to prove it can be a strong defender of Israel's security. The journalists stand behind a long rope as the mayor points to the three-story apartment house. "There was a small kin-

dergarten in the ground floor," he says. "Next time they may hit
when the children are still there to play." The civilians in Haifa and
other towns spend much of their time in shelters. Altogether, the attacks have left some twenty Israelis dead and hundreds wounded.
More than a thousand rockets have rained down on northern Israel.

Livni asks if I will speak to the press. I go to the many microphones that have been placed in front of the destroyed building and
condemn the firing of rockets that spread terror and suffering among
civilian Israelis. We then move on to our meeting in one of the main
hotels overlooking beautiful Haifa harbor. Livni has taken a suite at
the top floor. From her terrace the mayor of Haifa, Yahav, points
to all the synagogues, churches, and mosques and the large Baha'i
center that for generations have made Haifa a symbol of Middle
Eastern reconciliation and peaceful coexistence among all the major
religions and cultures. "The rocket attacks have undermined the
very moderate forces in Israel that I have been part of and who
argued for a withdrawal from Lebanon in year 2000 and who pro-
moted peace and reconciliation with Arab neighbors," Yahav concludes.

Then, suddenly, air raid alarms go off. Security agents yell that
everybody has to take shelter. I am pushed with the foreign minister
to the shelter, which turns out to be the stairwell. Here we cram in
some twenty-five Israeli diplomats, bodyguards, and UN officials. I
stand on the same step as Livni, who tells me, "It is the second time
today that we have had to stand in these stairs due to incoming Hezbollah rockets."

After fifteen minutes we are allowed back to the suite. Livni asks
me to sit at the small conference table. She looks tired and worried.
I can hear an adviser whisper to her that eleven Israeli soldiers have
been killed in today's fierce fighting in southern Lebanon.

"Let me repeat our condolences for the loss of civilian life here.
Hezbollah's indiscriminate rain of rockets is outrageous," I say. "We
appreciate that you agreed to have this meeting in Haifa. It is im-

portant for the world to know that the residents and population centers of northern Israel are being subjected to constant attack."

"Israel has no conflict with the people of Lebanon," she responds, "but we must defend our citizens after unprovoked attacks. It is our expectation that the international community will help the Lebanese government to confront the Hezbollah in order to enable Israelis and Lebanese to live in peace in the future. Israel is targeting Hezbollah, which may unfortunately result in the loss of civilian lives, while Hezbollah is targeting Israel's cities in order to target civilians. Israel expects the international community to recognize this crucial difference.

"I just spoke with the Canadian and Austrian foreign ministers," Livni continues. "We will work with you to enable the speedy recovery of the bodies of the four officers despite the ongoing fighting. Ehud Olmert and Kofi Annan also just spoke, but I want to register our concern. The SG should know better. Israel is of course not targeting UNIFIL [United Nations Interim Force in Lebanon], but in war terrible things like this may happen. The statement will affect relations between Israel and the UN."

The talk is drifting in a direction I had feared. Instead of focusing on how and why the IDF had attacked the UN post, the issue is becoming whether the first statement out of Rome was wisely phrased. "It was not a stray bomb in a chaotic war that killed our colleagues," I interject. "The bunker in which the four officers had taken shelter must somehow have been targeted. The pilot who pushed the button that ejected the precision guided missile clearly aimed at the tiny opening of that particular bunker."

"We all agree that there needs to be an investigation," Livni retorts. "And we need to be taking part in that investigation to determine what really happened and why," I add. "I note your request," she says. "In any case, Israel will provide details of what happened. You deserve to get a full and complete answer." Livni closes the subject.

I move on to the crisis in Lebanon: "We are struggling to set up a humanitarian lifeline to eight hundred thousand who are displaced or beleaguered in Lebanon. Your attack on Khiyam is just one of many examples that your air force has attacked civilians or other protected targets, even ambulances. If it is not deliberate, then one might wonder whether you are in control of what is happening or know the impact of what your armed forces are doing in Lebanon."

It actually is not a bad meeting. Livni does agree to my request to have a full-time UN liaison for humanitarian matters in the IDF high command. She reaffirms support for the corridors and the notification system for convoys. At the end of the meeting we talk about the deepening conflict with the Palestinians; the border closures at Gaza; and the roadblocks and growing barrier that encircle Palestinians in the West Bank. I tell her that in all my years of traveling to the Middle East I have never before seen this clearly that Israel is creating not only misery among the Palestinians, but also such deep hatred and extremism in Gaza and the West Bank that it undermines the very security of Israel.

As we end, Livni makes her final statement: "What I expect from Kofi Annan and the United Nations is an understanding that we are on the same side, fighting terrorism. We are facing the long arm of Iran in the region." I respond as I have in meetings with Siniora and Abu Mazen: "We need an immediate end to the hostilities. Continued fighting, missile attacks, and air raids will only lead to more civilian suffering on all sides." As we leave Haifa the police escort confirms that a Katyusha rocket from southern Lebanon had hit the city while we met with Foreign Minister Livni. It is close to impossible to get the Israelis to focus on the disproportionate damage they cause in Lebanon when these senseless and arbitrary attacks are causing an atmosphere of terror in Israel.

As we are on the road to a meeting with the embattled Labor Party chairman and defense minister Amir Peretz in Tel Aviv, Israel renews its bombardment in Gaza. A three-year-old Palestinian girl is killed. Altogether, 150 civilians have lost their lives since the conflict broke out in June. I had met Peretz many years ago when he was chairman of the main trade union Histadrut and I was state secretary in the Ministry for Foreign Affairs in the Norwegian Labor government. I thus would, in theory at least, relate more to him than to the right-leaning, former Likud politician Livni. But the meeting turns out to be less productive than the meeting with the engaged foreign minister.

Flanked by six high-ranking Israeli military officials, Peretz looks grumpy and seems disengaged. He speaks Hebrew and looks down at his papers as his translator speaks. "As you know, the escalation of the war started with the kidnapping of our two soldiers and then by Hezbollah's missile attacks on our towns. We have nothing against the Lebanese people, but the issue is one of sovereignty and responsibility. If the government of Lebanon only feels responsible for tourism in southern Lebanon, Israel has to confront Hezbollah herself and establish law and order. As regards the accidental killing of the four UN observers yesterday we are sending a letter of regret to the UN. We do not target the UN and it will not happen again. The event will be investigated and you will be informed. Finally, let me say to you as the UN humanitarian chief that we approve all the five corridors you have proposed. The coordination cell with people from your side here is also OK." Peretz looks at the general to his right, who nods and confirms that tomorrow we can put someone into their newly created "humanitarian coordination center" from our office in Jerusalem.

Trying to make eye contact with Peretz, I urge him to review the conduct of the air strikes and bombardments to avoid excessive use of force, which inflicts disproportionate suffering on the civilian population. "When there are clearly more dead children than actual combatants, the conduct of hostilities must be reviewed," I say. I add that we are afraid they may be attacking, by accident or lack of unity of command, our increasing number of humanitarian convoys struggling to reach the besieged towns in the south. "The only thing that can spare civilian lives and avoid further escalations and an uncontrollable situation that all will regret is our UN proposal for an immediate cessation of hostilities," I tell him. My plea has little impact. Peretz's thoughts are clearly wandering as he waits for the translation.

It is even more difficult to get the defense minister and his generals to focus on the ongoing conflict in Gaza and parts of the West Bank, even though it is, even now, costing many more lives among Palestinian civilians than the Hezbollah onslaught on Israel. I tell them that I saw the destruction of every single transformer of the power plant in Gaza. There is no public admission, but the body language among the Israeli officials shows that they now agree that destruction of this civilian installation was indeed unwise. "We will work with you to enable the import of new transformers," one of the generals says. They also recognize the importance of continued international assistance through the UN to the Palestinians, but my interlocutors become uneasy when I explain that the repeated destruction of infrastructure is making many aid workers give up. The produce from the greenhouses erected as part of former World Bank president James Wolfensohn's efforts was destroyed in the recent violence, as were the bridges built by UNDP with European aid over several years.

After all my meetings with Israeli officials in New York, Tel Aviv, Jerusalem, and Haifa, I sense that Israel increasingly understands that the misery of Gaza and many parts of the West Bank is a cradle for new recruits to extremism and terrorism. The problem is that they seem incapable of drawing the only sensible conclusion: end the futile military occupation and go systematically for trade, investment, and people-to-people cooperation. Only economic development and education will, in the long run, undercut the terrorists and the extremists.

• • •

On our last evening in Jerusalem we find time for a visit to the Church of the Holy Sepulcher in the Old City, which I had visited every week as a young fellow at the Hebrew University. The Christian communities who worship in the church have quarreled so much and for so long that the key to the church is kept by a neighboring Muslim family. As Europeans we have, since even before the time of the Crusades, brought so much suffering to the peoples of this region that we should be able to understand why the vicious cycle of violence between Jews and Arabs seems unbreakable.

I spend a good part of the night in the media center in Jerusalem, shuttling from the crowded CNN studio, where I am interviewed by the anchors of several of their international news shows, to BBC and their World Service and their domestic *Nightline,* to Al Jazeera, Norwegian and German television, and then back to CNN and the easygoing Wolf Blitzer with his *Situation Room.* "We have a few minutes. Have some coffee and a sandwich," Blitzer says. He is wearing a green military-style sports jacket. "You look like a ghost and I don't blame you."

After we take off the next morning for New York I sit with my entire luggage in my lap: a small and battered overnight bag stuffed with dirty laundry, and a chaotic pile of my daily briefing files and reports received from the people we met. I find a torn schoolbook I had stepped on when tramping on the rubble in South Beirut. In a little pocket with keys and credit cards I have also put a piece of shrapnel from the Gaza power plant and some of the vicious metal hail that the Hezbollah rockets are full of.

What should be my proposals to Secretary-General Kofi Annan and my main message to the Security Council? Hansjoerg and I sum up my public messages throughout the three war zones:

- The indiscriminate rain of rockets into Israel must stop.
- The excessive and disproportionate use of force by the Israeli Defense Forces in both Lebanon and Gaza must stop.

- The hiding of armed combatants and weaponry among the civilian populations in Lebanon and the occupied Palestinian territory must stop.
- Most importantly, we need a cessation of hostilities immediately.

However, repeating all of this would not only sound like a broken record, it would lead to very little as the war escalated and the refugee flows increased. So instead we came up with the idea that as a first step, I as emergency relief coordinator would propose a humanitarian truce of a minimum seventy-two hours for the sake of the children of Lebanon and of northern Israel, who all must agree, are innocent victims of this escalating conflict.

For the rest of the flight and then back in the office in Manhattan that evening, we worked on the presentation to the secretary-general for the next morning at 9 A.M., just before I would go to the Security Council and then to a press conference. By 8 P.M., which is 4 A.M. Jerusalem time, it has been twenty-two hours since we woke up at the American Colony in Jerusalem. I cannot go on and so take a cab back to my small apartment in Greenwich Village. My family has gone back to Oslo. The last clean shirt I put on that morning smells bad and I am afraid I will faint before I can open the door, drop everything, take a shower, and then collapse dead in my bed.

The next morning at 7:30 I am in the office reading a good draft of the Security Council statement that the OCHA team has worked on through the night, consulting with our teams in Beirut and Jerusalem. The seventy-two-hour humanitarian-truce proposal now includes a major operation in which the UN and partner organizations, as well as the International Red Cross and the Lebanese Red Cross, would be able to move freely in the combat areas, and do four things:

- First, relocate the children, the wounded, the disabled, and the elderly who have not been able to escape the fighting in the worst war zones.

- Second, resupply hospitals and health centers with emergency medical relief items and fuel for generators to avoid a complete breakdown of public health facilities caring for the thousands of wounded.
- Third, provide water and sanitation facilities, food, and other basic supplies to the tens of thousands of displaced who are seeking shelter in public buildings in the conflict zones.
- Fourth, establish an emergency communication system to vulnerable communities that allows us to address acute needs urgently where and when they arise.

"I like it," Kofi Annan says a half hour later. "You can tell the council it has my support, but be aware that you are sticking your neck again into a highly politicized issue since there are many proposals from many actors and they all blame each other for the lack of progress." We agree that the diplomatic stalemate might be broken if we make clear the need to evacuate the estimated twenty thousand children still within the intense war zones of southern Lebanon, along with other vulnerable civilians who have not been able to flee. The hundreds of thousands of traumatized children elsewhere in Lebanon and in northern Israel will get needed assistance and a respite from the terror.

Relieved, I take the elevator down from the secretary–general's serene thirty-eighth floor to the bustling Security Council chambers on the second floor, where several colleagues and many of the UN-accredited correspondents are waiting. It has been a gamble. If I had not had Annan's approval, there would have been no time to redraft the statement, which now has been provided to the interpreters to translate it into the six official UN languages.

"The Middle East is at a crossroads," I say to start the briefing. "My fear is that more violence, more missiles, more terror, and more destruction creates more anger, more hatred, and more disillusioned youths, and ultimately leads to less security throughout the region. Civilians on all sides are the losers of this endless cycle of violence."

I describe the effects of the war in some detail and our efforts to alleviate the suffering through convoys that now benefit from our having embedded a former U.S. military man as UN representative in the IDF high command. "Yet, Mr. President, it must be clear to all, the parties to the conflict and the members of the Security Council, that the limited and carefully controlled assistance we will be able to provide through this notification system with the IDF is not enough to prevent the excessive suffering of the civilian population. We need an immediate cessation of hostilities, followed by a cease-fire agreement, the deployment of a security force, and the political settlement of the conflict. As a first step, I am recommending to the secretary-general and through him to you, a humanitarian truce. We need at least seventy-two hours of tranquilities for the sake of the children of Lebanon and northern Israel who, I believe, we all agree are the innocent victims of this escalating conflict."

One-third of the statement is dedicated to the ongoing Israeli-Palestinian war, which is still overshadowed by the war in Lebanon. I propose the steps that can and must be taken:

First, the violence must stop. We must support the efforts of President Abu Mazen and international mediators to stop militants from lobbing Qassam rockets at Israeli settlements. Israel, in turn, must end its oftentimes excessive and disproportionate use of force, as was the case in the destruction of the power plant and the shelling that takes the lives of civilians. Second, we must rebuild vital infrastructure. We must help the Palestinian Authority to reestablish a social and economic infrastructure that will provide employment and hope, and help curb the extreme radicalization of Gaza's youth. Third, the border crossings must open. We encourage the Israeli authorities to establish a transparent and reliable regime at the key crossing point into and out of Gaza. In this respect, I *have proposed to Defense Minister Peretz a regular weekly working meeting between the IDF and the UN to facilitate the transport of humanitarian and other urgently needed goods into Gaza.*

I can see that my statement is having an impact. The often annoying small talk and even cell phone conversations that Security Council ambassadors indulge in during briefings are not happening. I hope the members will absorb the criticism of their lack of progress as I conclude:

As humanitarian workers, we are frustrated and feel that the work on the political and security agreements is too slow. We are afraid that the parties to the conflict are continuing the escalation, thereby prolonging the suffering of civilians and causing more hatred and sorrow today that they will regret tomorrow.

All the ambassadors exercise their right to speak after I am done. None are negative; most are in fact strongly supportive of my call for an immediate end to the fighting. I wish I had the same engagement and support from the Arab and Islamic ambassadors, as well as the Western powers, when we discuss Darfur.

The humanitarian truce proposal gets the traction we had hoped for. Nongovernmental organizations, diplomats, humanitarian colleagues, and the media pick up on the idea. Later that evening, I switch on Wolf Blitzer and his *Situation Room:* "Up first this hour, a new and dramatic call for a pause, a pause in the warfare here in the Middle East. The United Nations emergency relief coordinator is asking for a seventy-two-hour cease-fire to allow relief workers and humanitarian aid to get into crucial combat areas in Lebanon. Jan Egeland says this: 'There's something wrong with a war where there are more dead children than armed men.' "

The Israeli government is at first unwilling to agree to a humanitarian truce, but we get a green light for most of our convoys, which are bringing in supplies for expanding humanitarian programs under the leadership of the excellent new humanitarian coordinator in Beirut, David Shearer, whom we redeploy from Jerusalem. When the Russians state that they will table my seventy-two-hour truce proposal in the Security Council if there is no progress on a general cease-fire, the United States intensifies its diplomatic efforts for a UN force that can enter southern Lebanon as the Israelis leave and create conditions for a cessation of hostilities.

After a slow start, the UN under Kofi Annan's leadership works exactly as it should. We help coordinate a growing humanitarian operation, we get agreement for a greatly expanded and empowered UNIFIL peacekeeping force, and we recruit in record time the sufficient number of troop contributors. The senseless war ends with the UN-brokered cease-fire on August 14. But again, we fail to get a durable political solution. The deeply divided Lebanese parliament in 2007 failed to elect a new president when Émile Lahoud stepped down in November. Multiple new political assassinations added in 2007 to the worst political crisis since the civil war from 1975 to 1990.

Our appeal for humanitarian funding is well answered. But the ordeals of the civilian population in southern Lebanon are far from over. As most of the one million civilians who fled the war return, they not only find their homes and their infrastructure in ruins, but also an even greater threat, imbedded in the rubble: unexploded grenades, bombs, and other ordnance. As I prepare to go to a conference in Stockholm on September 1 that will focus on the rebuilding of Lebanon, I receive shocking documentation from our colleagues in the UN Mine Action Unit. They have identified 359 separate cluster bomb strike locations that are contaminated with at least a hundred thousand unexploded bomblets.

I ask my staff to reconfirm and reverify the information before I go to the noon UN press briefing to declare that we are seeing an end to the emergency phase and will now assist the Lebanese government in their rebuilding efforts. Toward the end I bring up the just-verified cluster bomb issue: "What's shocking and I would say to me, completely immoral, is that ninety percent of the cluster bomb strikes occurred in the last seventy-two hours of the conflict, when we knew there would be a resolution, when we really knew there would be an end to this. Cluster bombs . . . have affected large areas, lots of homes, lots of farmland, lots of commercial businesses and shops, and they will be with us for many, many months, possibly for years. Every day people are maimed, wounded, and killed by these ordnance; it shouldn't have happened."

Again there are mixed views on whether I have gone too far in criticizing our member states. Most colleagues are supportive. I am repeatedly approached in the cafeteria, elevator, and hallways by strangers who want to congratulate me that there "finally is someone telling the truth." But some conservative organizations that have supported me on Darfur are mobilizing against the statement, which becomes breaking news across world media. I am never in doubt myself. Cluster bombs belong in the garbage cans of history along with land mines and chemical weapons.

Twelve days later the Israeli newspaper *Haaretz* proves that I was, if anything, too soft on the issue: " 'What we did was insane and monstrous, we covered entire towns in cluster bombs,' the head of an IDF rocket unit in Lebanon said regarding the use of cluster bombs and phosphorous shells during the war. Quoting his battalion commander, the rocket unit head stated that the IDF fired around 1,800 cluster bombs, containing over 1.2 million cluster bomblets." Half a year later, my country, Norway, will call an international conference in Oslo to ban cluster bombs altogether.

Of all the wars and crises I have worked in over recent years, only three have gone from really bad to even worse: Iraq, Darfur, and the Palestinian territories. Most other conflicts, from Congo to Nepal and from Liberia to Lebanon, have seen progress or at least some degree of stability. We cannot allow defeatism and extremism to take over. There will be a greater ability to learn from past mistakes, certainly among Israelis and Palestinians. And we in the UN and the international community cannot give up. How can we give up on 1.4 million Gazans, half of them children? Or on Israelis and Palestinians who yearn for a life of security and prosperity? It is now, more than ever, that the occupied Palestinian territories and its neighbor Israel need our collective assistance.

"Don't give up. We have not given up," Allegra, the Israeli press secretary in our OCHA office in Jerusalem, told me as I left the Middle East in July 2006. She is an Israeli Jew married to a Palestinian. They live with their child on the West Bank, and each day she struggles to get through the many roadblocks to come to her office. Extremists on both sides criticize the couple and make it difficult for them to lead the family life they desire. There are many in the younger generation of Israelis and Palestinians, and in Arab nations, who want to break the cycle of violence. Herein lays the hope for ancient Jerusalem. The futility of violence and military options will emerge with younger generations. The benefits of mutual respect and cooperation was reflected in the letter and spirit of the Oslo Accord between Israel and the PLO in 1993.

One day there will be a return to that spirit and then there will be real and lasting progress toward peace among all people in these ancient lands. As the Bush administration managed to start a new round of peace talks between Israel and the Palestinian president at the end of 2007, we must learn from the mistakes and achievements of that historic first negotiation between Israelis and Palestinians on how to achieve peaceful coexistence. I was there when it happened and the next chapter tells that story.

7.

The Life and Death of
the Oslo Accord

S OMETIMES LIFE is more amazing than fiction. At least this was
our feeling, three small groups gathered in the Norwegian Government Guest House, address Parkveien 45, in Oslo on the night of
August 19, 1993. The main participants were four Israeli and three
Palestinian peace negotiators, hosted by our Norwegian facilitation
team of four. The evening opened with an official dinner hosted by
our then foreign minister, Johan Jørgen Holst, in honor of his Israeli
counterpart, Shimon Peres. The conversation revolved around general Norwegian-Israeli ties, but those of us who knew what was to
come after the guests had taken their leave could think of nothing
else.

My friends and co-facilitators—Terje Rød-Larsen, head of the
think tank Fafo, and his wife, Mona Juul, my foreign ministry assistant—and I retreated to one of the formal salons of this nineteenth-
century mansion. Just after midnight, the Norwegian Security Police
escorted the Israeli and PLO negotiating teams through the back
entrance of the then-quiet villa. They brought with them the final,
agreed version of the Declaration of Principles, signaling the first
joint effort to bring peace between Israel and the PLO.

The last points of contention, on how to establish the Palestinian
self-rule authority in Gaza and part of the West Bank, had been re-

solved only two nights before. Minister Holst had presided over a marathon nightly mediation session at Haga Castle outside of Stockholm, Sweden, between Shimon Peres and PLO Chairman Yasser Arafat and his "kitchen cabinet," who were linked by phone from Tunis. The bulk of the historic Declaration of Principles we were to baptize that night had become a reality through more than a dozen secret rounds of negotiations in Norway over eight hectic months. Not even the Israeli intelligence agency Mossad had detected the extremely active back-channel communications as far north as Oslo. As late as the day before, it was still unclear whether we would have a green light from all the leaders involved to formalize the deal in a solemn act.

At one in the morning Foreign Minister Peres rejoined our group to act as an observer when the heads of the two negotiating teams, Ahmed Qurei (Abu Ala) of the PLO leadership and Uri Savir of the Israeli Foreign Ministry, initialed the Oslo Accord. There were short speeches from the three sides present. A greeting from Chairman Arafat was read aloud. The security police photographer took video and some group photos. The atmosphere was hushed and solemn. There were no more than twenty of us present, and most of us had regarded one another as bitter enemies only a few months before.

The following day, the two parties again sat down in a large suite in the Oslo Plaza Hotel, where we had sealed off an entire floor to continue work on an agreement that was equally revolutionary, a Declaration of Mutual Recognition, to transform Israel and the Palestinians from enemies into political partners and peaceful neighbors. Further rounds of secret negotiations would ultimately lead to Foreign Minister Holst's very public shuttle diplomacy between Tunis and Jerusalem with the letters of recognition between Prime Minister Yitzhak Rabin and Chairman Arafat during the first week of September 1993. The few of us who had been present in Oslo gathered with three thousand well-wishers when the agreement was signed in splendor in front of the White House, and Rabin and Arafat shook hands for the first time with a smiling President Bill Clinton between them.

The Oslo five-year framework agreement on Palestinian self-government in Gaza and the West Bank took the world by surprise. *Time* magazine quoted an Israeli diplomat in Washington: "It is so unreal. Next we'll hear that Rabin and Arafat are meeting Elvis Presley in a UFO." One wondered how Palestinians and Israelis could quietly agree on a plan to settle generations of bitter conflict, when the official negotiations and the strife on the ground had brought only bad news since the Madrid Conference in October 1991. Commentators noted, correctly, that the parties had only agreed to start on the road to peace, since they had agreed to a postponement of negotiations on such fundamental issues as whether there would be a Palestinian state, the status of Jerusalem, the future of Palestinian refugees, and the Israeli settlements in the occupied Palestinian territories. How did a small country like Norway, "of all places," as *Time* wryly commented, come to be at the center of an international political drama?

The story of the secret negotiations changes fundamentally depending on whether it is told from an Israeli, Palestinian, American, or Norwegian perspective. There would have been no such talks if there had not been independent peace initiatives on all four sides that came together in the Norwegian channel. My account is as one of the original Norwegian facilitators and hosts.

I had hoped to play a role in Israeli-Palestinian reconciliation ever since I had studied Middle East conflict as a visiting fellow at the Truman Institute for the Advancement of Peace at the Hebrew University in Jerusalem in 1984. On the invitation of its director, peace activist Edward "Edy" Kaufman, who was also my colleague from the International Executive Committee of Amnesty International, I spent several months at beautiful Mount Scopus, which overlooks the synagogues, mosques, and churches of Old Jerusalem. Living and walking in the ancient Holy City and crisscrossing the West Bank of the Jordan River made it abundantly clear to me—and to anyone who wanted to see—that political contacts could not remain frozen between the two closely related peoples living virtually on top of each other. At the Truman Institute I read hundreds of articles and reports on previous attempts to bring Arabs and Jews to agreement on the urgent issues of peaceful coexistence, recognition, the end to occupation, and the future of the Palestinian refugees who I could see firsthand were living in miserable conditions as they had done since the 1948 and 1967 wars.

Not long after I joined the Norwegian Ministry of Foreign Affairs in late 1990, I received permission from Foreign Minister Thorvald Stoltenberg to travel to the region twice with Mona Juul and other colleagues in 1991 to test the waters for a more active Norwegian bridge-building role. In April 1992, we invited Israeli war hero Yitzhak Rabin for breakfast in the Norwegian ambassador's residence in Tel Aviv. Rabin was the candidate of our sister Labor Party in Israel for prime minister in elections scheduled for June. Rabin was a man of few words and even fewer smiles. He took note of our Norwegian offer of "confidence-building efforts" but emphasized that he saw the United States, "which sends us billions of dollars every January upon which our security relies," clearly in the lead for any mediation efforts. It would take some time for him to realize that a back channel was needed to complement and later even substitute for the U.S. front channel.

The very public and high-profile official Middle East peace process had proved too large, noisy, and indirect to produce any deal between enemies. We would see that when Mona Juul and I traveled uninvited to the inaugural Madrid Conference in October 1991 to try to meet the Israeli and Palestinian delegations at the peace talks, which U.S. Secretary of State James Baker had initiated. It was a cir-

cus. Thousands of security guards, reporters, and lobbyists surrounded the Israelis, the Syrians, and an unmanageable combined
Jordanian-Palestinian delegation. To make progress virtually impossible, the PLO, the undisputed de facto leadership of the Palestinian
side, was banned from participating in the talks. We met Gaza doctor
Haider Abdel Shafi, who led the Palestinian team, and Benjamin
Netanyahu, who was acting Israeli delegation leader. None of them
were optimistic about any progress in the intensely charged atmosphere. After Madrid I was more convinced than ever that there was
a role for discreet small-state reconciliation and confidence-building efforts.

A precondition for any effective third party in conflict resolution is to gain the confidence of the two opposing parties. It was
Norway's close historic ties with Israel in general and the Labor
Party in particular that made Norway so interesting for the PLO.
Our direct contact with Chairman Arafat enabled us to offer Israel a
direct back channel to the leader of the PLO when the Israeli government would finally be ready for that.

After the Second World War, the Norwegians, who had seen
Jewish friends and neighbors rounded up during German Nazi occupation, felt a special sympathy for the state of Israel when it was
established in 1948. Our wartime foreign minister, Trygve Lie, became the first secretary-general of the United Nations and worked
with the Norwegian delegation in New York to promote and protect the Jewish state. Our Labor governments forged close ties with
their Israeli counterparts. When I visited Jerusalem in 1991 and
1992, older Israeli officials told me stories of how in the 1960s,
Prime Minister Golda Meir wept and embraced the visiting Norwegian Labor Secretary General Haakon Lie, who had helped the
Zionist movement at crucial moments for the young Israeli nation.

However, after the Israeli occupation of the West Bank and Gaza,
sympathy for the plight of the Palestinian people gradually increased
as aid workers, diplomats, journalists, and Norwegian UN peace-

keepers saw how the Palestinian refugees were living after the 1967 and 1973 wars. Through the 1970s and 1980s our Labor governments began to build direct relations with the Palestinian Liberation Organization, which was allowed to open an office in Oslo. After the Gulf War in 1990–91, a weakened PLO was ready for peace and needed a third party through whom they could approach the Israelis. The outgoing Swedish foreign minister, Sten Andersson, had close relations with Yasser Arafat, and had even succeeded in organizing indirect contacts between the United States and the PLO. When the Swedish Social Democrats lost the national elections, Andersson advised the PLO to look to Oslo, where Thorvald Stoltenberg was the new foreign minister. No fewer than four high-level Palestinian delegations were sent to Oslo in 1992 to ask for a more activist Norwegian role in the Israeli-Palestinian peace process in meetings with Minister Stoltenberg and myself. These included Faisal Husseini, Abu Ala, Hanan Ashrawi, Nabil Sha'at, and Bassam Abu Sharif.

Abu Ala, the "finance minister" of the PLO, came in February to ask for Norwegian funding and support for an ambitious development plan in the Palestinian territories, but it was something we could not offer. After our meetings in the ministry, Mona suggested that Abu Ala see Terje Rød-Larsen in Fafo. It was, however, Bassam Abu Sharif, with his deep facial scars and fingerless hand from a bomb attack, who on August 18 arrived with the most explicit appeal from Arafat himself for a Norwegian bridge-building role. After appealing to Foreign Minister Stoltenberg to become personally engaged in reconciling the two parties, Abu Sharif went out of his way to talk to me privately in the elevators and corners of Bristol Hotel when I hosted a lunch for him and two PLO diplomats. "Go straight to the Israelis and say that now is the time to talk and make historic compromises for which the PLO is now ready. When you hear back from the Israelis on a possible contact between us and them via you, do not tell anyone, only me. Don't even tell the Oslo PLO office!"

Official Israel had not yet changed positions and was not interested in any contacts with the PLO. "We will not even contemplate meeting the PLO, and strongly discourage even you to have any contacts with them," the Israeli ambassador to Oslo told me when I invited him to the ministry after the Abu Sharif meeting. It was therefore to be a much more indirect route that would ultimately produce what we sought. Those contacts were with a new generation of Israeli "doves" who had emerged within the Israeli Labor Party. A crucial link was established in May between Rød-Larsen and Yossi Beilin, a young Labor member of the Israeli Knesset. "I think we have the man we have been looking for on the Israeli side," Rød-Larsen, always the optimist, told me on the phone after coming back to Oslo. Beilin would become the operator we had hoped for as Labor and Rabin won the elections in June 1992 with a clear peace mandate.

I had known Terje Rød-Larsen for some time as both the husband of Mona and as the dynamic leader of Fafo, a think tank set up by the large Norwegian Confederation of Trade Unions. He is a brilliant man, always full of new ideas and ambitious initiatives. I felt that he was the one who could help bring forward our still-vague ambitions.

In September, Stoltenberg agreed that it was time for us to approach the Israelis with a more formal offer of facilitation of contacts on the Palestinian side. On September 10, 1992, I was back in Israel to meet my new Israeli counterpart, our new friend Deputy Foreign Minister Yossi Beilin. My message was simple: "The official peace talks are, as you know, going nowhere because PLO is not at the bargaining table. We can connect, with discretion, PLO or non-PLO Palestinians on any level with Israeli representatives at any level, anywhere." The message was delivered at a late-night meeting

in my hotel suite after an official dinner in Tel Aviv that Beilin had
hosted for my delegation. We were visiting Israel after talks in Syria
and Lebanon and a visit with the Norwegian UNIFIL peacekeepers. Not even the Norwegian ambassador to Israel knew of my
meeting with Beilin.

Terje and Mona had prepared the ground for the meeting with
help from Beilin's old friend and colleague, Professor Yair Hirschfeld,
the only other Israeli present. I explained that we were able to provide the perfect camouflage for the proposed channel: the extensive
standard-of-living studies being carried out by Fafo in the West
Bank and Gaza. These required frequent contacts and meetings with
Israeli and Palestinian counterparts. Beilin still felt it was too early
for him to have direct contact with the PLO, but he confirmed his
interest in indirect contact, for example via Hirschfeld. We agreed
that one possibility for indirect contact would be in connection
with a meeting between Beilin and the Jerusalem Palestinian leader
Faisal Husseini in Oslo. Beilin and Hirschfeld did not tell us that
they had already met with Husseini in Jerusalem. They wanted an
Oslo meeting because Husseini, who was not officially a member of
the PLO, could bring others with him.

I was so convinced we would be able to connect Israel and the
PLO in some way that a new problem arose: what would the Americans, our most powerful ally, who had invested so much in the Middle East peace process, say of our freelance back-channel efforts? I
traveled with Mona to Washington, D.C., in early November 1992
to brief the State Department about our plans. The first Bush administration was preparing to hand over to the incoming Clinton
team. Thus my most important meeting was with the career deputy
assistant secretary of state for the Middle East, Daniel Kurtzer. "Norway may be able to use our unique relations to both sides in the Israeli-Palestinian conflict, including by involving the PLO, to the
benefit of the overall peace effort," I told Kurtzer and his colleagues.

They listened to us politely and neither encouraged nor discouraged us. "Keep us informed if you get anything going," Kurtzer told me. "But let me make it clear that the incoming Clinton administration will almost certainly not alter the Washington framework for talks. Nor will they want to speak to the PLO."

We did in the end not manage to get Beilin and Husseini to Oslo at the same time, but Terje was able to arrange for Hirschfeld to see Abu Ala in London in December as a prelude to a first meeting in Norway. It was still a criminal offense under Israeli law to meet with the PLO when the two courageous Israeli academics, Yair Hirschfeld and his younger colleague Ron Pundak, confirmed their willingness to come to our first meeting in January 1993. The law was changed only days before they arrived in Norway to meet Abu Ala and two colleagues from the staffs of Chairman Arafat and Abu Mazen. A secluded country house in Sarpsborg, a hundred miles south of Oslo, was the venue.

Both teams were determined to break from the tradition set by earlier Israeli–Palestinian talks and by most Jewish–Arab discussions. They agreed *not* to dwell on the past. I remember both essentially saying at the first evening meeting, "If we are to quarrel about the historic rights to these holy lands, about who of us was there first, or about who betrayed whom and when, we will sit here quarreling forever. We must agree to look to the future."

Abu Ala, Hirschfeld, and Pundak were all experts in economy and development. After the first meeting of minds in Sarpsborg they agreed to a second meeting in February. The logistics were arranged by Mona, Terje, and his Fafo assistant Even Aas. For the second time we were embarrassed by overzealous police in the passport controls who held back Abu Ala and the Palestinians for an hour even though I had booked the VIP lounge services for them through the Foreign Office. I had to start my meetings with the fuming Abu Ala by apologizing on behalf of the hosts. Nevertheless, the atmosphere at the

Borregaard mansion in Sarpsborg remained excellent. The hard-working, no-nonsense, pragmatic approach of the two teams of ne-gotiators produced results.

Based on draft papers from the PLO team and especially the two Israeli academics, the teams arrived at provisional agreement on three strategic papers: a fourteen-point Declaration of Principles on basic arrangements for Palestinian self-rule and a framework for fu-ture negotiations; a six-point proposal for major infrastructure and development programs on which Israel, the Palestinians, and Arab neighbors could cooperate; and, third, an ambitious "Marshall"-style international assistance plan that would engage the Group of Seven greatest economies (G7) and the Organization for Economic Co-operation and Development to the benefit of the Palestinian areas in particular, and the wider Middle East in general. Impor-tantly, they also agreed that self-rule could start in Gaza and gradu-ally grow to include the West Bank. The latter was an old proposal of Shimon Peres that previously had been rejected by the PLO. I got a copy of the text through Terje, who was, as the chief organizer, stay-ing with the two teams at the manor house. The two sides were still far from working toward an "Oslo Accord," but it was suggested in the preamble to the draft texts that "the U.S. Secretary of State will go to Jerusalem and will submit to the Government of Israel on one hand, and to the Palestinian leadership (Faisal Husseini and Hanan Ashrawi) on the other hand, an American draft" for the three docu-ments mentioned above.

After a third session in the seclusion of the country house, the two teams agreed on a further developed draft Declaration of Prin-ciples, which included many of the elements that would remain until the final, signed agreement. We were amazed and elated. The academic contact point we had established held greater potential than we had originally assumed. However, the paper had one major drawback: there was still no official backing from the Israeli side. "Who are they really? And who do they really represent?" Abu Ala kept asking us. When I met separately with Hirschfeld and Pundak I conveyed the Palestinian concern that their high-level delegation, sanctioned by Arafat and Abu Mazen, might be wasting their time on two Israeli private citizens. "Well, that is their dilemma," Pundak commented. "It may take some time before they know whether they are negotiating with the Israeli government or wasting their time on two monkeys. But I think they cannot afford to not keep on going in this channel."

It took several weeks through April and early May 1993 for Beilin to secure the support of Foreign Minister Peres to the channel his private emissaries had managed to establish in Norway. Peres had become increasingly impressed by the constructive, businesslike, and moderate "Gaza-first" text drafted in Sarpsborg, and in the end he also managed to get Prime Minister Rabin to see the potential of the Norwegian channel and the Sarpsborg document. With hundreds of telephone calls, Terje and Mona kept Jerusalem and Tunis informed about the other side's questions, answers, threats, and propositions. Beilin reported back that Israel had agreed to upgrade the talks to an official level, provided we could guarantee that the talks remained secret.

Similar discussions took place in what the Palestinians described as the "Arafat kitchen" in Tunis. Only a handful of Palestinian leaders participated, including Chairman Arafat, Abu Mazen, and Abu Ala. For the Palestinian leadership, Israel's willingness to initiate direct talks with the PLO was a breakthrough, since it meant de facto recognition of the organization as the legitimate representative of the Palestinians. The draft agreement also said the PLO could start to govern at least parts of Palestinian territory immediately as Israeli forces withdrew.

The director-general of the Israeli Foreign Ministry, Uri Savir, was sent to Oslo in May to "test the seriousness" of Abu Ala and his two colleagues. Thorvald Stoltenberg had left Norway to become a full-time peace mediator in the wars in the Balkans, and Johan Jørgen Holst took over as foreign minister in April. With the Israeli government now participating, secrecy became even tighter. We never used hotels or other public venues for the negotiations, nor the real names of our guests. We always used our VIP facilities at the airport to prevent our guests from meeting anyone they might know in the waiting areas—officially they were on business elsewhere in Europe.

When the official negotiations started in June, with Israeli lawyer Joel Singer joining as the fourth Israeli, on Rabin's initiative, we used the two-hundred-year-old Heftye House, which belongs to the Oslo municipality. I called a representative of the Oslo Town Hall and said I needed the villa for internal "Foreign Ministry seminars." As I prepared to leave the ministry and join the negotiators, our press spokesman, Ingvard Havnen, rushed into my office with a dispatch from the Washington correspondent of Agence France-Presse claiming that there was a secret Norwegian channel between Israel and the PLO. "The Norwegian press wants to know what this is. My God, Jan, what are you up to now?" he asked. I was totally taken aback, but managed to tell Havnen that he should inform the Norwegian and international press that the AFP story must be based on a misunderstanding, and probably referred to a multilateral meeting on Palestinian refugees in Oslo in May. This had actually taken place as part of the official U.S.-sponsored peace process and our elaborate smoke screen.

At the house I met Savir and Hirschfeld first. They read through the AFP report, which quoted anonymous State Department sources. "I think we can deal with this, but don't tell the Palestinians since the negotiations are in a crucial phase," Savir told me as Singer was interrogating the PLO representatives about their intentions. Ten minutes later I gave the same dispatch to Abu Ala, who calmly said he knew the story through PLO intelligence and had already instructed Tunis on how to deal with it. "But don't show it to the

Israelis," he said. "The negotiations are difficult now and the Israelis could become more nervous."

Because the leak had clearly come from the U.S. State Department, both parties asked me to discontinue the regular briefings to Washington about progress in our channel that I had agreed to provide when I met with Daniel Kurtzer in November. After each of those meetings I had walked the two blocks from the ministry to the U.S. Embassy to use their "safe phone," which scrambled the transmission to Kurtzer on the other side. In Washington they carefully took note of our efforts; Secretary of State Warren Christopher had been eager to receive a copy of the "Sarpsborg" document from Stoltenberg in March. In a major error of judgment, however, the American diplomats did not believe the Israel-PLO channel in Norway would lead to anything. Being left deliberately out of the loop from June onward meant that the Clinton administration would be unprepared for the breakthrough in August.

In June and July, Rabin and Peres and Arafat and Abu Mazen were following the negotiations closely and imposing increasingly strict terms for their negotiators. Their goals were ultimate and ambitious, but not mutually exclusive. The Israelis wanted maximum security for all their citizens indefinitely; the Palestinians wanted maximum self-rule, territory, and economic development immediately. In July we experienced a first breakdown in the negotiations. It was in the middle of the holiday season and nearly impossible to find the right kind of secluded "safe house" that could accommodate the increasingly large set-up. I called many guest houses and mansions that normally would be for rent, but they were all closed for the summer or under renovation. In the end we rented a large country estate through a colleague of my wife some 150 miles north of Oslo overlooking Norway's greatest lake, Mjøsa. We also brought for the first time the Norwegian security police to guard a session we hoped would see the final breakthrough.

As the talks turned official I realized that our guests—in particular the Palestinians—were running an increasing security risk from extremists who would not tolerate fraternization with the enemy. With the consent of the parties and Minister Holst, I told the head of the security policy the necessary minimum about the channel. A team of eight policemen was assigned to help us with security and the growing logistical demands, since the sessions were organized more frequently, often with only a few days' notice.

The owners of the estate were told that we would bring a group of eccentric Middle Eastern academics working around the clock to finish a book. We knew that the Israelis had received the go-ahead from Rabin and Peres to initial a text then and there if it met a series of new Israeli demands. Terje, Mona, and I spent the last night half asleep on sofas hoping that the final pieces of the puzzle would fit together in the next few hours.

Instead, due to far-reaching new Israeli demands, there was a growing anger on both sides and the two teams broke off their talks at 5.30 A.M. and asked to be taken either to their Oslo hotel, or in Savir's case straight to the airport. They had spent thirty-five of the forty-four hours at the house negotiating. When the owners of the estate awoke to prepare our breakfast, we had all gone. After both teams left Oslo to report home we did not know whether there would be any further negotiations.

But both sides needed a political breakthrough, and the negotiators were soon back. During July and August both sides engaged repeatedly in brinkmanship even as they saw that an agreement was within reach. Leaders would instruct their negotiators to introduce new demands, and give them little flexibility to accept new language. Stalemates were always followed by daily contact with the parties by telephone.

Rød-Larsen and Juul kept their mobile phones within reach on round-the-clock watch. They talked to Uri Savir and Abu Ala frequently with questions or accounts of developments. This was an important part of our facilitation: keep momentum by urging and begging for new positions, clarifications, more talks. Having learned in the ministry that all phones may be tapped at all times, I had suggested in June a primitive code. We tried to avoid all references to names and countries. The prime minister level (Rabin and Arafat) was termed "the grandfathers," the ministers (Peres, Abu Mazen, and Holst) became "the fathers," and deputy ministers (Beilin and me) "the sons." A typical call could be: "They have already briefed their grandfather and will soon have news back, have you informed yours?" "No, but the son sees his father today as he will talk with the grandfather tomorrow morning."

In tough negotiations the final points of contention are lifted to the highest levels and left for the last hours. Shimon Peres's official visit to the Scandinavian countries in mid-August became our perceived deadline for initialing the agreement. In the early morning of August 17, Peres called Foreign Minister Holst, who was in Iceland: "Can you meet me discreetly in Stockholm tonight? It is now or never." That night Holst sat for eight hours with a phone at the Haga Castle in Sweden and transmitted messages from Peres next door to Arafat, who was in Tunis. At 5 A.M. the final wording was agreed to on security for Israeli settlers, and on the location and authority of the future elected Palestinian Council. The negotiators embraced in Tunis as well as at the Swedish castle. Two days later we would witness the late-night, official initialing of the Declaration in Oslo.

To take part in the inner circle of the successful mediation effort between Israel and the PLO was a dream come true for me as a young Norwegian diplomat. I have taken part in more than ten conflict resolution efforts, from Guatemala and Colombia to Sri Lanka and Sudan, but never have I worked with such committed, hardworking, and able negotiators. The whole "Norwegian channel" cost Norwegian taxpayers less than a million U.S. dollars from the first sessions to the final agreement. It would equal less than one

day of expenses in the large and inconclusive "front-channel" negotiations in Washington, D.C., Madrid, and elsewhere. I had autho-
rized expenses for all talks, writing on the applications I got directly
from Terje Rød-Larsen that "this has been cleared by the ministry's
political leadership," before it went to the Political Office, in charge
of humanitarian funding. It was all presented as "consultations" connected to Fafo's standard-of-living survey in the Palestinian areas.
But as inexpensive as our mini-channel was, it clearly could not
have gone on much longer without any visible outcome before we
would have had to put the brakes on humanitarian funding.

During the magic months of intense conflict resolution work,
friendships were forged among negotiators and facilitators. We were
all loyal to our sworn secrecy, to the collegial spirit, and to our goal
of achieving a compromise solution to one of the most difficult
conflicts of our time. After the channel became a huge international
sensation at the end of August, it all changed, and mostly for the
worse. There was a rush for the stage by actors on all three sides as
history was rewritten and retold countless times in press accounts,
books, and television dramas. Some original participants were side-
lined while others assumed roles that the rest of us could not recall.

The Nobel Peace Prize was awarded to Rabin, Peres, and Arafat.
Such high honors were by necessity given to some actors only, but
tension quickly rose among the participants in our once-so-cordial
channel. I often felt it would have been better if the Norwegian
channel had remained secret and the Oslo Accord had been fed into
the official Washington talks. This was indeed what we had envis-
aged for most of the time during the secret talks. If Secretary of
State Christopher had not insisted that the true story come out
when he was presented with the agreement by Peres and Holst just
after it had been initialed, we might indeed have kept our secret.

"The soap opera became a love story," Johan Jørgen Holst commented self-critically to me in September, after the Washington
signing ceremony. He was referring to how his original press brief-

ings had given his wife and home a prominent role in the talks, but
had forgotten his predecessor and my own role. That was overtaken
by a British television documentary that presented Terje Rød-
Larsen and Mona Juul as a lonely couple organizing and initiating
the whole channel. The news media, particularly in Norway, could
not get enough of the secret negotiations. For Holst, who had gotten little credit as defense minister and a brilliant foreign policy ana-
lyst, it was an unexpected gift to get the Norwegian channel in his
lap when he took over as foreign minister from Thorvald Stoltenberg in April 1993. "There is a reason for all my travel and all my
interviews in the wake of the signing of the agreement," he told me.
"The global attention is coming at the best possible time since the
government wants me to be a candidate for secretary-general of
NATO when [German] Manfred Wörner steps down next year."

Sadly, Minister Holst would not realize his dream in NATO. On
January 13, 1994, I was met at the Cairo airport by the Norwegian
ambassador to Egypt when I landed on the way back from talks
with President Bashir in Khartoum on possible peace talks with the
SPLA rebels in South Sudan. I took an urgent call from Siri Bjerke
in Oslo, the other of Holst's two deputies. "I wanted you to know
before you hear it from the media that the foreign minister died
early this morning from a massive stroke while asleep in his hospital
bed," Siri said in a sad and formal voice. I stood for some time looking numbly at the black Egyptian phone booth. Minister Holst had
worked around the clock to advance the Norwegian channel, traveling constantly for more than six months. He had suffered his first
stroke on November 28, but had insisted on going back to work in
early January. We had only just started implementation of the Oslo
Accord and losing Holst was a terrible personal and professional
blow to all who worked with and for him.

After the signing of the Oslo Accord on the White House lawn
in September 1993, the Norwegian role was gradually transformed
from principal bridge-builder between Israel and the PLO to facili-

tator of economic assistance and the establishment of the first Palestinian police force. Importantly, Norway was asked by the United States and the European Union to chair the donor group that started its work in Washington in October 1993, and that still exists with the participation of the Palestinians and the Israelis. I chaired many of these large and very public international meetings and felt a strong and united international desire, from the United States to Russia and from the European Union to the Arab Gulf countries, to bring development to the Palestinian territories. It was internal rather than external forces that failed to implement the peace plan.

We also continued as occasional mediators in crisis situations. When an Israeli settler killed thirty Palestinians who were praying at Abraham's grave in Hebron on February 25, 1994, the PLO froze all participation in talks on implementation of the Oslo Accord. It was only when agreement was made on a "temporary international presence in Hebron," with 150 international observers led by Norway, that the negotiations could resume. On the one-year anniversary in September 1994 of the signing of the agreement, we also managed to get the stalled talks back on track temporarily when both Arafat and Peres came with their teams to Oslo to participate in a large peace concert.

But the forces of gravity and international politics made the United States, Egypt, and other global and regional powers again the main actors in the Middle East peace process, as they had been before the Norwegian channel. On September 28, 1995, the so-called Oslo 2 agreement was signed in Taba, Egypt. Terje Rød-Larsen also helped make the United Nations a significant political participant after Kofi Annan named him special coordinator for UN efforts in the region.

The violence and crisis of confidence between the actors in the Middle East peace process showed that the understanding and trust that was reached between Rabin/Peres and Arafat/Mazen did not filter down to the ordinary man and woman as we had, perhaps naively, believed in 1993 would happen. With the Oslo 2 agreement a new effort was launched to promote cooperation between Israeli and Palestinian citizens in fields such as economics, cultural affairs, and education. This people-to-people exercise was intended to do away with the stereotypical images of Israelis as "brutal occupiers" and Palestinians as "terrorists." Norway was asked to facilitate these programs, and more than a hundred bridge-building projects were initiated with youth groups, businesspeople, academics, and local politicians.

What are the lessons learned through the Norwegian channel? I believe our secret meetings proved to have several advantages over traditional conference diplomacy:

First, the news media, which tends to focus on what divides rather than unites, was not involved. As a former news reporter and a strong believer in free speech and open societies, I was struck by how disruptive the news coverage was at public peace negotiations on the Middle East. As soon as the delegates would arrive in Washington or another official venue, journalists would confront them with the hostile comments or acts of violence on the opposing side, which would elicit aggressive responses.

Second, there was no time-consuming diplomatic protocol that had to be followed, no speeches to the gallery. Participants in official public sessions spend almost 100 percent of their time blaming one another, whereas the negotiators in Norway spent 90 percent of their waking hours in real negotiations. Even mutual provocation did not stall their efforts as it did in the official channels.

Third, an atmosphere of trust and affinity developed among the handful of individuals who spent hundreds of hours working, eating, quarreling, and joking. With only seven negotiators at the table the dialogue was direct. Since the inception of the official negotiations in June, the negotiators were, except for the change of one Palestinian midway, the same individuals. This provided for continuity and institutional memory.

Fourth, a close partnership between the Foreign Ministry and Fafo, the nongovernmental organization, allowed us to offer the parties "deniability." If anything leaked we could and would explain the meetings as academic seminars. The small size of our team helped. Our promise to keep our secret forever if the negotiations broke down was a precondition for the participation of the Israeli side, but both sides feared that news of secret negotiations with the enemy without any agreement would have disastrous results at home.

The process that culminated in the Oslo Accord and the subsequent negotiations was followed by numerous crises and setbacks, but also by some historical breakthroughs as the Palestinian Authority that was set up in Gaza and Jericho gradually extended to most of the West Bank. Enemies of peace on both sides repeatedly tried to derail the process, mounting terrible terrorist attacks in Hebron, Jerusalem, Tel Aviv, and elsewhere. New settlements and border closures were obstacles to the peace process, and have prevented the two Oslo agreements from being implemented. The process was soon far behind the original Oslo schedule and the mutual confidence built during the Norwegian channel slowly but surely eroded. The counterforces were stronger than we originally expected.

Less than two years after Holst died, another of the main actors, Prime Minister Yitzhak Rabin, was murdered—shot in the back on November 4, 1995, by a Jewish anti-peace fanatic during a peaceful demonstration in favor of the Oslo agreements. After Rabin died, a steep downhill slide took place. Rabin's successor, Peres, lost the elections in May 1996 and Benjamin Netanyahu of the Likud Party took over on a platform hostile to implementation of the Oslo Accord. Since the mid-1990s living conditions have eroded and violence has mounted steadily in the Palestinian areas, hitting rock bottom, I could only hope, when I visited Gaza in 2006 amid the bombing and killings.

In 2007 there were finally some renewed efforts by Israeli, Arab, and Palestinian leaders to break the deadlock. The "Quartet"—the United Nations, the United States, European Union, and Russia—restarted a diplomatic effort to search for a negotiated outcome. Former British prime minister Tony Blair became their new envoy as the United States, the most important peace broker in the region since the Madrid Conference, promised to refocus on this conflict. In Annapolis, the Bush administration in November 2007 succeeded in getting Israel, the Palestinian administration led by President Abbas, and other Arab leaders to restart peace talks. The first direct meetings took place in December and involved our old Palestinian friend Ahmed Qurei, Abu Ala, as chief Palestinian negotiator, meeting with Foreign Minister Livni as head of the Israeli delegation.

There are steps that can and must be taken. Most important is a return to real negotiations on final-status issues such as the creation and recognition of borders of a Palestinian state, effective recognition of the state of Israel by all Arab states and movements, the right of return of Palestinian refugees, and the future status of Jerusalem and the Israeli settlements in the Occupied Territories. Maximum pressure must be exerted on all actors in the Israeli-Palestinian and wider Israeli-Arab conflicts for progress to be made on these burning issues. There is not much time. When I returned to the Middle East in November 2007 to address the annual UNRWA (UN Relief and Works Agency) conference on assistance to Palestinian refugees, the aid workers were very clear: We either see a clear departure from the downward spiral for the Palestinians, or we see a collapse worse than anything we have seen so far. The sense of confinement and despair in the West Bank is growing and Gaza is more locked in than ever, with a defiant and isolated Hamas at the helm. Nothing can be more important than breaking the spiral toward the abyss.

8.

"Tents Are for Arabs"

ZIMBABWE'S PRESIDENT Robert Mugabe looks older and frailer than I remembered him from photographs and film footage. He moves slowly and is thinner. He leans on the right arm of his chair for support as he speaks. As someone who campaigned against apartheid during my student years, I am slightly in awe of the hero of the liberation struggle against Ian Smith's white minority regime as he peers at me through thick glasses. I feel like a student undergoing an examination by an eminent professor.

The president is notorious for keeping people waiting and I think we have done quite well to see him by 9:15 A.M. this rainy Tuesday, December 6, 2005, after only fifteen minutes in an anteroom of the presidential palace in Harare. I know this will be one of my most difficult missions and meetings ever. Nearly three years earlier, my predecessor as UN relief coordinator, Kenzo Oshima, a more polite and diplomatic envoy than me, had been kept waiting for hours in the presidential antechambers before being lectured for an hour about UN shortcomings. This time, probably because of the international publicity surrounding my mission, we do not have to wait and it seems I will be allowed to speak uninterrupted. It is a unique opportunity to speak truth to power.

Zimbabwe was called "the jewel" and "the bread basket" of Af-

rica after its liberation from white minority rule in 1980. The economy, the infrastructure, and the educational system were among the
best on the continent. Twenty-five years later it is synonymous with
economic collapse and political repression. It started at the end of
the 1990s. Large and productive farms were nationalized and white
farmers were forced to hand over their estates to ill-prepared veterans from the liberation struggle and political activists from Mugabe's
party, the Zanu-PF.

The need for land reform in a country where a few white colo-
nizers had claimed the best farming land is indisputable. But reform
was brutally enforced in the worst possible manner for the farmers,
the agricultural sector, and the population at large. Production
plummeted, the black farm laborers lost their jobs, and little food
made it to the markets or to foreign exports. A country that had had
a large food surplus could not feed itself, and had to rely on foreign
emergency aid and remittances from the growing number of Zim-
babweans who have to leave the country to make a living.

As both domestic and foreign investors fled the country, a general breakdown in the rule of law fueled the economic crisis.
Mugabe's government was however undeterred and continued to
fund ambitious public programs that principally benefited the political and tribal groups that supported the government. To cover the
enormous state budget deficits the National Bank was instructed to
print additional money that created inflation, and later hyperinfla-
tion. Today the Zimbabwean economy is arguably more misman-
aged than any other in peacetime.

I am primarily going to discuss the massive homeless problem
Mugabe has created almost overnight through his "Operation Restore Order," a brutal eviction campaign that began seven months
ago. I spent hours yesterday walking among some of the seven hundred thousand destitute and homeless people who are living under
makeshift plastic sheeting or in the open after being evicted from
shantytowns across Zimbabwe. The evictions were not only partic-

ularly brutal and chaotic in the way they spread throughout the country, but profoundly political, turning out many who did not support the government party and leaving urban areas to regime supporters who would like cleaner and leaner cities and less competition for jobs. Those evicted were not only among the poorest and most vulnerable in the country, many were sick with AIDS or tuberculosis.

I saw and spoke to dozens of families who had lost everything when their tiny "illegal" brick houses were bulldozed, or their small vending shacks burned and torn apart by security forces in an operation that began in May.

The presidential office is smaller and nicer than the grotesquely oversized staterooms that so many African presidents preside in. As planned, I start our discussion by describing the shocking scenes I saw in the slums of Hopely Farm, and the Whitecliff and Hatcliff suburbs on the outskirts of Harare. I explain that we need to discover how we can most rapidly and effectively help with food and shelter for the homeless.

President Mugabe carefully enunciates each syllable in his academic English as though addressing someone who does not speak his language. He is immediately on the defensive. While acknowledging his awareness of "a problem," he seems intent on downplaying a situation that has scandalized the world with its callous indifference to human suffering. His most outrageous comment comes as I try to impress upon him the urgent need for emergency shelter for the thousands of families with children who are at great risk with no shelter, no food, and no income. The UN is willing to supply tents immediately as a short-term answer to the problem.

As I press, the tenor of Mugabe's calm, lecturing tone rises. There is a hint of barely repressed anger as he says, "We do not feel comfortable with the term 'shelter.' Shelter has connotations of impermanency and we build for permanency." As I seek to return to the need for immediate action he is clearly angered. "Keep your tents, we do not need them. Tents are for Arabs!" Stunned, I ask him to repeat what he said. "We want to give real houses to our people. Tents are for Arabs," he says again. It is a phrase that in its absurdity will reverberate through my office.

"We may have an accommodation problem," Mugabe continues, "but the 700,000 figure is exaggerated. People can be sheltered by their families." He embarks on a semantics lecture, suggesting the term "shelter" sends the wrong meaning: "The word connotes impermanency. We want permanent housing here. In terms of humanitarian needs it is not even as bad here as in South Africa. The South Africans have sent delegations here to learn from our housing programs.

"When I was a boy herding my godfather's cattle and it rained I looked for 'shelter' where I could find it—under a tree or in a nearby hut. That is shelter. You can provide food if you want to and build permanent houses with us, but not provide 'shelter' in the form of tents."

It is one of those situations when you do not know whether to cry, laugh, or shout. With the UN resident coordinator Agostinho Zacarias and my OCHA colleagues Agnes Asekenye-Oonyu and Hansjoerg Strohmeyer, I am failing to get the head of state to admit the gravity of the situation in his country—that his people are in desperate need of precisely the things we offer. Through the UN agencies, the International Organization for Migration, and excellent local and international NGOs, we can help meet acute emergency needs. But instead of saying "How can we help you help our people," the man wants to lecture me about the shortcomings of official UN terms and concepts!

I try to explain that there is no money for any form of more permanent housing since the donors are reluctant to help even with temporary shelter. They regard Zimbabwe's problems as the direct result of Mugabe's evictions, and his agricultural and economic policies.

"Donors will only pay for temporary shelters. They think it's indefensible that there are no tents allowed. Disaster victims accept tents in Louisiana, Florida, and in Europe. Why not here?" I ask.

"The UN is politicized," Mugabe says. "You want to provide an image of refugee camps here. Our attitude to tents is negative." Nodding from the nearby black leather sofa in Mugabe's small, white-walled office are the permanent secretary of the President's Office and the ministers of foreign affairs and defense. It is difficult to know whether he believes what he is saying because the nodding ministers never seem to tell him what he does not want to hear.

The UN is politicized, Mugabe says, because it is dominated by Britain and its stooges—among whom I, a Norwegian, am soon lumped. Mugabe is particularly angry with the UN because a field visit several months earlier by Anna Tibaijuka, the African head of UN Habitat, our organization for urban issues and housing, had first alerted the world to the full extent of Zimbabwe's housing disaster.

He suggests that Tibaijuka would be better advised to visit Nigeria, which has a far greater "cleanup" program under way than Zimbabwe. "It is clear to us that the UN is being used by Britain for political purposes," he repeats. "That is why we are sensitive to your own presence."

Mugabe's body language and that of his ministers express their profound skepticism about the motives behind the UN's work in Zimbabwe. Mugabe speaks slowly. "We are beginning to lose confidence in the United Nations and even the secretary-general."

Urban renewal campaigns and removal of unauthorized buildings and squatters take place all the time all over the world. I had, however, called Zimbabwe's eviction program "the worst possible thing at the worst possible time" when it was at its brutal height in May, June, and July. I had no interest in castigating the government of Zimbabwe. Apart from protesting against apartheid, I supported our Scandinavian assistance to the liberation struggles against the white minority regimes of both Rhodesia and South Africa. But we

have to tell the truth about what is taking place in the country that
President Mugabe rules.

I lean forward, seeking eye contact, and try again: "The purpose
of my mission on behalf of your fellow African, Secretary-General
Kofi Annan, is to discuss how we can more effectively contribute to
meet humanitarian needs in Zimbabwe. The challenges here are, as
we all know, daunting: There are more than three million who need
food assistance. There are one million orphans caused by AIDS. We
are willing and able to assist the people if we know whom you will
cover and if you will do more to enable the work of the humanitarian organizations. We are less effective here than in most other places
due to all the restrictions on our work. We use tents in the emergency phase for the homeless in Europe, America, and Asia. Tents
will only be one of the ways we would like to provide shelter to
the most needy of the hundreds of thousands who are homeless. I
saw thousands yesterday who have nothing. Your government
housing programs are small and still not completed. Those who live
under plastic sheeting or out in the open want the tents that we can
provide."

"Yes," he says, fixing me with a challenging stare. "Kofi Annan is
an African, but he and the organization are being used politically, or,
more specifically, manipulated by Britain and Blair. Even the innocent Prince Charles is now being manipulated."

Mugabe says his government embarked long ago on a "massive
housing program" at a time when people were living in shanties and
housing was scarce.

"Everyone in Zimbabwe has somewhere to go, everyone is
rooted somewhere in the country, in rural areas. Harare is never a
permanent home and those who come from outside behave like
people from other countries. We have a situation here but even in
terms of humanitarian aid our needs are not as bad as South Africa's.
South Africa sent a delegation here to look at our housing program,"
he repeats.

I tell him that I spoke to an old woman yesterday who was looking after her daughter's children because their mother had died of
AIDS. I met the old lady in a hut made of plastic sheeting and
branches that she had built with her grandchildren on the same spot
where the security police had bulldozed her brick house. Operation
Restore Order had failed to send her back to "where she came
from." She had nowhere else to go. His campaign had only managed
to raze the result of a lifetime's toil.

Mugabe is tired of discussing the eviction campaign and moves
on. "The food system is under control. All we need," says the president of a country that was once the breadbasket of Africa, "are the
agricultural imports. The situation is not as severe as people make
out. We give food to everyone despite the propaganda stirred up by
NGOs for political reasons. We can organize food for our people
although perhaps not always of the kind that they like the most," he
says. "We even provide assistance to others. We also have cattle. We
sent beef to Europe ..."

When I urge that his government enable the work of the essential NGOs, Mugabe remains unimpressed. "The problem with
NGOs is that they cannot accept that Zimbabwe can do it better.
They want to bring in their own people, outsiders, and we don't like
outsiders. We have invested a lot in education and have the most
highly skilled workforce in Africa."

My mission has been planned in detail with Kofi Annan and
Ibrahim Gambari, former Nigerian foreign minister and currently
UN undersecretary-general for political affairs. If in the course of
my visit, progress can be made on providing assistance to the victims
of eviction, Annan might later visit Zimbabwe to deal with political
issues. At first Harare had rejected my mission, but Gambari spoke
to Mugabe at an African Union meeting in October and managed
to convince him to agree to see me in Zimbabwe.

Relations between the United Nations and the government are
at an all-time low. Anna Tibaijuka's report concluded that the evic-

tion campaign had made more than 110,000 families, or close to 600,000 people, homeless. More than 100,000 others had lost their principal source of income, leading to the widely quoted figure of 700,000 victims of the operation.

Relations between the donor nations and Mugabe are even frostier. The United States, United Kingdom, and other Western nations have had repeated diplomatic rows with the government. In my meeting with the ambassadors of donor countries two days earlier there was resentment against government policies. Some of the longest-serving ambassadors were even expressing a deep personal anger against the government. "We will not give any money, ever, to build housing for the evicted people," one ambassador said. "Why should we pick up the bill for the atrocities committed by the government?"

The donor meeting concluded that we could have money for tents, but not for permanent housing. Again, we humanitarians find ourselves in a political crossfire: Mugabe will not agree to tents, and the donors will only fund tents!

Ignatius Chombo, Mugabe's minister for local government, was even more blunt when I met him yesterday in my hotel: "Anna Tibaijuka is nothing but a tool in the hands of those who want to undermine us. The report is a fabrication of facts. It is the same people who attack us for taking land from the rich." The meeting with Chombo in my hotel had been an open confrontation. He refused to admit any problems when I insisted that the Tibaijuka report was the official UN line based on available facts and that the situation would only deteriorate unless there was a government policy change.

After an hour and a half in Mugabe's office, we are running out of time. We are due this afternoon to meet church leaders in the southern city of Bulawayo, where opposition to government policies has been strong and suppression of dissent brutal. I ask the president for a few private minutes, to which he agrees immediately. As his ministers and my UN colleagues leave, Mugabe leans forward for the first time to listen to me. "The situation is very bad and it is my impression that it will get worse unless you move from confrontation to finding common ground and new policies between yourself and international actors, including donors and the U.K. Can we in the UN help facilitate such a dialogue under the leadership of the secretary-general?"

In private Mugabe becomes less a headmaster and more a real interlocutor. "We did not want confrontation, neither with the U.K. nor with other Western powers," he says. "If you in the UN or other international actors can help provide dialogue among equals, we want to make progress." In the next few minutes we agree to set up a task force of the government, UN agencies, and selected donors to look at the reasons for Zimbabwe's disastrous food production. We agree to facilitate access for humanitarian agencies, and to start a pilot program for 2,500 temporary shelter "units" for the evicted. It is not what I had hoped for, but it is a step toward a working climate that can only improve.

I have a final issue to raise: "As you know there has been a lot of interest in my mission. I have avoided speaking to international media while here in Zimbabwe. Tomorrow in Johannesburg I will, however, have to report on what I have seen to a press conference. You may subsequently find the coverage tough, but I hope the improved dialogue to seek policy change can continue?"

"As long as you speak the truth and do not undertake the errands of others it is all right," Mugabe says. We have been talking for thirty minutes. He rises to shake my hand.

My journey to Bulawayo in a tiny single-engine plane is a nightmare as we fly through intense turbulence, falling through deep air pockets in driving rain. I arrive exhausted to a scene of misery as bad as anything I saw in Harare and accompanied by an atmosphere of suffocating political oppression. As I am meeting courageous priests and spokesmen for the homeless and poor in our hotel, my local UN contacts interrupt us with a message: "The authorities say that we must either allow them to sit in on the meeting or they will send the police to break it up."

We quickly agree that I will leave by the back door, and the clergymen will go out through the front door. In this way, I hope to avoid putting them at risk by appearing with me.

The media attention for our mission and the political fallout will soon be even greater than expected. The following day, we travel to South Africa and urge the South African deputy foreign minister to do more to encourage and enforce policy change in Zimbabwe.

Before I fly back to New York, the OCHA regional office sets up an international press conference at Johannesburg Airport. Forty journalists, including from all international news agencies and most large television networks, are in the room as I enter. As always, and as I promised Mugabe, I try to tell the simple truth, what I saw, heard, and smelled: the dramatic realities of Zimbabwe.

There is a freefall in life expectancy from more than 60 years in the early 1990s to between 30 and 40 today. The eviction campaign and the agricultural policies of the government have been "the worst possible things at the worst possible time" and have contributed to changing the country from being the breadbasket of the region, with admirable standards of living, to a place of widespread starvation—unless there is massive international assistance. I try to end my remarks on a note of optimism: "I believe the country has a real chance to turn the corner as there is more awareness nationally, regionally, and internationally, but we have to work together to change the situation."

I am then asked to characterize the social decline. I reply that the halving of life expectancy can only be described as a "meltdown." I repeat this word in a long interview with the BBC, which has set up a temporary studio next door. Harare has banned the BBC from reporting inside Zimbabwe and I know that Mugabe will not like what he hears on its television and radio broadcasts.

The president is indeed unhappy with the next day's banner headlines in the international and South African media: "UN envoy: Zimbabwe in meltdown." Two days later, in a stormy address to activists in his Zanu-PF party, Mugabe calls me "a liar and a hypocrite." "He came here to see our achievements, we receive him, and then he goes away telling lies about Zimbabwe to Western media. He did not even speak proper English," he says in a parting shot at my Norwegian accent. Several thousand party activists stand to cheer with raised clenched fists.

The public shouting match notwithstanding, my colleagues in Harare afterward report increased dialogue on policy change in the failed Zimbabwean agricultural sector, and improved access for humanitarian organizations, including to the victims of the eviction campaigns. The World Food Programme continues its very effective and well-funded food distribution and South Africa engages more actively in helping Zimbabwe improve its dialogue with international financial institutions. But hard-liners remain in control of most policies and neither the evictions from unauthorized housing nor the equally disastrous evictions of many farmers from their well-organized farms has stopped. Kofi Annan did not go to Zimbabwe.

"I see you called it a 'meltdown,'" the secretary-general says when I call him to report. "Yes, it was actually a term that a leading Zimbabwean diplomat had used to describe the situation in his country. I thought it was a good word, considering what has happened," I answer.

Since my visit to Zimbabwe, the deep social and economic crisis has continued to worsen, while Robert Mugabe's regime has solidified its grip. It is the only peacetime economy that has suffered a dramatic decline of some 30 percent in recent years. Inflation has grown from 100 percent in 2003 to several thousand percent in 2007. Perhaps as many as three million have fled the economic turmoil to seek work in South Africa, Europe, and elsewhere. When I visited a clinic for people with AIDS in Zimbabwe in December

2005, I was told there are more trained Zimbabwean nurses in Manchester, England, than in Harare.

The political opposition has for years been harassed, persecuted, and detained. But the political parties are also weak because of infighting that prevents the formation of any real alternative to the Zanu-PF and Mugabe. This former hero of the struggle against white minority rule has succeeded in maneuvering so that neither the African Union nor the Southern African Development Community (SADC) can or will challenge the terrible governance in Zimbabwe. In mid-2007, when its mismanagement was glaringly evident for all to see, the summit meeting of the SADC in neighboring Zambia concluded that Mugabe was doing his best to solve the problems of Zimbabwe. Since then the Zanu-PF "unanimously" selected the eighty-three-year-old Mugabe to be the only candidate for the upcoming presidential elections in 2008.

Zimbabwe is thus yet another case where those who could press for positive change, its African neighbors, look the other way. Conversely, those who once refused to support the struggle against apartheid, and still have little moral authority in this part of the world, the U.K. and the U.S., are spearheading the attacks against Mugabe. At the 2007 summit between the EU and Africa, U.K. prime minister Gordon Brown was alone in boycotting, while the African leaders felt compelled to "stand by" the symbol of Africa's inability to get rid of its worst rulers.

The international paralysis and the internal rivalries among opposition groups signal continued crisis and collapse in Zimbabwe. Mugabe is greeted with applause in many African countries because of his image of "standing up" to unpopular and rich Western powers and white estate owners. Only a united, effective, and democratic national opposition movement, supported by principled African neighbors in the SADC, and international organizations such as the AU and the UN, can foster real change. Only then can Zimbabwe regain its position as the jewel and breadbasket of Africa.

9.

Uganda's Twenty Thousand Kidnapped Children

"I AM CAPTAIN Sunday of the Lord's Resistance Army," says the man in the olive-green uniform leaning into our vehicle and flicking his eyes over the flak jackets, helmets, and water bottles covering the floor of our car. "No white faces can carry guns from here. We don't trust them—we only trust black faces."

I had never thought of Wellington boots as sinister but I do now when I meet Captain Sunday and his crew of guerrilla fighters. We had caught sight of him as our car rounded a corner on the narrow track we were following through the Sudanese jungle. He was standing by a tree lying across our path. He looks about twenty-five, with a Kalashnikov slung across his chest and a cascade of dreadlocks scraping the collar of his uniform. The rubber boots on his feet would have lent his guerrilla-issue outfit a somewhat comical air had it not been for a group of heavily armed teenagers lounging nearby. The only piece of attire most of them have in common are Wellington boots, worn to protect against water, snakes, and bugs by members of one of the most sinister and ruthless guerrilla forces in Africa.

Marcus Culley, a New Zealander in charge of UN security in southern Sudan who is traveling ahead of us with five colleagues and was stopped seconds earlier, walks back to our car looking grim.

"I'm sorry but I think you should hand over your guns," he tells my Romanian bodyguards. "It is not worth spoiling the whole mission over three guns." We only have a few more hours before we have to return to the UN helicopters to reach our base in Juba, Sudan, by sunset. Automatically I check my watch and look for the tropical sun, which has already passed its zenith as it filters through the jungle trees. It is just past 1 P.M. on Saturday, November 12, 2006, and we are on the first UN mission to meet the Lord's Resistance Army (LRA) and its leader, Joseph Kony.

"Do you agree with this?" asks the bodyguard sitting next to me incredulously. I feel sorry for him. He and his colleagues have flown from Khartoum to protect our mission and have been watching over me for the last forty-eight hours. They sit outside my tent at night, and during the day guard the door of the container that doubles as our meeting room in Juba, where we planned this controversial meeting with the LRA and its leaders.

Now, when there is a real and very visible security risk, they are ordered to hand over their guns. I just nod and ask them to be quick. Too much is at stake.

The LRA has kidnapped more than twenty thousand children from northern Uganda and southern Sudan in two decades of fighting. The kidnapped children have been brutalized, tortured, and raped while being forced to join this self-styled army and attack their own villages and families in a forgotten war. Some of the abducted boys and girls are probably among the underage, impassive guerrilla fighters who surround us here at the Sudan-Congo border. Nearly two million men, women, and children, the majority of the proud Acholi people, have been driven from their ancestral lands in northern Uganda to live in the miserable overcrowded camps that I know only too well from previous visits.

I have taken a huge risk on behalf of the UN in grabbing a rare opportunity to speak directly to the reclusive Kony. I am hoping that it may help prolong the most promising cease-fire in the course of twenty years of strife and untold suffering. We should be willing to take big risks for that.

"I feel naked," says my bodyguard anxiously. "How do we defend you now if there is a fight? By running behind you as you try to flee?" After a late start from Juba, on a journey of nearly two hours by helicopter and then twenty minutes by car through jungle and head-high grass to this roadblock, we have lost a lot of time. UN security rules state that we must be back in Juba before nightfall. We have no more time to argue. One of our Toyota Land Cruisers is driven back to the three waiting Russian-made Mi-18 helicopters along with the handguns, bulletproof vests, and helmets that Captain Sunday is refusing to allow the "white faces" to keep. I feel as vulnerable and suspect as an African at a European border control. It makes no sense that they should be threatened by our standard UN protection gear, but the LRA leadership is among the world's most paranoid. The International Criminal Court (ICC) issued warrants in 2005 for the arrest of five commanders, including Kony and his deputy Vincent Otti, with whom I have been negotiating. The charges are war crimes and crimes against humanity. The LRA leaders fear we might try to arrest them on behalf of the court.

During my last visit to northern Uganda, seven months earlier, the situation had improved to the extent that even the overprotective UN security officials let me stay overnight in a camp; I slept in one of the small mud huts that the displaced have shared for half a generation. I had been deeply moved by the experience of talking with families about their hopes for peace, security, and a better future when they could return to rebuild their homes, their farms, and their herds. We swapped stories and talked about their dreams over a *wang-ho,* a traditional Acholi bonfire, late into the night. At one point an old lady began to weep quietly. "It is fifteen years since I could happily enjoy a *wang-ho,"* she said. "I was then a young mother. Now I have nothing. My children have been stolen by the rebels. The government has done nothing for me. Happy memories of bonfires with my murdered husband and my missing children are coming back."

I remember the poignancy of that night as I watch the LRA fighters who have caused such misery, and who may well include some of those same kidnapped children, lifting the tree blocking our path. They wave us on and we plunge down the barely visible track which has narrowed to a point where we are driving through tall grass while jungle foliage smashes against our windows. At one point the track turns into a deep pool of mud, water, and rotting leaves, which causes our driver to stop. Gripping the steering wheel and muttering to himself, he guns the engine and plunges in at full speed. Just as the bow wave threatens to drown the engine we start to climb out of what has become a swamp to emerge into a clearing. According to the Cessation of Hostilities agreement, this is the assembly point for LRA fighters scattered throughout western Sudan and Congo.

I am in a place as remote from my office in Manhattan or my home in Oslo as it is possible to imagine. Ri-Kwamba is an abandoned, destroyed village on the border between southwestern Sudan and northeastern Congo. Our party, including Vice President Riek Machar of the new South Sudan government and twenty of his armed guards, have flown in three helicopters from an airstrip in Juba, the main town in South Sudan. The Sudan People's Liberation Army (SPLA), protecting Machar and his entourage, have been allowed to keep their weapons after an extended yelling match between their commander and Captain Sunday. The SPLA, having "more trustworthy" black soldiers with a long history of guerrilla warfare, are in a somewhat more persuasive position than our UN bodyguards. Our convoy of ten Land Cruisers also includes a team of mediators, UN colleagues, Ugandan government officials, LRA negotiators, and a dozen foreign journalists. The journey from Juba to the remote village of Ri-Kwamba—and, we hope, back on the same day—is a massive logistics operation involving the movement

of sixty people through some of the most inaccessible and dangerous territory in Africa.

My journey to this place had started more than three years earlier when, in September 2003, as the new undersecretary-general
for humanitarian affairs, I asked a group of the most experienced
OCHA field officers in our Geneva headquarters to identify "the
most forgotten and neglected humanitarian crisis in the world."
Most of the twenty-member group had more than ten years of experience in humanitarian fieldwork. It was a question they had not
expected. After an extended pause, Ayo Fowler, an African colleague,
raised his hand: "I think it must be the war of northern Uganda," he
ventured. "Nowhere else are so many people terrorized, brutalized,
and displaced with so little attention, so little assistance, and so little
protection. Nobody seems to care that a whole generation of children is perishing . . ." I decided then and there to go to Uganda on
my first field mission as emergency relief coordinator.

It took two months before I reached northern Uganda, since the
UN's attention was diverted to Iraq following the bombing of our
offices in Baghdad. When I finally arrived in Kampala it was early
November. Our very experienced OCHA head of field office,
Eliane Duhoit, wisely suggested that I ask the heads of all UN agencies in Uganda to accompany me to the war-torn north, an area
with which some of them were strangely unfamiliar.

What I saw around the towns of Kitgum and Gulu was an outrage. Hundreds of thousands of men, women, and children lived in
appalling conditions in overcrowded, filthy camps. With the exception of the UN World Food Programme and a handful of courageous Ugandan and international nongovernmental organizations,
humanitarian workers were absent in the midst of the misery. The
contrast with the empty refugee camps and well-stocked warehouses that I had just visited in Iraq and on its borders was stark.
Why had no one in the international community woken up to the
carnage of northern Uganda? Where had I been while in charge of

the Norwegian Red Cross and during many years of humanitarian, human rights, and peace work? It was incomprehensible. The capital, Kampala, was bursting with UN and other aid officials since Uganda was one of the darlings of Western governments and development agencies. Few, it appeared, had looked far beyond the horizon at the outrage being visited on the children of the north.

The scene in Kitgum, the heart of the area experiencing the worst LRA terror and Ugandan government neglect was one of the most profoundly disturbing I have experienced in all my years of humanitarian work. Daylight was fading as we arrived at the village school that doubled as a health post. As the sun set over the hills the first of more than a thousand children, some as young as two or three, accompanied by their mothers, began to shuffle into the grounds to spend the night lying huddled together in rooms and corridors and on the pavement outside. They were just a small proportion of the estimated forty thousand children, so-called "night commuters," who gather every evening at several impromptu "safe" meeting points in local towns and villages. They hope to avoid being kidnapped by LRA press gangs that for nearly two decades have been pillaging and raping their way through the countryside for provisions and "recruits." As dawn breaks the children begin their journeys back to their scattered huts and shelters, only to return that same evening.

All the children told similar stories of living in continuous fear of attacks on their settlements while being utterly neglected by the Ugandan government and the international community. Some blankets are passed around by NGOs and church groups but there is no food, no medicine, no counseling, no registration, and no journalists—only sadness and lost childhoods. My African colleague was right when he said this was perhaps our "number one forgotten failure."

The next morning I asked my UN colleagues to meet me on the veranda of our guest house. I was angry and still reeling from the desperately sad scenes of the day before. Some of those I was addressing had worked in Uganda for months, even years, but had never bothered to make the daylong journey north. "I hope you all agree we cannot continue like this," I told a group of nodding heads. "We have failed utterly here. You and your organizations have to step up action dramatically and I will do all I can to wake up donors and headquarters." They were rightly embarrassed.

Now, three years later, as I come to the last few weeks of my time as undersecretary for humanitarian affairs at the UN, I return to the issue that became my first priority. "Welcome!" says Vincent Otti, Kony's deputy, striding toward us. A tall, elderly man in camouflage uniform with elaborate Soviet-made red epaulettes, he has taken the title of lieutenant general. He is waiting to greet us at the assembly point in Ri-Kwamba together with a dozen silent LRA officials. A huge UNICEF canvas tent that is to be our "meeting room" stands in the middle of a large open grass field. An advance UN team has prepared the site in recent days. Otti presents the rest of the LRA "high command" as we sit down on red plastic chairs in the tent, its side flaps rolled up to allow some air.

My group consists of Vice President Riek Machar; Martin Mogwanja and David Gressly, the UN's humanitarian coordinators in Uganda and South Sudan; and Hansjoerg Strohmeyer, my chief of staff from New York. It is an unprecedented meeting. No ranking UN official has ever met the LRA leadership in the twenty years they have been in hiding.

Machar is at ease. He chats and jokes with some of the LRA commanders whom he has met several times before. His old contacts from the shifting alliances of the southern Sudan liberation struggle helped him set up historic peace talks that began in July 2006 and led to the current cease-fire. I neither smile nor chat. The night before and that morning I had a yelling match with Otti on the satellite phone during which I threatened to cancel today's meeting. Otti had reneged on a verbal agreement that our meeting would conclude with the announcement that the sick and wounded in LRA hands would be handed over for care in our hospitals, that LRA children would be identified so they could attend schools organized by the UN, and that women and other noncombatants would be separated and receive special assistance when they arrived at assembly points under the cease-fire. My team and the LRA negotiations team had even agreed on a draft text in Juba the previous afternoon. But Otti had backtracked when the final text was read to him at 9 P.M. that night. "You have no credibility with anyone now. Do something good for once and we might start trusting your word!" I shouted at him on the phone this morning. "You just demand and press us—we get nothing!" Otti screamed back before the satellite link was cut.

"Where is Kony?" I ask Otti as we settle down to talk. "We have little time." "The chairman has empowered me to do the negotiations on behalf of the LRA," Otti says, so quietly that I can hardly hear him. "What?" I exclaim. "I travel across the world from New York to this place to meet Kony after your people tell the BBC that he wants to see me. And now you tell me he stays away!" It is an intensely uncomfortable moment. I have talked on the phone numerous times with Otti. I can call him by satellite at any time. How do I convince them that Kony has to be present without wasting more time quarreling? It appears that he is somewhere close by in the jungle, within an hour's walking distance. One of the LRA's greatest strengths in avoiding capture or defeat has been their insistence on never using vehicles. Vehicles can be tracked.

After a quick exchange with Machar, I tell Otti, "We will not start without Kony. Tell him the next chance for such a meeting may be in twenty years. In two hours we will have to leave."

"But he is far away. It is not safe for him here," answers Otti. "You should not have your guns in this place," he says to the South Sudanese vice president. It is obvious they are still deeply concerned that we might try to catch Kony and bring him to the ICC.

"How can you still fear us after being my guest here in South Sudan for months," exclaims Machar. "You know my soldiers by now. But, if it makes you happy let us remove our men, both of us, one hundred paces from the tent. OK? And now, tell Kony to start walking."

Otti responds by getting up and walking off. He is not amused. He had probably tried to get Kony to come this morning and had given up in the face of his leader's intense paranoia. Now he has also failed to convince us that he would be an acceptable counterpart. He goes to a hut some hundred yards away and begins to call Kony on his satellite phone.

I feel uncomfortable in my plastic chair chatting with Machar, who tries to convince me that I can "relax" and that Kony will come. But my UN team reminds me the clock is ticking. We have only two more hours before we have to leave to reach the helicopters at 4:30 and Juba before sunset.

By the time Otti returns, the SPLA fighters have withdrawn, but he has done nothing about ordering the withdrawal of his own heavily armed LRA teenagers who surround the tent. "The chairman is on his way. But he is far away and does not know whether he will make it in time. He asks us to start the talks."

I am inclined to accept. We will at least have half of the LRA high command present as I try to convince them of the necessity to respect the cessation of hostilities; demand the release of women and children; and warn that we are watching them for any signs of a return to abuse of the civilian population. But Machar puts his hand on my shoulder. "Tell the chairman to hurry up because we are not starting without him." Otti gets up again to walk to the hut as Machar whispers that he is convinced Kony will not appear if we start with the others. "Trust me," he says, sitting back in his chair with a smile.

Another hour passes. My chief of staff, Strohmeyer, and some journalists who have been allowed to record the event try unsuccessfully to engage Captain Sunday and his armed boys and girls in conversation. With only half an hour to go before we have to leave I decide to ignore Machar's advice and agree to start the meeting on "humanitarian matters" with Otti and his commanders. At least we can hope that they will pass on my message to the rest of the leadership.

Just as I have finished listing our concerns and demands, we see Kony approaching in his Wellingtons at the head of a group of some twenty-five soldiers. At exactly 3:56, he hesitantly extends his arm for a handshake. The journalists plunge forward to record the meeting. I do not smile. Many of the LRA victims will see the photo and I am fearful of sending out the wrong signals. My first impression is of a more reserved, quiet, indecisive, and boyish-looking man than I had expected. "Can you leave us now?" I shout to reporters, soldiers, and bystanders, and look at my watch, hoping our security officers will give us some space. We have already passed the "absolute time limit for returning."

"Thank you for coming," says Kony.

"We have been waiting. There are a number of things to discuss and time is short," I answer.

Kony asks to speak in Acholi and one of the educated LRA negotiators from Juba comes forward to translate. I expect him immediately to bring up the ICC, but his ten-minute speech is devoted to describing how the LRA feels chased by the Ugandan army, how disappointed they are that the other side still attacks them, that there is no security for them in southern Sudan, where they are supposed to assemble under the cease-fire agreement, and that their own respect for the cease-fire is not being reciprocated. "We are seriously engaged in trying to end the war and find a just and peaceful settlement. But even the day before yesterday some of our people were attacked by the Ugandan army," he concludes.

I am relieved by what I hear. These are security issues that can be dealt with in the talks. Some of his charges may actually be true. The Ugandan Army is indeed in southern Sudan. The difficult and time-consuming issues of constitutional reform, a referendum, and a federal structure for northern Uganda that had been brought to the negotiations table in Juba by the LRA have thankfully not been raised. Kony has not even raised the ICC indictments.

When he is finished I take the opportunity to address him without interruption for ten minutes in English, which he understands. He listens and, as I always do in these kinds of meetings with men of power on questions of life and death, I try to keep continuous eye contact. I need to be sure that our message sinks in. My sole purpose is to get him to understand how much is at stake.

"If you continue to respect the cessation of hostilities and assemble your forces as prescribed, we will help ensure that you will get food and other supplies at all assembly points. We will continue to work to make the talks more effective and will get international support for a peaceful settlement of the conflict and reintegration of the LRA fighters in northern Uganda. We will also monitor the cessation of hostilities. But if the cease-fire collapses and you return to your old ways of attacking the population, there will be a war that will be worse than ever. That will be terrible for all, including you in the LRA!" I warn.

I end with an appeal for our right to care for children and women as they assemble and demand the immediate release of those recently abducted in northern Uganda and southern Sudan. I decide not to hand over a list of about twenty boys and girls we know have been kidnapped by the LRA from neighboring South Sudanese communities following village-to-village investigations by UN officials. I have been warned by one of our team that the list may backfire and threaten the lives of the abducted. If the LRA continues to deny attacks on civilians they could simply kill anyone whose name appears on the list. I do, however, end with a direct question to Kony that I have planned in advance: "What do I tell the weeping mothers in northern Uganda and southern Sudan who have asked me to bring back their beloved children?"

Unfortunately, Otti interjects before Kony can answer. He repeats what he has already told me twice on the satellite phone in recent days: "We have no women or children here in Ri-Kwamba, only our wives, our own children, and combatants. But I will speak to Commander Cesar Achello on the Sudanese-Ugandan border as he assembles later in the month. If he has weak children or wounded people with him, we will hand them over to you." I look at Kony, who only nods.

I then offer to send Ugandan UN teams to the bush to present our demobilization, disarmament, and reintegration package as the LRA soldiers assemble. The whole purpose of our new efforts to bring supplies, people, and mediators to the assembly points is to get the leadership in the field to engage and make decisions on how to end the senseless conflict. While Kony agrees to future contact, voices are hissing in my ear: "We really, really have to leave."

As I gather my papers Otti suddenly raises the one issue that has been a sticking point in all discussions with the LRA and over which I have no say. "The ICC indictment will not make it possible for us to give up our arms. What can you do to stop them?" Kony stares at me as I tell him that the ICC is a totally independent body. "I cannot influence them. But you can influence how the world regards you. Make peace, stop all attacks, release the abducted, and influence your case positively. Then we will see how justice can be served." I rise and approach Kony and Otti while holding up a sheet of graph paper on which every single attack, kidnapping, and armed clash they have been responsible for in recent years is recorded. I want them to feel that they are being watched continuously, that we will know if they return to terror and that we will hold them accountable in the future. At this point the journalists burst through the

LRA security cordon screaming questions about what has been discussed.

"The peace process in Juba," answers Kony in cautious English. "Did you agree to release women and children?" asks a BBC reporter. "There are no women and children in the LRA, only combatants," replies Kony in the monotone of a pilot trying to reassure passengers that nothing is amiss as they plummet through turbulence. It is the last message I hear before we scramble for the cars. "Get everybody to mount," I yell, jumping into a vehicle. As we drive off I see journalists running for the cars while Machar takes an additional minute with the LRA leadership.

When we reach the helicopters, an hour and a half late, the Russian UN pilots are clearly impatient. The journalists want a statement before leaving the area. "I think it was an important meeting," I say. "For the first time ever we could impress on the LRA leadership that they must keep to the cessation of hostilities and never again start abusing civilians. There is only a negotiated end to this long and brutal war. We made progress in being able to do this today by building trust through face-to-face meetings with the leadership, an essential step in any negotiation process."

As we fly back to Juba the sun is setting and we are again struck by the immense size and beauty of Africa. I reflect on the events of the past three days as I gaze out the helicopter's window. It has been worthwhile, of that I am convinced. The BBC will predictably portray the lack of agreement on release of some of the kidnapped as a setback and here I acknowledge that I should have presented the meeting differently to the media. Instead of saying that I would only meet Kony if it led to the release of the kidnapped women and children, the precondition of our meeting should have been to discuss their condition and their release. The LRA leadership is not a rational negotiating group and, living as outlaws for the last twenty years, it does not react well to unenforceable deadlines. However, by saying that I would only meet with Kony if they released some of the abducted I had managed to get their attention away from something I could not and would not give: support in lifting the ICC indictments. At the same time we focused the minds of the leadership on the fact that they are being watched and pursued as long as they keep the many kidnapped.

To have the abducted released had been an obsession of mine ever since I met some of the kidnapped children who had escaped. In November 2003, I visited the World Vision center for former LRA child soldiers in Gulu, northern Uganda. A sixteen-year-old girl, her eyes cast to the floor, had told me in a quiet, unemotional voice how she was abducted one night from her family's hut and brutally driven into the bush. "We were several children from ten to fourteen years. One girl could not keep pace. At gunpoint a boy and I were ordered to club her to death. A month later another girl, a small one, tried to flee. This time all of us were forced by our commanders to kill her by biting her to death. It took a long time . . ." As she finished talking she raised her head to gaze at me with blank, sad old eyes. I felt as though I was going to be sick. How does one respond to such pure evil, to such terror?

One of the other girls at the center, who had been given to one of the commanders as an additional "wife," gave birth that morning. The care center leader asked me the first name of my wife. "Anne Kristin," I said. "According to our tradition we always name a newborn after a prominent visitor. We will call her Anna Christina. The mother will be very happy."

As we land in Juba I wonder how Yoweri Museveni, the Ugandan president, will react to the LRA meeting. Before I left New York for Africa, the Ugandan ambassador to the UN had come to my office to protest about the proposed meeting with the "criminal" Joseph Kony. I managed to speak to the president by phone the same day and got him to take a neutral stance on my mission. I would only know whether Museveni was going to attack me again when I arrived in Kampala in two days. In 2004 Museveni sneer-ingly called me "Mr. England" in an Independence Day speech to the diplomatic community, accusing me of distorting the situation in Uganda to the world's media.

However, I get the president's views sooner than expected. After landing at Uganda's Entebbe airport we are whisked through the VIP lounge to waiting UN cars. With blue lights flashing and sirens blaring, two police cars lead us at breakneck speed into Kampala, defying all traffic laws, frequently using the wrong side of the road. We reached Kampala in thirty-five minutes instead of the usual two hours or more.

For the first time that my UN colleagues can remember, we do not have to wait for hours in hotels and waiting rooms before being received by Museveni, but rather are taken straight through a back door in the Parliament Building. The president has clearly been waiting for us as he sits at the end of a long table, his key advisers to his left. He grimly takes my hand and I sit down at his right, facing the foreign minister; chief government negotiator, Minister Ru-hakana Rugunda; and several other senior ministers.

Skipping the courtesies, the president begins on an ominous note: "You were just wasting your time in the bush with them. I told you so."

"No, I think it was useful to meet them. It was good for peace and therefore to your benefit," I reply.

"No, those talks were not to our benefit. Let me be categori-cal—there will only be a military solution to this problem."

"But we have, for the first time, an absence of fighting and terror due to the peace process!"

"No, that is only due to the efforts of our army!"

I draw a breath and look at the president. The ministers watch nervously, but Museveni appears to be enjoying the disagreement. I know him from several similar exchanges. He is one of the most significant elder statesmen in Africa, a warrior who ended the horrors of the Idi Amin regime, which were followed by a long and cruel civil war. Once we had sat for three hours talking under a tree at his large cattle farm. Another time he insisted that I take his helicopter to see the skulls of the tens of thousands among his own people who died in the 1970s to "get perspective" on my criticism of the government's policies in northern Uganda. He is an impressive leader, but he has become increasingly authoritarian and has so far failed in northern Uganda, where the Acholi people feel alienated and where neither civilian nor military authorities have managed to avoid some twenty years of horrors. The LRA has not been the only bloody rebellion in the north.

I explain at some length why the international community now supports the Juba-based peace process: why six nations now give funding to the South Sudanese–mediated talks through OCHA; and why the UN Security Council, after my many briefings, has for the first time come up with a presidential statement of support for the talks. Six months of negotiations have done more to provide peace and quiet than half a generation of military offensives.

"I don't mind peace talks as long as pressure is maintained. But the talks cannot go on forever as a business for the negotiators," says Museveni. The meeting continues for another two hours and more common ground is established between us. We agree that the talks must produce tangible agreements that can lead to disarmament, demobilization, and reintegration of the LRA and that a true process of reconciliation and rebuilding must follow the peace process. Museveni, who had asked the ICC to indict the LRA leaders, was of the opinion that he could stop the international judicial process if a good agreement to end the war was reached. I try to tell him, as the chief ICC prosecutor had asked me to stress, that the decision was no longer in the hands of the Ugandans. The court would itself have to assess what would serve the cause of both peace and justice.

Museveni seems pleased with the tough and direct exchange. He clearly enjoys the verbal jousting. Within his own government nobody dares to argue with him. Not once in three hours do any of his ministers interrupt. The president even agrees to withdraw the Ugandan army from two bases close to the eastern assembly point; the army is currently blocking access for LRA fighters who should gather there according to the cease-fire agreement. During the last two hours of our meeting he is only angry once, when I bring up our growing concern with widespread violence in the eastern Karamoja area, where civilians are being killed in battles between cattle rustlers, tribal militias, and army units. "Do not lecture me on how to disarm illegal armed groups and cattle rustlers. On that I am an expert," he says forcefully.

The next day I hold a press conference with the archbishop of Gulu and the Catholic relief organization Caritas, attended by the Ugandan media and international stringers based in Kampala. We want to give positive recognition to the Catholic and Anglican churches, which have shown immense courage in defending the rights of the people of northern Uganda. Only Caritas had the guts to help when I asked the UN and nongovernmental organizations to provide food, water, and sanitation to encourage the LRA to congregate at the two assembly points in southern Sudan.

The press conference goes well. "I leave Uganda after my final mission as UN emergency relief coordinator more optimistic than at any previous point. I think we see the beginning of the end to the abject suffering of the children of northern Uganda." The archbishop of Gulu agrees: "Thank you for bringing the suffering of northern Uganda to the attention, for the first time, of the international community. As you return to your family in Norway we, the people of the north, want to thank you and the United Nations for speaking up when we needed it the most." It is the best thing anyone could have said to me.

More than at any other place, I feel that what my colleagues in OCHA and I have done for northern Uganda has had an impact. The peace talks will almost certainly go through crises and breakdowns, but the people of the north have already voted with their feet. The "night commuters" have all but stopped and hundreds of thousands of displaced have returned or are planning to return and rebuild their ancestral land.

I am deeply moved when, later in the week, I am asked to support preschool for little Anna Christina, the child born to the LRA girl during my 2003 visit and named after my wife. Nothing could better symbolize the renewed hopes for northern Uganda.

10.

The Generation That Can
End the Suffering

WHETHER THE one billion poorest and most oppressed on our watch get any help at all is still an immoral lottery. We are only on the first leg of a long marathon toward coherent and predictable multilateral action for all vulnerable communities. The besieged minorities in Ivory Coast I described in the first chapter are neither a strategic concern nor a public opinion priority in most of the leading capitals. Its population is not only African, but French speaking, and can easily lose out in the dominating English-language Western media, and in Washington, London, and the Scandinavian capitals that are best able to place humanitarian priorities on the international agenda. After conveying to the Security Council in early 2006 the desperate appeal for help from the displaced and persecuted in Guiglo, the short-term outcome of the deliberations among the powers is blankets and Band-Aids rather than justice and protection.

It took weeks of local desperation before the agencies, the UN peacekeepers, and African Union and UN reconciliation efforts were able to reestablish themselves in western Ivory Coast. But the world is, in spite of all the setbacks, moving slowly in the right direction for most of us. Even in a place like Guiglo there were in the end enough national, regional, and international efforts to improve security and living conditions for the displaced and the minorities.

In March 2007 a peace agreement was brokered by neighboring Burkina Faso and tension decreased as the two sides in the north and the south agreed on a joint army and a unity government. Within the western parts of Ivory Coast, international relief groups and peacekeepers facilitated the return, in safety and dignity, of the displaced Burkinabe people I had met in the camp to their old farmland or to new land that they can call their own.

The men, women, and children of Guiglo are on the front lines of our collective humanity in the new millennium. The slow and unpredictable progress for international compassion and solidarity in this little-known corner of multilateral work represents all that is now at stake. It had long been evident that French assistance or military force was too controversial to allow the former colony to escape the vicious cycle of discrimination, strife, and violence. It was as doomed as U.S. unilateralism is in Iraq. Only internal efforts combined with united pressure and assistance from West African neighbors, the United Nations, and the African Union has helped, and will help.

There was no lack of early warnings from the United Nations about the growing conflict in Darfur, but most member states were not interested. There were early cease-fire agreements facilitated by neighboring Chad and UN envoys, but the international community did not care to enforce them. For years important Asian and Arab nations were more interested in protecting the brutal regime in Khartoum than defending the defenseless women and children in the bloodstained western desert. We humanitarian workers were, as in Bosnia in the 1990s, asked to feed and shelter millions while armed men around the 140 camps planned their next massacres with impunity. It is as if Srebrenica and Rwanda are ancient history.

In the buildup to the invasion of Iraq in 2002–2003, there were countless warnings from those working in and on Iraq against the irresponsible inability of Security Council members to agree on how to deal with Saddam. There were equally clear warnings that the use of force by the U.S.- and U.K.-led coalition could have disastrous results. Those politicians who chose to rely on speculative, unsubstantiated, and false intelligence rather than the warnings of UN staff on the ground, or of Secretary-General Annan, can now hardly sleep well at night. In the highly respected British medical journal *The Lancet*, American and Iraqi medical experts have documented that an estimated 650,000 Iraqis died in the forty months that followed the invasion. In no other place on earth have so many been killed by blunt violence during the last five years. Millions died in the Congo and in the Sudan from preventable disease and malnutrition, but Iraq is, like no other place, the contemporary home of murder and massacres.

Nearly a decade without coherent international efforts to solve the Israeli-Palestinian conflict, or to end Israeli occupation and border closures of Gaza and the West Bank, caused what I called a "ticking time bomb" when I visited Gaza in 2006. Less than a year later Gaza exploded in the worst internal strife ever, and we got what our inaction called for: more fertile grounds for new extremism. When you lock 1.5 million people in a cage smaller than an average Norwegian municipality, and deprive hundreds of thousands of angry youth of hope, you do not get Boy Scouts or choir girls; you get long lines of new terrorists.

There would not have been a relentless increase in natural disasters and extreme weather if this global generation had managed to curb greenhouse gas emissions after we first agreed to do so at the 1992 global summit in Rio de Janeiro. The slide into climate change would have been slowed down. The first scientific prediction of man-made climate change was published as early as 1896 in the article "On the Influence of Carbonic Acid in the Air Upon the Temperature of the Ground," by the Swedish chemist Svante Arrhenius. Decades ago the world's leading scientists agreed through the United

Nations climate panels that policy and behavioral change were urgently needed. Even the "kindest" of the climate panel predictions indicates permanent flooding of entire island states, provinces, and large coastal cities, because the ice on the two poles will be melting. If Europeans, North Americans, Chinese, and others had started the process of real change in the 1980s and 1990s, we would have had positive results earlier and at lower cost.

Even now, seven times more livelihoods are devastated by natural disasters than by war. Humanitarian field-workers cannot believe their ears when politicians and industrialists argue that our explosive global economic growth has not changed the climate. For many years we have seen increasing numbers of vulnerable people have their lives devastated by extreme droughts, hurricanes, and floods. The scale of human lives lost and devastated are, as always, much greater in poor developing countries than in the affluent North. But even in Europe, the extreme heat wave of 2003 took more than thirty thousand lives. The World Health Organization has estimated that we annually suffer 150,000 climate-change-related deaths. This number will be doubled by 2020. The spread of epidemic disease, of hunger due to failed crops, and of polluted and inadequate drinking water will also be linked to warming levels. Those who still believe this is all part of periodic changes in weather patterns should climb Africa's tallest mountain, Kilimanjaro. The snow and ice that have covered the peaks for twelve thousand years will have melted by 2020.

In spite of these brutal challenges, I believe there is reason for optimism. The coming years can and will see a revival of multilateral action, because the largest disasters, wars, and crises cannot be handled by any nation on its own. In this regard no nation is exempted. I saw graphic evidence of this in 2005, which started with the tsunami, brought Hurricane Katrina in August, and ended with the devastating earthquake in Pakistan in October. Pakistan had nearly three million people homeless after the quake and immediately requested and received, as did tsunami-stricken nations, effective international relief. The partnership between Pakistani civilian and military relief efforts and our international assistance provided shelter, food, health care, and basic education to the hundreds of thousands of needy in time. Surveys showed no marked increase in disease or malnutrition. More girls went to primary school than in any previous year. This remarkable achievement could not have happened if the Pakistanis and the UN had not entered into an immediate operational partnership.

As emergency relief coordinator, I offered to "lend the support of the United Nations to the United States' relief effort in any way possible" when the full extent of the Hurricane Katrina disaster in New Orleans became evident on August 31. The letter was delivered to Ambassador John Bolton in the U.S. mission to the UN. It took five days before we were asked to send the first team of experienced disaster relief managers to work with U.S. institutions in Washington and at the Gulf Coast. The United Nations and other international humanitarian institutions have experts who handle the consequences of such enormous catastrophes every year. But as we saw in Louisiana, for an individual nation these are often "once in a generation" events that can overwhelm the administrative capacity of even the world's number one country in logistics, materials, and military hardware.

I believe in a renaissance for the United Nations and multilateral cooperation because this decade has proved the costly futility of unilateral force. Since 2003 the United States has spent the incomprehensible sum of more than $500 billion on its continued war and unsuccessful nation-building project in Iraq. That is five times more than the combined bill of all United Nations humanitarian, developmental, environmental, peacekeeping, peacemaking, and democracy-building efforts in more than a hundred countries during the same years.

Clearly the age of investment in joint, collective, and coherent action through the United Nations has come for its rich and powerful member states. As we move from a unipolar world of U.S. dominance to a multipolar world where China and India are also superpowers, it will be as important to recognize the political importance of Beijing and New Delhi as to demand they assume their part of political and economic burden sharing. Just as the United States cannot shrink from its obligation to push for a peaceful settlement of the Israeli-Palestinian conflict, China cannot pretend to be a developing nation when it is the dominant investor in Africa and, as such, must play a leading role in forcing an end to the carnage in Darfur. In the new world the Security Council and the Group of Eight nations should reflect economic and political realities and not the world as it was in its Eurocentric and Western-dominated past.

Just as Iraq is a symbol of unilateral impotence, the momentous positive change in the worst war zone of our generation, the Democratic Republic of the Congo, is a symbol of multilateral potency. During six terrible years of war, from 1998 to 2004, nearly four million Congolese died of malnutrition, preventable disease, and violence, according to surveys done by the International Rescue Committee. That is a loss of human life as great as the population of Norway, or five Rwandan genocides, or nearly twenty times the human toll in Bosnia in the 1990s.

When I visited the Congo in 2003, a dozen or more armies were fighting in eastern Congo. Armed groups and militias consisted of hundreds of thousands of ruthless, undisciplined men from neighboring states, from the main ethnic groups, and from organized crime fueled by the illegal exploitation of Congo's vast natural resources. Among them there were some thirty thousand child soldiers. In the crossfire was the defenseless civilian population. We went by helicopter and jeep to see how peacekeepers and humanitarian workers negotiated or enforced the access for relief and reconciliation efforts. Seeing the drunk, drugged, and heavily armed militias, and meeting some of tens of thousands of sexually abused and mutilated women and children, I felt, like most, that the Congo was the closest one could get to a hopeless case of chaos and societal collapse.

When I came back in the autumn of 2006, massive change was taking place. More than 2 million of the 3.5 million displaced had returned home. A series of militias had been disarmed. In conflict-prone Katanga, Ituri, and North and South Kivu we met many who were impatiently waiting for the small sums of money and support that are given by the World Bank and the UN for the demobilization and reintegration of men who had specialized in living by the gun, and who now told us they wanted to join in a peaceful society as working men. My humanitarian colleagues had access for the first time to nearly all major communities. The mortality rate, more than one thousand deaths each day in 1998–2004, was finally coming down in 2006–2007.

How did things turn around in the Congo? After years of inde-cisiveness, neglect, and penny-pinching lack of investment in United Nations operations, there was finally in 2004 a concerted effort by a united Security Council to provide a more robust peacekeeping force; there was a generous and long-term push by the European Union to fund the enormous UN-led electoral process; and there was more money for our efforts to provide coordinated relief in all parts of the country. On the front lines of this increasingly effective operation were the good efforts of dozens of Congolese and inter-national nongovernmental organizations, all the UN humanitarian agencies, and a peacekeeping force that received its soldiers primar-ily from the Asian and African nations that today bear the brunt of global UN peacekeeping. These soldiers have, with little publicity, courageously helped pacify and secure increasing parts of these enormous territories.

•   •   •

In the coming generation much greater global progress can be achieved. It is beyond doubt that we can end the massive, collective suffering of entire populations that we have seen throughout human history. Even with the less than generous investment of previous generations in peacemaking and peacekeeping, there has in recent years been momentous progress. The Human Security Reports document that there are 50 percent fewer wars in 2007 than when the Berlin Wall fell in 1989. While there were ten unfolding genocides in 1989, there was one in 2006. World Bank economists could in 2007 for the first time record that there are under one billion people who live on less than the index-linked one dollar a day even in a growing world population of 6.7 billion. Those of us in the exploding global middle and upper classes have fewer absolute poor to lift out of abject misery and fewer wars and genocides to end. And we have at the same time infinitely greater resources at hand.

We have superior technology and information. When in the spring of 2004 the regime in Khartoum blocked our access to the civilians in Darfur for months, our experts could plan the future relief operations with the help of advanced satellite imagery that identified where the displaced and refugees in Darfur and Chad had fled, and how many they were. We could use other satellite data and computer projections to determine whether there was underground water in the region, and whether the roads to the camps would be usable in the coming rainy seasons. The UN specialized agencies make use of sophisticated models projecting weather patterns, livestock availability, migration trends, and local and regional tension. We have advanced early warnings for hunger, disease, and conflict that make it impossible to claim we did not know what was brewing.

At our disposal we now have the biggest and best network ever of like-minded intergovernmental, governmental, and nongovernmental organizations as channels of future investments in peace and development. Humanitarian agencies can feed, vaccinate, and provide primary school for children for a couple of dollars a day even in the remotest areas. Such investment is, dollar by dollar, more cost-effective than anything I know of in the private and public sector in any Northern or Western society.

These nongovernmental and UN organizations will also speak up more for neglected peoples. Through three and a half years as UN emergency relief coordinator I had a pulpit from which I could advocate more effectively than I had dreamed of before taking the job in 2003. Every working week for more than three years I could speak to the major international media on unmet relief needs in exploding natural disasters, such as the droughts on the Horn of Africa; forgotten emergencies, such as northern Uganda, where twenty thousand children had been kidnapped; and the abuse of civilians and especially women, who are raped and abused in conflicts around the world. Several heads of state from Zimbabwe to Sudan came after my scalp. In previous years I may not have been able to keep my job, but Kofi Annan, a secretary-general of great integrity, always defended my right to speak the truth.

The several hundred humanitarian and human rights organizations will be mobilized in coming years to hold leaders around the world accountable as never before. I see three major advocacy campaigns building:

First, the political leadership in an increasing number of industrialized and affluent nations will have to fulfill the United Nations–agreed goal that at least 0.7 percent of Gross National Income should go to foreign assistance. It is now only 0.3 percent among the twenty-two major donors in the Organization for Economic Co-operation and Development (OECD). The goal of providing 0.7 percent to combat poverty, disease, and hunger has been reaffirmed several times by world leaders meeting in New York; in Monterrey, Mexico; and, importantly, in the European Union. It is

not an overambitious goal. Given that economies from Singapore to
Saudi Arabia, from Qatar to the United States, and from Italy to Iceland show exploding consumption of luxury goods, it is simply
stingy that most of these states have endorsed no realistic domestic
plans to achieve the 0.7 percent goal. The generous private donations of many individuals in these countries cannot make up the
lack of predictable and adequate public allocations. Countries such
as Sweden, the Netherlands, and Norway have, in spite of unmet
domestic needs, overfulfilled this goal for decades and enjoy public
support for providing 1 percent in aid to the poorest.

The Group of Eight (G-8) nations, the self-proclaimed collection of the world's leading economies, agreed at their summit in
2005 to pledge an additional $50 billion in foreign assistance by
2010, of which half would go to Africa. In 2006 these same leaders
and countries gave less, not more. Except for the British summit
hosts, all others failed to honor their commitments. The OECD reported a decrease of 5 percent in foreign assistance from 2005 to
2006 and the G-8 rich were no exception.

But it is not only the G-8 nations that must be the objects of aggressive advocacy campaigns. The newly rich nations of Southeast
Asia, the Persian Gulf, and elsewhere should be held accountable. If
the affluent in Asia, the Americas, Europe, and the Middle East used
half as much on ending wars, abject poverty, and epidemics as they
spend on vacation travel, pets, and ice cream we would have more
than enough. Each year from 2003 to 2006 I launched the global
humanitarian appeals with Secretary-General Annan for 25–30 million of the most vulnerable war and disaster victims in the world.
We did not ask for more than $3 billion to $4 billion in each of
these years, the equivalent of less than two café lattes per person in
the industrialized world or less than two days of global military
spending. We always received less than two-thirds of what we asked
for, even in appeals for lifesaving assistance. With the exception of
the tsunami and the Lebanon war appeals, no emergency appeal was

fully funded. Many places, such as Somalia or the Congo, where children died in the thousands for lack of funding, did not get more than 50 or 60 percent of what our field-workers said they needed to save lives.

The second major campaign that is building will be to hold world leaders accountable in their obligation to protect otherwise defenseless civilians in lawless places around the world. World leaders from the United States, China, Russia, Europe, the Islamic world, Asia, and Africa—some 190 heads of state and governments in all—solemnly swore at the United Nations summit in September 2005 to uphold a "responsibility to protect" vulnerable communities when national authorities cannot or will not provide such protection.

I was there when it happened. For many months diplomats from all UN member states had sat in the windowless basement meeting rooms to ponder the "millennium plus five years" summit declaration. For the first time there was a decisive majority of states who rose above the medieval principle of not "interfering in the internal affairs of sovereign states," and the following text was agreed by consensus when the kings, presidents, and prime ministers met in the General Assembly Hall of the UN:

". . . [W]e are prepared to take collective action, in a timely and decisive manner, through the Security Council, in accordance with the Charter, including Chapter VII . . . should peaceful means be inadequate and national authorities are manifestly failing to protect their populations from genocide, war crimes, ethnic cleansing, and crimes against humanity."

This "responsibility to protect" is more revolutionary than many world powers and third world leaders seem willing to admit. They can no longer be passive bystanders to carnage. The campaign we need to undertake will aim to see this responsibility translated into action for beleaguered and threatened communities. In my seventh and last briefing to the Security Council on the protection of civilians, in December 2006, I appealed to the members to make sure that "your responsibility to protect must be depoliticized, become a truly shared interest and translate into joint action by all members of this council and our global organization."

What does this mean? It means that more countries must give more forces to peacekeeping and peace-enforcing operations undertaken by the United Nations or the African Union. These forces need to be operationally capable. It also means that more governments will enforce protection by international forces where and when the national elites fail to end the abuse. It means that these and other UN member states will enforce economic sanctions and individual judicial accountability on political and military leaderships who attack civilian populations. If the new and emerging powers do more to defend women and children worldwide, the Western powers, with their questionable global image post-Iraq, could step back and not always spearhead such moral causes. More than anything, it means the end of standing by when they know that there is killing, rape, and mutilation of civilians or noncombatants. Individuals and nations have a responsibility to act immediately, forcefully, and coherently with UN members to end the abuse.

Third, there must be stronger international efforts to control proliferation of small arms and light weapons, in particular military-style automatic firearms. Even though there has been a marked decline in wars and full-scale genocides since the fall of the Berlin Wall, the number of violent attacks against civilians has increased. Parties to conflict have demonstrated a willful disregard for the basic tenets of humanitarian law of armed conflict. I have seen firsthand how mass murderers, mafias, and terrorists in Colombia, Darfur, northern Uganda, eastern Congo, Iraq, and elsewhere in the Middle East never lack the tools to maim, kill, and terrorize civilians. There is an increase in government-sponsored and private illegal armies, ethnic militias, and nonstate guerrilla forces. And they are supplied as never before with lethal automatic military weapons, often the most sophisticated kinds overflowing from the East and the West and the cold war. Today there are an estimated 640 million small arms and light weapons in circulation worldwide. In recent years arms suppliers from the South, with no scruples, rival the warlord-friendly suppliers in Eastern Europe. Only a concerted effort to curb production, to control and publish all weapons sales, and to vigorously prosecute the networks of illegal arms brokers will reverse the supply of our generation's weapons of mass destruction.

Indiscriminate weapons are another deadly plague. In August 2006 I was shocked when our UN mine-clearing teams reported that, weeks after the end of the Lebanon war, they were wading through a million unexploded bomblets from Israeli cluster bombs as the Lebanese civilians were returning to their homes, farms, schools, and clinics. Cluster bombs, like land mines, are indiscriminate weapons that kill long after hostilities are over and belong in the garbage can of history.

A precondition for the effective future multilateral action is real reform of the United Nations system from today's old-fashioned model to a more operational structure. The UN can no longer reflect the world as it was seen by the victors after World War II. Japan is the second-largest contributor to the regular budget of the UN, as big as four of the five veto-wielding powers of the Security Council (France, Russia, United Kingdom, and China) combined, and barely behind the much larger United States. Yet like the biggest country of Europe, Germany, they are still not given a seat in the Security Council. India, Brazil, and Nigeria are among the most populous and influential countries in the world, but also without a permanent seat in this council. I saw after nearly three dozen briefings to the current fifteen-member council that its Eurocentric structure is not only a source of alienation for the rest of the world, but also a hindrance to effective multilateral action. When less relevant nations take the seats that could have been occupied by some of the contemporary world's most influential powers, we get weaker sticks and smaller carrots.

It is not only the membership-governing structures that should be radically reformed—including the General Assembly, which spends much of its time discussing issues and resolutions nobody notices—but the Secretariat's structure and operations also need to be shaken up. Coming from the Norwegian government and the Red Cross to United Nations Headquarters, I could not believe how cumbersome UN procedures are, and how little executive power the secretary-general and his chief executives have. It takes more than a year to fill a post. It is virtually impossible to move staff or units around in the system, or eliminate posts or create new ones. Too many of the more than 190 member states, from the South as well as from the North, behave like control freaks when they review plans and budgets in the unwieldy committees, boards, and panels that have a right to review and hold up everything and anything before it becomes a reality.

Some Northern donors have added controls because they are obsessed with the danger of corruption, even though evaluations and investigations of the UN, such as the massive "Oil-for-Food" investigation, show that the system is less plagued by corruption than by ineffectiveness due to bad management and slow and cumbersome procedures. Representatives of developing countries on committees and panels are even less inclined to delegate executive responsibility, because they believe, wrongly, that this will increase Western influence. The net result is that even internal control mechanisms and internal risk aversion grow, and the poor and abused suffer because the UN is not there with the right response when it is most needed.

Secretary-General Kofi Annan provided detailed and well-argued proposals for change to the crucial 2005 General Assembly of member states. In most areas, Northern or Southern member states came together as spoilers and blocked progress. Historic opportunities for change were lost. The United Nations is today more often than not an effective tool for the international community not because of, but rather in spite of its structure. Fortunately, the humanitarian area became an exception.

In 2005 I initiated an ambitious humanitarian reform process because our slow response to the humanitarian needs in Darfur was ample proof that the old system for funding, preparedness, and coordination did not work. We were simply too slow to come to the rescue of the one million displaced when in June 2004 we succeeded in lifting many of the Sudanese government's restrictions on our access to Darfur. Even with the so called "CNN effect" working on our side and numerous development ministers coming to our fund-raising meetings, it took months before we received the necessary funds to jump-start the large and expensive operation. Even though all the main operational organizations agreed on the priority to deploy relief workers massively to the field, inside Darfur we had too few experienced logisticians, water engineers, camp managers, and protection experts for many months. And even though we agreed on which lifesaving services were the highest priorities, we did not get the organizations to provide, together and jointly, first things first.

Knowing that it is usually easier to get forgiveness than permission, I decided to start the reform process with humanitarian colleagues immediately and ask for formal approvals later. A Humanitarian Response Review was first undertaken by experienced experts interviewing operational organizations and field-workers. The question was simple: how could we best ensure the provision of at least a minimum of lifesaving relief and recovery assistance to all those with emergency needs irrespective of time, place, and cultural background? The reform was first discussed in the Inter-Agency Standing Committee, consisting of the UN, the Red Cross, and the NGOs, and which I chaired as emergency relief coordinator. Here we agreed that the reform should improve the effectiveness of humanitarian response by ensuring predictability, accountability, and partnership. We aimed at reaching more beneficiaries with more comprehensive needs-based relief and protection, in a more effective and timely manner.

The humanitarian reform program was launched at the end of 2005 with four key pillars:

First, we agreed through the Inter-Agency Standing Committee to establish a series of operational partnerships that we dubbed the "cluster" approach. These clusters improved coordination and accountability in providing humanitarian services in the key aspects of emergency relief, including such gap areas as water and sanitation, emergency health, and protection of the civilian population. We asked individual operational agencies to take the lead in each of these clusters and ensure that materials and expertise are planned, mobilized, and applied to good effect. Before the reform, our response capacity varied hugely from one area and population to the other. More often than not, we were great at providing food, because the World Food Programme is a highly effective, well-resourced, and dedicated organization for this purpose. But tons of corn or lentils are of no use to a mother if her child is dying from the lack of clean water, so it was of great importance that UNICEF, partnering with NGOs such as Oxfam, took an accountable leadership role for providing water supplies and latrines in a more predictable manner. The cluster approach is slowly, but surely, having the effect of more predictable assistance for more people in more places. Some good donors have given the cluster leaders, the UN organizations, the NGOs, and the Red Cross and Red Crescent Movement the funds to build preparedness in the key subject areas and in all geographic regions.

Secondly, we needed more predictable overall funding for this improved response capacity, not only in emergencies such as Darfur in 2004, but equally in the neglected emergencies where there is no

"CNN effect." We had an old UN central emergency revolving fund that was launched in 1992 after the Kurdish refugee crisis. But more than a decade later this was still a modest $50 million and could only provide loans to relief organizations, which in turn were afraid to indebt themselves. I suggested to the secretary-general that he include in his package to the 2005 summit a proposed new Central Emergency Response Fund (CERF) with $500 million in voluntary contributions. We secured important allies for this through the British minister for development, Hillary Benn, as well as Sweden, Norway, and Luxembourg. They were willing to invest in and campaign for a fund that guaranteed we had "water in our hose when a fire was detected," to quote Benn.

When the proposal to dramatically upgrade the emergency fund was brought to the General Assembly in late 2005, it was already an uncontroversial fait accompli and the first element of the secretary-general's reform package to be agreed on. All regional groups had been consulted, donors had promised sufficient money to get going, and humanitarian organizations had been included in the planning process. Only four months later the CERF was launched with an impressive initial $260 million from forty-eight governments and private-sector groups, representing all continents and as many traditional as nontraditional donors. In the first four months of activity we allocated more than $100 million for 130 relief projects in nineteen war- and disaster-stricken countries. By August 2007, the CERF had committed over $450 million to 522 projects in fifty countries. From the start, the fund has given two-thirds to jump-start operations in sudden-onset emergencies and one-third for neglected and underfunded ongoing crises. From East Timor and Somalia to the Congo and Ivory Coast, the CERF has helped make humanitarian relief more predictable when it is most needed.

There will, of course, be neither successful operational clusters nor efficient use of funding if there is no guarantee of effective leadership on the ground. The third element of the humanitarian reform was therefore a systematic effort to recruit and train a standby pool of highly qualified "field marshals" for emergency relief operations. There has for many years been a system of humanitarian coordinators to facilitate the work of relief groups and to stimulate cooperation among humanitarian agencies. The work of these key representatives under extremely difficult circumstances has been laudable, but they have varied in terms of leadership and creativeness. Some UN resident coordinators had continued business as usual when they were also given emergency responsibilities. The roster of experienced candidates from inside and outside the UN system of experienced leaders will now be ready for immediate deployment and can replace those coordinators who are not up to the challenge.

Finally, we started a process of broadening partnerships by trying to be less "UN-centric" and less "Northern." The United Nations system is engaged in larger and more numerous relief and recovery operations than ever before, but its relative share of the total humanitarian response is shrinking. The UN is needed for standard setting, coordination, facilitation, and seeing that political, security, and humanitarian efforts come together in a coherent whole. Most of the actual delivery of assistance on the ground is undertaken by the growing number of non-UN public and private actors in humanitarian response, including NGOs from the North and increasingly—and impressively—from the South. During the uniquely generous and global response to the Indian Ocean tsunami in 2004–2005 more than ninety governments and millions of individuals and companies from all over the world donated some $13 billion to relief and reconstruction in the affected communities. Some four hundred international relief groups in total converged on Aceh in Indonesia and Sri Lanka in the first month of the relief effort. This was clearly too many—perhaps two or three hundred too many—for the local communities to bear since they had their own organizations and authorities who were too often pushed aside and not consulted as recovery and reconstruction was planned and carried out.

In the future we must think more strategically, and more locally, in the way we undertake our long-term efforts to make societies resilient to hazards and strife. We must work more closely with local governments and civil society to strengthen their capacity for handling crises and exercising good governance. We must find better ways to forge coordination and partnerships internationally, nationally, and locally. Thus we will be able to tap local resources and local expertise better. Time and again we see that more lives are saved in earthquakes, floods, and tsunamis by local groups than by expensive airborne fire brigades. Similarly, it is usually local and regional actors who are make-or-break for peace-building efforts and reconciliation.

Recognizing the need to discuss a new deal in forging effective partnerships beyond borders and artificial organizational barriers, in Geneva in 2006 we called the first of several meetings of executive leaders of leading humanitarian organizations from the North and the South, and from UN and non-UN agencies, to form a "Global Humanitarian Platform."

The growth in high-quality civil society movements, especially within third world societies, is probably the single most important trend in global efforts to combat poverty and conflict. They are vastly more important than governments and intergovernmental organizations such as the UN tend to recognize. All over Asia, Africa, Latin America, and the Middle East, I could see how religious groups, women's groups, peasant groups, student groups, and trade unions stand up for human rights, for local development, and for peace and reconciliation. They represent great hope for the one billion who struggle to survive every single day as we embark as the generation that has in its hands the power to end massive misery and prevent conflict and disasters.

Acknowledgments

I HAD NO plans to write a book during my years of overwhelming crisis management in the United Nations, the Red Cross, and the Norwegian Ministry of Foreign Affairs. When I ended my term as global emergency relief coordinator for the United Nations in December 2006, many encouraged me to write my story; and the first among these was the literary agent, Annabel Merullo, in London.

I am indebted to my editor at Simon & Schuster, Alice Mayhew, for her help, advice, and patient and professional stewardship of my book. Roger Labrie and Serena Jones have ably coordinated our cross-Atlantic process. I got valuable assistance from Mr. Bjørn Klouman Bekken at the Kennedy School at Harvard University with documentation, research, and scholarship.

I have been honored to hold important positions in my country Norway and within the United Nations. Foreign Minister Thorvald Stoltenberg invited me to join in a new era of Norwegian foreign policy activism in the post–cold war period. UN Secretary-General Kofi Annan offered a similar opportunity to join his team at the helm of the UN in a challenging time for that organization, the first decade of the new century. None of my previous employers have any part in the observations, conclusions, or proposals in this book.

That responsibility is mine. I am now the Director General of the Norwegian Institute of International Affairs and can comment freely as observer and researcher.

I have benefited by working with immensely talented and hard-working colleagues in the Office for the Coordination of Humanitarian Affairs and elsewhere. Often, in the United Nations and elsewhere I have been given credit for actions or advocacy that was prepared by others.

I cannot thank anyone more than my wife, Anne Kristin, and our daughters Ane and Heidi. Over many years my travel absences have been a strain on our little family. I am forever grateful for their support and understanding.

Selected Bibliography

Global Challenges: War and Peace

Annan, Kofi. 2005. *In Larger Freedom: Towards Development, Security, and Human Rights for All.* This is the ambitious package of proposals from the Secretary-General to the 2005–06 General Assembly—where much of it was shot down. www.un.org/largerfreedom

Secretary-General Annan's most important speeches are found at: www.un.org/News/ossg/sg/stories/AnnanKeySpeeches

Human Security Reports. Yearly reports providing global overviews and trends on human rights abuse, genocide, internal strife, armed conflicts, etc. www.humansecurityreport.info

Stockholm Institute of Peace Research (SIPRI). SIPRI's yearly reports provide comprehensive annual reports on war and armed conflicts worldwide. http://yearbook2007.sipri.org

The United Nations: Reform Efforts

Annan, Kofi. (2006). Investing in the United Nations. For a Stronger Organization Worldwide. www.un.org/reform/investinginun/investing-in-un

Kemal, Dervis, with Ceren Ozer. *A Better Globalization: Legitimacy, Governance, and Reform.* Washington, D.C.: Brookings Press, 2005.

Kennedy, Paul. *The Parliament of Man: The Past, Present, and Future of the United Nations.* New York: Random House, 2006.

Security Council Report. Publishes data and analysis on the work of the Security Council: www.securitycouncilreport.org

Thakur, Ramesh. *The United Nations, Peace and Security: From Collective Security to the Responsibility to Protect.* London: Cambridge University Press, 2006.

Traub, James. *The Best Intentions: Kofi Annan and the UN in the Era of American World Power.* New York: Farrar, Straus and Giroux, 2007. Traub was allowed by

Annan to follow the work of the Secretary-General from the inside for more than a year while I was there.

The UN Charter is the legal foundation of the organization: http://www.un .org/aboutun/charter

United Nation's Web site on UN reform efforts, in general: www.un.org/ reform

UN High-Level Panel on Threats, Challenges and Change. 2004. *A More Secure World, Our Shared Responsibility.* This global group of "elder statesmen and women" was asked to do a report on UN reform, which was a basis for Annan's proposals to the General Assembly (see above): http://www.un.org/secure world

UN High-Level Panel on System Wide Coherence. 2006.—*Delivering as One.* Report of an international high-level panel on reforming UN development, environment, and humanitarian work: http://www.un.org/events/panel/

United Nations Handbook. An annual summary of what is going on in the UN, published by the Ministry of Foreign Affairs of New Zealand.

Humanitarian Challenges

Egeland, Jan. A number of the briefings and speeches I made during 2003–06 are found at: http://ochaonline.un.org

OCHA, UN Office for the Coordination of Humanitarian Affairs: http://ocha online.un.org

    IRIN is OCHA's news and feature service: www.irinnews.org

OTHER HUMANITARIAN WEB SITES

Amnesty International: www.amnesty.org,

Federation of Red Cross and Red Crescent Societies: www.ifrc.org

Human Rights Watch: www.hrw.org

International Committee of the Red Cross: www.icrc.org

International Crisis Group: www.crisisgroup.org

International Rescue Committee: www.theirc.org

Reliefweb is the largest collection of reports, news items, and appeals from the whole humanitarian community: www.reliefweb.int

Responsibility to Protect—Engaging Civil Society: www.responsibilitytoprotect .org

UN Central Emergency Response Fund (CERF): http://cerf.un.org

Tsunami

Tsunami Evaluation Coalition. 2006 and 2007. A comprehensive series of evaluations were undertaken by teams of independent experts: www.tsunami evaluation.org

Small Arms and Light Weapons

International Action Network on Small Arms: www.iansa.org
Small Arms Survey, annual reports: www.smallarmssurvey.org
UN Yearbook on Disarmament: http://disarmament.un.org/e-yearbook.html

Trends in Economic and Social Development

Human Development Reports by United Nations Development Programme: http://hdr.undp.org. The statistical basis for these are also found online: http:// hdr.undp.org/hdr2006/statistics/
Millennium Development Goals 2007, an annual UN reports, describes progress (and lack of such) in achieving the Millennium Development Goals: www .un.org/millenniumgoals
UN Millennium Project. 2006. The report of the group of experts examining whether and how the Millennium Development Goals (MDGs) can be achieved by 2015: http://www.unmillenniumproject.org/reports/index.htm
World Development Indicators, the World Bank: http://publications.worldbank .org/WDI

Climate Change

British Government commissioned independent report on climate change (the "Stern-report"): http://www.hm-treasury.gov.uk/independent_reviews/stern_ review_economics_climate_change
Reports of the International Panel on Climate Change: www.ipcc.org
The UN System's Web site on climate change: http://www.un.org/climate change/

UN Resolutions and briefings

Security Council Resolutions since 1946: http://www.un.org/Docs/sc/unsc_ resolutions
General Assembly Summit Resolutions. 2005. "Millennium Plus Five": http:// www.un.org/summit2005/documents
So-called Millennium Declaration at the UN World Summit. September 2000: http://www.un.org/millennium/declaration/ares552e

Darfur

Security Council Resolution 1769 (2007). Establishes a robust peacekeeping force of 26, 000 soldiers and police, a joint African Union and UN force to replace the smaller and lighter Africn Union force supported through resolution 1590 (2005).

Summaries of my press conferences on Darfur May 19, 2006: http://www.un
    .org/News/Press/docs/2006/sc8724 and November 22 2006: http://www
    .un.org/News/Press/docs//2006/sc8875
"Save Darfur," a coalition of NGOs: www.savedarfur.org

The Middle East

Security Council 1701 (2006) is the basis for the cease-fire between Israel and
    Hezbollah.
Summary of my press conference of July 18, 2006, on the humanitarian conse-
    quences of the war between Israel and Hezbollah: www.un.org/apps/news/
    infocusnewsME.asp?NewsID=1085&sID=35

Uganda

Security Council Resolution 1653 (2006) condemns the LRA and other armed
    groups for their human rights abuse.
Summary of press briefing on September 16, 2006, on Northern Uganda and
    Eastern Kongo: http://www.un.org/News/Press/docs/2006/sc8831

Index

About the Author

JAN EGELAND is Director General of the Norwegian Institute of International Affairs. He was the UN Undersecretary-General for Humanitarian Affairs and its Emergency Relief Coordinator from August 2003 to December 2006. From 1999 to 2002, he was the UN Secretary-General's Special Envoy for war-torn Colombia. As State Secretary in the Norwegian Ministry of Foreign Affairs he was initiator of the Norwegian channel between Israel and the Palestine Liberation Organization that led to the Oslo Accord in 1993. Egeland lives in Oslo, Norway, with his wife and two daughters and is frequently in the United States.